THE
ACTIVIST ENTREPRENEUR

TO: RICH – –
WE GO WAY BACK!

Nov 13, 2013

THE
ACTIVIST ENTREPRENEUR

What I learned About Business at the Urban Coalition and My Proven Keys to Personal and Career Success

WALT
DOUGLAS

with ANTHONY NEELY

NEELY MEDIA GROUP, LLC

Printed in the US by Lightning Source
Typesetting by *www.wordzworth.com*
Cover Design by Stephanie Lewis, 23 Exchange LLC

This book is dedicated to **Retha Hughes Douglas**, my faithful companion, wife, friend and critic for fifty-plus years. Her wise and loving counsel has helped to soothe the many rough edges of life and provided countless hours of everlasting joy.

CONTENTS

Chapter 12 Worthy Reflections and Closing Thoughts **217**

FIGURES

QUOTATIONS

"You need to find something for Walter to do because he's not college material. He will never make it in college."

— MRS. EMMA CHAPMAN
Hamlet, N. Car. — 1950

"Waste no tears on me. I didn't come along too early. I was right on time."

— BUCK O'NEIL, AGE 91
Negro League Baseball Star
Quoted in USA Today July 7, 2003

"Man does not decide his future, but he decides his habits, and his habits decide his future."

— JOE TAYLOR
Florida A & M Football Coach
Quoted in New York Times, Nov 8, 2009

"Life is about vision and impact; one follows the other."

— WALT DOUGLAS
Detroit, Michigan 2004

FOREWORD BY EDSEL B. FORD II

The life story of Walter Douglas epitomizes the quintessential American Dream, with an added element of triumph. He gracefully came from an era and an environment that was deliberately designed to ensure that a success story such as his would never be written.

That's why it is with immense admiration for my good friend that I invite you to experience his life, in his eloquent and honest words, on the following pages.

Walt showcases and celebrates how, upon a foundation of family, faith, education and determination, he blazed a trail among our nation's first African American automotive dealers.

While enjoying tremendous success as owner of Avis Ford in Southfield, Michigan, Walt also committed his time and talent to the economic, political and social improvement of Detroit. Inspired by the 1967 "rebellion," Walt has for decades served on countless boards that continue to enable him to make a positive imprint on our world.

His ability to excel in business and simultaneously uplift our community was only made possible by the rock-solid foundation of a loving home in which he and his wife, Retha, raised three children.

When I first met Walt many years ago, we began to enjoy a friendship that is rooted in the many parallels of our lives. We share a commitment to life-long careers with Ford Motor Company, and together we served on the Skillman Foundation's Board of Trustees.

Walt and I soon discovered that we hold two significant beliefs that guide our lives in every way. First, that family is the bedrock of life, and second, that Detroit has infinite potential to rise as a world-class city.

Now, as the economy reshapes our local and national landscape, I must say that Walter Douglas could not have chosen a more relevant time to share his life story. It testifies to the power of the entrepreneurial spirit when backed by hard work, discipline and faith.

How fortunate we are now, to glean nuggets of wisdom and inspiration from Walt's extraordinary life. I commend and congratulate my friend for leaving this literary legacy that will continue to inspire countless generations to come.

[signature]

EDSEL B. FORD II

Figure 1.   Edsel Ford II and Walt Douglas on the showroom floor of Avis Ford

ACKNOWLEDGMENTS

I start by thanking Claudia Corbin, who got me started and did a number of initial interviews with me, plus many friends and family, which she taped and transcribed. Claudia asked many insightful questions that got me started; thus, this book began to emerge. After completing the first draft of the manuscript, Claudia and I asked the Wayne State University Press to give us an assessment of our work. After reviewing their comments, the book layout and text went through the first of a number of revisions.

An additional revision occurred when I shared the text with my sister Shirley's daughter-in-law Angela (who is married to Shirley's son, Eric). I credit Angela with introducing a refreshing writing style as she edited the first portion of the text — a style I then followed in rewriting the remaining text. To Angela I offer my thanks and appreciation, for her efforts put this book on a better track. I also want to thank Dr. Jeffrey Sammons, PhD, a history professor at New York University and fellow golfer; and Dr. Delores Coles, PhD, a senior executive at the U. S. Department of HUD. Both are friends who read a sampling of the text and made very cogent suggestions. Again, thanks for helping me with the nuances of documenting one's life.

Tesse and Jim Sharpe, family friends, and Patricia Douglas-Evans also volunteered to read an early version of the manuscript. Together, the Sharpes and Patricia provided great comfort with their encouraging remarks. Finally, needing some professional help in polishing my book after continuing to correct and clarify many parts of the text, I asked Detroiter Elizabeth Atkins, an author and professional writer, to review the book and make the changes she thought necessary. What a splendid job she did. I cannot thank her enough.

And as luck would have it, I was contacted by an old colleague from the Economic Development Corporation (EDC) who happened to find me while he was searching for a repository for his important papers covering the EDC/ICBIF era. Mike Weston, EDC's third president, provided enormous insights and documents that helped clarify many points regarding the troika of New Detroit, EDC and ICBIF. Mike provided me with a copy of the 1972 EDC Annual Report that helped me pinpoint the involvement of the participants during that era. Also, Karl Gregory, PhD, a distinguished professor emeritus of economics who taught at Oakland University in Rochester, Michigan, and Walter McMurtry, ICBIF's former president, provided me with information about the EDC and ICBIF era.

Many others have played roles and have helped me to clarify the involvement of individuals I mention in the book. Those include Alex Luvall, who worked with me at the Detroit Police Department years ago; Chacona Johnson, who has twice read this text; Glenn E. Wash; and V. Lonnie Peek, Jr. — all part of the New Detroit family. They helped me recall many events during my years at New Detroit and the Detroit Police Department. Howard Sims, during our occasional reflections about names and events from the seventies and eighties, has helped me immensely in recalling events, names and situations detailed in this book.

I also wish to thank Tiger Woods for the quote he provided for inclusion in the book's section detailing my service on his foundation.

Before his death, I asked Dr. Arthur L. Johnson to make some introductory comments for my book. Agreeing, he joined with Federal Judge Damon J. Keith in writing a descriptive and insightful prologue — the two of them speaking as close friends whom I have known since shortly after my arrival in Detroit. Retha and I consider them both remarkable individuals and two people who in their demonstrative lives capture the soul of the City of Detroit.

While wintering in Florida, I twice asked my friend Lois Munson to take a look at the text. I thank her for her thoughtful comments.

We all have respectful friends who make our lives meaningful, and two of mine are Debbie and Wilson Copeland, who not only read this text, but Wilson — in his baronial style — offered his insight about two organizations to which we both belong. I thank both him and Debbie.

I thank Alan Mulally for taking the time to read this text and for providing a quote in the manner that only he can do — portraying his dynamic style of speaking and leading.

I wish to thank Edsel B. Ford II, who without prodding quickly agreed to write the Foreword for this book. Edsel and I have known each other for years, beginning with my relationship with his father, Henry Ford II, and our mutual involvement with the Ford Motor Company.

But most of all, I want to thank my wife, Retha, who has read each version of this book and has helped immeasurably in clarifying many points, since she has traveled most of the years of this journey alongside me. I am eternally grateful to her for her encouragement and the tireless hours she spent in supporting me in this effort.

I also wish to thank my children and their spouses: Petra (Derek); Edmond (Van); and Mark (Tiffany) for their support and insights as I have labored to complete this book. What wonderful thoughts they have shared with me.

Finally, as the text needed final editing and major rearranging, I asked Anthony Neely, former *Detroit Free Press* reporter, press secretary to former Mayor Dennis Archer and General Motors speechwriter, for help. Anthony did a splendid job of rearranging and rewriting the text to its present form. Anthony, words do not express the appreciation I owe you for your splendid work!

WALTER E. DOUGLAS, SR.
Southfield, Michigan
December 31, 2012

THOUGHTS FROM TWO FRIENDS

THE WALT DOUGLAS STORY

In producing this rich and inspiring autobiography, Walter Douglas personifies grace and dignity. His story is about work, family, love, achievement and triumph over the racial barriers that are common in the life struggle of African Americans. In painstaking and intimate detail, Douglas tells us all that needs to be told about his early childhood and formative years.

Wrapped in the protective love and high aspirations of an entire family, he grew into manhood listening to the sage teachings of his mother and father, including in particular, the admonition not to work for white people, but rather to be independent and self-reliant. His family was rooted in the spiritual culture of the Methodist Church, a proud tradition that has remained strong in the life of this remarkable Black man.

A distinguished record of achievement, to which Walter Douglas points with pride, characterizes all the members of the Douglas family. They are living proof that with education, determination and shared belief, an entire family can triumph and live with honor. Douglas rose to the heights of successful business and professional enterprise, including data management in the IRS, leadership of the nation's largest urban coalition, school transportation services and finally owning and operating a profitable automotive dealership. It is a remarkable demonstration of human spirit and will. He makes no false claims or apologies for the bold positions that he has taken on the most significant issues of the day. He learned that the path to greatness is reached in doing more than what was required in every job and position that he held. To his credit, he has shared the gifts of his success with a generous regard for the needs and trials of others.

Following the footsteps of his friend and mentor, Larry Doss, in the presidency of New Detroit, Inc., Douglas offers readers an intimate view of the social forces and opportunities that have shaped his life. With a self-assured grasp of the political dynamics of change in urban America, he illuminates on a grand scale his sense of duty and purpose. Ultimately, he becomes the consummate insider and one of the most trusted individuals serving the Detroit community. His integrity, courage, and perseverance in the face of adversity provide a vivid example for all to follow. In Walt Douglas' story, we find a clear reflection of this truth and reality.

ARTHUR L. JOHNSON
(1925-2011)
Vice President University Relations and
Professor of Educational Sociology
Wayne State University

THE HONORABLE DAMON J. KEITH
Senior Judge
United States Court of Appeals for the Sixth Circuit

CHAPTER 1

PRELUDE

INTRODUCTION

I arrived in Detroit on July 11, 1966 — 377 days before the 1967 rebellion that turned a proud city, universally admired for its ingenuity and industrial might, into something very different: an international symbol of urban unrest, decline and decay.

I choose to use the term "rebellion" instead of "riot" when I refer to the events of July 1967, because I believe the chaos the world saw on the streets of Detroit was caused by an eruption of long-suppressed emotions, rather than a reaction to an event — which generally causes a riot. Years after the 1967 event, Howard Beale, a character played by Peter Finch in the movie *Network,* captured the sentiment of inner-city Detroit with his classic line: "I'm as mad as hell, and I'm not going to take this anymore!" I saw, and continue to see, the Detroit uprising of 1967 as a rebellious act that announced Detroit's African Americans were not going to take their second-class status anymore.

The 1967 rebellion was a seminal moment in the city's history and in my own career. I was a college-trained, computer systems specialist for the federal government — which was one of the few organizations willing to hire African Americans for white-collar jobs. Very shortly, I would become an active volunteer for the Inner City Business Improvement Forum (ICBIF), formed by a self-determining group of black leaders in Detroit whose purpose was to advocate for increased business opportunities. Through that organization, I and others began to work somewhat in tandem with New Detroit Inc., the trailblazing organization formed by the city's business, political and community leaders in response to the rebellion, which shortly would become the model for action-oriented urban coalition organizations across the country. Approximately one decade after its formation, I would become the organization's president.

What New Detroit taught me about successful business formation and management; community development; politics; race relations; and most importantly, leadership — would help me advance to the next phase of my career. Indeed, those lessons have made it possible for me to enjoy success as an entrepreneur, principally as majority owner of Avis Ford, in the Detroit suburb of Southfield, Michigan — one of the nation's top auto dealerships.

A more significant point is the fact that the course of my professional life since 1967 has mirrored the progress made and lessons learned as America's business and political leaders acted to correct long-standing economic obstacles and inequities against African Americans and other people of color, as well as women. Moving to Detroit thrust me right into the middle of this historic initiative. As an activist coalition builder, I influenced public policy and the creation of private programs that made communities and their economies stronger. Having used newly open doors to become a business owner myself, I've been pleased to engage in job creation, wealth building and public reinvestment — important issues, all of which are essential to the health of any community.

I believe my experience is worth reliving and describing now for three important reasons. First, the history of the progressive, wealth-creating and community-building initiatives that businesses and metropolitan governments created together, in response to America's urban unrest, is a largely untold story. The average citizen is totally unaware of it — and that's certainly true for those too young to have lived through it. For whatever reason, there is faint public memory of a time when business leaders viewed rebuilding communities as a top priority in their short and long-term planning.

The Detroit story stands out because just as Detroit's rebellion was the worst civil disturbance of the decade, the response of the city's business, government and community leaders was one of the most inspired and action-oriented. The auto industry's acknowledgment of its critical role as America's leading economic engine was a primary reason for Detroit's national leadership on the issue of diverse business development and improved employment opportunities for people of color.

Detroit's automakers established standards for diversity and inclusion that the rest of corporate America continues to adhere to today. That leads me to the second reason the history of forming community and business development programs in the 1960s and 1970s is important. Initiatives that were successful need to be continued; they should be made bigger and better. We should certainly avoid repeating programs that failed, but if they had any merit whatsoever, those good elements should be preserved and reintroduced as part of new job-creating initiatives.

The third reason this decades-old history must be dusted off and clearly understood is to counterbalance an aggressive campaign now underway to denigrate all sixties and seventies initiatives — local and national — that fought discrimination and promoted diversity. Conservative politicians and pundits who belittle such programs as a waste of time and money must be challenged and set straight. The fact is my success, chronicled by this book, proves their twisting of history is flat-out wrong.

Progressive programs that build the U.S. economy from the bottom up have never been needed more than they're needed now, in the twenty-first century's second decade. I'm happy to share my odyssey with you as a reminder of how awful things were, how bold our action can be, what remains to be done, and what is possible when we stop pointing fingers and begin to give each other a hand.

STARING DOWN AN ICON

The man sitting across the table was enraged. His face was red and seemed to vibrate with anger. From the neck up, his muscles were as tight as a clenched fist. I thought he might actually leap at me at any moment; but on my side of the table, there was a "beat-down" waiting for him! Here we were, two businessmen in suits, meeting for the closing of a major deal — yet ready to fly at each other like pit bulls.

My adversary was Sid McNiece, top lieutenant of Warren Avis, the iconic founder of Avis Rent a Car. Avis, a legendary figure in the world of retail auto sales, had launched both the rental car company and the dealership bearing his name in 1946, following his service in the Air Force during World War II. Forty years later, my business partner Ed Brown and I arranged for the purchase of Avis Ford, which had become a national leader among Ford dealerships once Warren Avis relocated it from Detroit to Telegraph and Twelve Mile roads in the Detroit suburb of Southfield.

The fact is, the purchase was well underway before Avis and his team realized that I — an African-American professional with scant experience as an independent business owner — had partnered with Brown, a white Detroit-area dealer well known and respected for his leadership of Bill Brown Ford. That didn't go down too well with some of the Avis people, and if his body language, comments and constant actions were any indication, certainly not with McNiece, General Manager of Warren Avis' business empire, which included Avis Ford.

Avis had put his dealership on the market only after the tragic death of his business partner, Richard Turner, who died in a plane crash in March 1986. Ed and I agreed to buy Turner's 49 percent share of Avis Ford, with a contractual provision that after five years of successful management, Warren Avis' 51 percent of the company would be ours, as well. We paid a hefty premium in 1986 to buy Avis Ford, so five years down the road — with plenty of headaches and scars to show for our good results — we were in no mood for foot-dragging. But that's exactly what we were facing.

It had become clear that Warren Avis did not want to sell. I believed he had always assumed that Ed and I would not succeed and the dealership would be returned to him. And, seeing that we had persevered and done well, he attempted to present a case to Ford Motor Co. — writing letters and otherwise advancing his position — encouraging Ford to intervene on his behalf and convince Ed and me to retain him as a partner. Warren acknowledged our successes to Ford, suggesting that our "team" needed to be "kept intact."

None of his espousals worked, for what he had forgotten was that he had no deal with Ford. His deal was with Ed and me. Finally, six months after the contractual deadline for the dealership to transfer to us, Warren realized he had to sell his remaining 51 percent to us.

But that didn't stop him and Sid from flinging obstacles in our path, trying any maneuver that might possibly discourage us from closing the purchase. For instance, Warren insisted on payment for continued use of his name once we assumed full ownership of the dealership. Having founded Avis Rent a Car through the dealership, Warren wanted extra compensation for the Avis name, recognizing it was a valuable asset. Obviously, our position was that the name came along with all the other Avis Ford corporate assets at the time we purchased the first 49 percent of the dealership's stock. Yet that did not stop Avis and his minion McNiece from attempting to copyright the name "Avis Ford," and then force Ed and me to pay for its use.

In response, on November 12, 1991 — five years after our takeover and during the period we had anticipated that we would be closing on the purchase of Avis' remaining 51 percent; Sid called a formal board meeting to legally change the dealership's name. He exercised his authority to vote Warren's majority ownership; and although Avis General Manager Jim Witmer and I were in attendance, Sid prepared minutes reflecting the convening board's action as if we were not present — ramming through an action to change the dealership's name to "Southfield Motors." Because Warren's "team" took no further action to change dealership signs or marketing materials, we figured Sid's action was just another irritating bluff and stalling maneuver. But on the day of the deal closing, we discovered that Sid had, indeed, submitted the name change — through their attorney Tom Roach — to the Michigan Department of Commerce in Lansing. Of course, at the dealership we had done nothing and had continued to operate as Avis Ford. Sid didn't realize that a name change of the dealership required the approval of Ford Motor Co. Our lawyers cancelled the switch to "Southfield Motors" once the dealership purchase was final.

Sid and I had our ultimate confrontation two days before the closing. Warren Avis' lawyers met ours at their offices at Avis Farms — the Avis Enterprises offices, which were located on a tract of land owned by Warren Avis just east of I-94 in Ann Arbor, Michigan — to iron out any last-minute issues. This was the meeting at which Sid looked like a man about to explode from internal combustion, and I became just as furious. More importantly, I revealed myself as a man who had finally had enough. My true personality was now in play and I was no longer Mr. Nice Guy who for five years had silently tolerated Sid's abrasive comments — and an action he once took in an attempt to disallow $30,000 of business expenses I had incurred. Sid had never used a demeaning word in addressing me; yet, the message of contempt behind each of his paternalistic comments — spoken in a deep Southern accent — could not be missed.

After a contentious comment by him, before I knew it, I was standing over him in that converted conference room that was once a barn, determined that my next move was going to be physical. "Sid, I'm sick of you," I said, adding a few choice four-letter words for full effect as I told him how pathetic his bullying tactics were. I finished my remarks by inviting him to stand so I could knock him on his ass. He did not move, but I knew I had frightened him. My actions changed his demeanor.

Two days later at the final closing at Manufacturers Bank in downtown Detroit, things went more smoothly. Yet, Sid again brought up the Avis name and the need to compensate Warren for its use — to which I responded: "Here's what you can do. Just write Ed and me checks for our initial investments and for the time and energy we've expended over the last five years, and you can have the damned dealership back." At that point — after an anteroom conference between Sid and their lawyers, he backed down. He agreed that we could keep the Avis name without compensation, and the closing moved swiftly to its final conclusion. Two-party cashier's checks were all countersigned; then we all shook hands and left.

It was over! Ed and I now owned the entire dealership — fifty percent each. I never saw Sid again.

★ ★ ★

My partnership's purchase of Avis Ford in 1986 and the dealership's performance during the ensuing five years had proved beyond a shadow of doubt that I could successfully make the transition from the not-for-profit to the for-profit sector. If there had been doubters, they were now convinced that Walt Douglas had skills beyond those I had employed as an advocate for social change during my career at New Detroit, the influential (and once revolutionary) urban coalition organization I had led as president for eight years. Those who had known me as an information technology specialist at the Internal Revenue Service learned that I wasn't limited to government work, either. I was showing I could manage a profitable business that for several years produced more than $100 million in annual sales, and which also scored impressively in customer service rankings.

Although in my early fifties, I was proving that I was still young and agile enough to change careers — and successfully make a complete transformation.

Perhaps most significant was the fact that becoming an entrepreneur proved I could practice — and validate — what I had preached for so many years: African Americans with the skills, experience and means to own businesses and create jobs should do so. Furthermore, once-closed doors should be opened to give qualified black entrepreneurs those opportunities.

My success at Avis Ford also validated my strategic decision to leave the East Coast and distance myself farther from my native South, when I moved to Detroit in 1966. Detroit had somehow continued to be for African Americans an oasis of fortune; a place to start fresh and remake oneself, in ways not as evident in other U.S. cities. This was despite the dominance of assembly-line industrial work and little else for people of color and those with limited education and training; the scarce career choices for educated black professionals even in the early to late 1970s; and the fierce racial conflict still evident today throughout the region.

Any observer would have to conclude that with my dealership purchase, I had become a full-fledged Detroiter. Like so many of my colleagues and predecessors, I treasured the hard knocks, trials and triumphs up North that had changed my life and shaped my character — no matter how fondly I remembered my friends and formative years down South.

CHAPTER 2

CAROLINA ROOTS

FROM THESE ROOTS — A LITTLE TOWN CALLED HAMLET

If you travel 77 miles southeast of Charlotte, North Carolina, on U.S. Highway 74, before long you will reach Hamlet an aptly named little city in the southern central portion of the state, close to the border of South Carolina. Hamlet is my hometown. It is part of North and South Carolinas' Sandhills region, an ancient territory whose grainy soil indicates the area was once underwater or was an oceanfront beach.

Hamlet was founded in 1873 by an Englishman named John Shortridge. Its principal industry developed from the urgings of Shortridge; he convinced The Raleigh and August Railroad Company to choose Hamlet as the site for its major crossing. In 1876 the company's engineer, William Moncure, was directed to install tracks and map out the town's lots and streets. Thus, the town of Hamlet's future was set to be that of a railroad hub — paving its way to prosperity during the turn of the century and into the first half of the 20th century. Because of the railroad, the town flourished, especially during the period leading up to World War II, attracting new workers throughout the region.

At its peak, Hamlet was a major connection point for trains traveling north and south from New York to Miami, with a spur that ran from Wilmington, North Carolina, on the Atlantic coast through Hamlet to Atlanta — and finally Birmingham, Alabama. During the heyday of railroading, as many as twenty-five passenger trains passed through Hamlet each day, along with countless freight carriers hauling livestock, produce, mail and anything else that could be carried by rail.

The Seaboard Railroad Company was a major employer of people who worked at its large maintenance and repair facility or in the many support and adjunct businesses that grew up around it. Jobs were so plentiful that even my father, the principal of a local elementary school, worked part-time sorting mail at the train station during the war years.

Everyone in our town loved trains, and talked for years about visits by President Franklin D. Roosevelt, whose private train passed through Hamlet on its way to his therapeutic retreat in Warm Springs, Ga., in the late 1930s; likely, more than once. On one occasion, his private train stopped in Hamlet for refueling and he toasted the crowd gathered around his Club Car at the tail end of the train.

Another well-chronicled railroading story was the time Booker T. Washington changed trains in Hamlet on his way to Washington, D.C., to receive an award. In 1901, Seaboard Railroad Co. alerted the town of Mr. Washington's travel schedule and arrangements were made for the famous black educator and his party to dine at the Seaboard Terminal Hotel. This presented protocol issues for a racially segregated city, of course. A solution was devised whereby a hotel bed sheet was hung down the center of the hotel's dining room. Mr. Washington and his group were served on one side and the regular hotel guests on the other.

Clearly, the railroad was the most notable thing about Hamlet. Not once did I ever imagine that I would remain long in Hamlet once I became an adult. When I finally left for good, I can't say I ever bragged about my hometown. Yet, I did learn later that there were several prominent Hamlet natives. One was Tom Wicker, the noted *New York Times* writer; another was John Coltrane, the popular jazz musician; and a third was Frederick Clinton Branch, the first black commissioned officer in the U.S. Marine Corps. On July 9, 1995, years after Branch's retirement, the Marine Corps named its education building and Officers Candidate School at Quantico, Virginia, in his honor.

Yet, growing up in Hamlet was fun for a young boy. I could hike into a nearby forest less than a half mile from our home, lie on the pine straw beneath the tall pines, gaze at nature and daydream of my future. During summer spells I would sit out front under the china-berry trees that afforded great shade, while daydreaming of what my life might become.

At times, I would lie in bed at night, dream of far-off places and know the time by listening to the whistles of the arriving passenger trains that ran with spot-on accuracy — maintaining their schedules during the era when railroading was king in America. Arriving and departing trains always reminded me of places I longed to visit; places where I might someday live.

FAMILY

Hamlet is just north of the area in South Carolina where my parents grew up. My father was from a rural farming community near the "Wire Road," a community that took its name from the electric line that first brought electricity to the northern border of South Caroli-na. My mother grew up some fifteen miles farther south in a farm community called Clio, just east of Bennettsville, South Carolina

Both of my parents were raised as Methodists, with each claiming a home church in their communities: my father's was Aaron's Temple; my mother's was Clio Methodist.

Education always seemed important to my father; and was first demonstrated by actions he took early in his life. Because his quest for education was beyond that offered by the local schools in rural South Carolina — no high school education was available — my father urged his father to allow him to attend William Penn High School in High Point, NC, some eighty miles away.

His father demurred and never gave him a straight answer. Therefore, with the assistance of his younger brother Edward, my father devised his own plan. His brother Edward was asked to accompany him on a wagon loaded with cotton to the local cotton gin. Once the cotton was ginned, my father headed north to High Point with the proceeds from the cotton sale and his suitcase of clothes that he had hidden under the load of cotton. His brother Edward returned home with the empty wagon.

I am sure that his plan had been discussed earlier with his father Scippio, whose family consisted of sixteen children — some older than my father (brothers Earnest and Arch) and the rest younger; a brood born of three wives. [No one in my family ever mentioned how my grandfather received his name. Scippio or "Scipio" is a classical name — dating to the Hellenistic and Roman World where Publius Cornelius Scipio Africanus (236-184) was hailed as the greatest Roman general.]

Figure 2.   Childhood in Hamlet

My father's plan had been to return home once he had completed his education and assist his father in managing his 1,000-acre farm. However, before his schooling was completed, his father, who was not yet fifty, dropped dead of a heart attack, resulting in the loss of the family farm. Scippio Douglas left behind a widowed wife and a house full of children. The year was 1919.

It then became the responsibility of my father and his older siblings to help raise their younger siblings. He assumed leadership of his family; yet, he also continued his schooling and succeeded in attaining his college degree. Eventually, he earned his master's degree in education.

It was in 1924 that my mother and father discovered their love for each other. My mother, Inez Theresa Highland, was born in 1900. She lost her mother, Ethel, as a teenager in 1914. After assisting her father in caring for her younger siblings, she attended a boarding high school — Browning Home Academy in Camden, South Carolina — from which she graduated in June of 1924 in a class of nineteen students. She was twenty-four years old.

My father was more than six feet tall, slender in build and dark brown in color. My mother was just the opposite — very short (less than five feet tall), light skinned and attractive. Striking mixed-gray hair was her trademark; at middle age it became much grayer. My father was a music lover who enjoyed singing; my mother loved to read and was a student of geography.

Over the objection of my mother's father, Thomas Highland, she and my father were secretly married on February 1, 1925. It was not until after his death later that year that they began to live together as husband and wife. A marriage that began secretly was to last 56 years, produce three children and end with the death of my father on January 11, 1981. My mother died two years later — in the very same month that my father had passed — on January 2, 1983.

My parents moved north to Hamlet after Thomas Highland died, bringing along a handful of their nearly adult-aged siblings, who lived with them for several years before dispersing: my mother's brothers Richard and Henry moved to Pinehurst and Rockingham, North Carolina; not far away; her two sisters, Alonia and Mary, moved to Newark, New Jersey; my father's brother James to Newport News, Virginia, where he joined two of his older brothers already living there. My mother's brother Cottingham died as a young adult, while living with her and my father.

My parents started their own family in Hamlet, which consisted of my older brother Frederick, Jr. — three years older than me; and my younger sister, Shirley, born prematurely sixteen months after me. I was born August 22, 1933.

We lived in a T-shaped, three-bedroom clapboard house at 308 Monroe Avenue, a street three blocks long, in the more prominent part of Hamlet's black community. We had no indoor plumbing until the early 1940s, when my daddy remodeled our home, adding a bedroom as well as modern plumbing. We lived there until he built a new home next door following the war.

Our street dead-ended into a large field adjacent to our house that lay fallow for years. It was a favorite site for flying our homemade kites and playing all sorts of games, including baseball — and where a homemade hoop was rigged to play basketball. Later, on this open space would be built a senior high school for black students. When Hamlet's schools were integrated, it became the site of the junior high school that served our side of town.

My father owned a Model A Ford — later replaced by a Pontiac, and then by several Ford models in later years. My father was not a good driver, but tended to avoid accidents. While driving, it seemed that he was not always alert to his surroundings — road bumps and such — which made riding with him something of an adventure. When I became old enough to drive, I always drove my dad when we went places together. As children, we rode with him sparingly; mostly to church at Saint Peters Methodist church each Sunday.

Also, several times a year on Sundays and holidays we visited our mom's grandmother and other relatives who lived in Laurinburg, North Carolina, some fifteen miles away; as well as her brother Richard and his family who lived in Pinehurst, North Carolina, her brother Henry and his family in Rockingham; and our dad's relatives who lived near the Wire Road in South Carolina. Other than church and these occasional family trips, we rarely rode in his car. We walked most places we went, including trips downtown — a mile away — and to the schools we attended, which were close. As we grew older, many of these meandering trips were made on our bicycles.

At Saint Peter's Methodist church, my father sang in the church choir while my mother sat near the front in the center section with my sister Shirley — always keeping an eye on Fred, Jr. and me in our pew, which was adjacent to a window near the right rear of the sanctuary. Church attendance was a ritual most families like ours followed. It included Sunday school, occasional church skits at Christmas and Easter time, and the annual vacation Bible School.

Everyone called my daddy "Fess" — short for professor — as he was principal of the East Hamlet Elementary School across town, some two miles from our home. He possessed a rangy gait and elegant stature. He was a gifted educator who took time with people, made personal inquiries about their welfare and assisted any number of them in need.

His penchant for education was apparent in everything he did. It was from him that my brother, sister and I received friendly but pointed lectures about the future he expected of each of us. Assuming we would all grow up to become teachers, he reminded us that an educational specialty like music would always guarantee employment; thus, he encouraged and planned for all of us to take music lessons. I never developed an ear for music while my brother and sister became talented musicians, eventually playing in their respective college bands.

During the time of our births, my mother taught at a nearby country school; but, after bearing the three of us and at the urging of my father, she enrolled full-time at Fayetteville State College (Now Fayetteville State University) to complete her college training — living away from home for nearly two years, while my father cared for us, with the help of his sister Odessa. The custom of the day allowed my mother, who was just a high school graduate, to teach at the rural school, but not in the local schools of Hamlet. Thus, she was motivated to attend college and complete her degree.

Once my mother completed her college training, she joined my father at his school in East Hamlet where she taught fifth grade. They worked together for more than thirty years — retiring in the late 1960s. I have often wondered how difficult the period must have been for the two of them when they were away from each other, while she completed her college work. At the same time I marveled at their strength of mind and determination to make the sacrifices needed to fulfill their personal visions and prepare for successful careers. Years later, my mother also earned her masters' degree in education.

Figure 3.   Early childhood with my brother Freddy (middle), and sister Shirley (right)

My siblings and I all grew up knowing full well who our parents were and that they were held in high regard throughout our community — being acknowledged for their accomplishments by both blacks and whites alike. We knew our family was special and we received recognition and respect because of their accomplishments. Our activities were constantly monitored by the broad community, with feedback given either to us or to our parents anytime we committed mischievous acts or displayed behavior not considered appropriate. Sometimes, this constant community vigil made it difficult for us Douglas kids to grow as normal children — considering the spotlight on us as we grew up in Hamlet, a small town where everyone knew everyone else.

THE CASTE OF COLOR

It seemed that at times, I was particularly singled out as I, like my father, was dark-skinned while my brother Fred, Jr. was much lighter — a male version of my mother. He was also more outgoing than me and seemed favored by all. So was my sister Shirley, who was also fair like my mother.

It seemed that as folks observed me in family settings, their non-verbal language depicted a notably different perspective of me because of my skin color. I felt that some pitted me against everyone else as the "black sheep" of my family.

Perhaps it was my skin color that caused some town's people to think that nothing good might come of me. Skin color was often mentioned when ascribing competency to individuals when I was growing up. Skin color and hair were often used to describe individuals and its use was well understood among blacks. I learned early that blacks assigned each other an "acceptance quotient" based on skin color, hair texture and facial features. And the lighter the skin, the straighter the hair, the keener the features — and the more closely a black person's features resembled those of whites — the higher he or she "ranked" among other blacks. Long and straight hair, for example, scored higher on the acceptance strata than short 'n' nappy hair. And lighter skin seemed to make a person inherently more beautiful and acceptable.

In cultural discussions during my youth, observations about skin color and hair texture were omnipresent and undergirded an informal ranking system that measured the attractiveness of individuals — in many instances influencing one's choice of life mate. Indeed, a preferred mate for a dark-skinned person was one with lighter-colored skin so that their children would be endowed with lighter skin color. And above all, hair texture seemed preeminent, or unsurpassed as a personal trait.

Since these topics were often mentioned in family and social settings, I began to understand the parameters of hair and skin color, and much more. At the same time, I was realizing that the entire South was viewed as inferior by Northerners. Southern whites were often referred to as "rednecks" and their language skills were mocked and ridiculed. The same was true of blacks; Northern blacks viewed themselves as both different and superior to Southern blacks, who were looked upon as possessing a rural, cotton-field mentality.

Yet, what was confusing to me about skin color was the concept that light-skinned blacks were viewed as being superior because of their white blood mixture. This notion contradicted my personal experiences. I had observed that my father, born of uneducated dark-skinned parents — and being himself quite dark — had "boot-strapped" himself from rural farm beginnings to become a successful educator.

"How could that be, if skin color drove achievement?" I wondered. And, as I grew older I learned of many successful and high achieving dark-skinned blacks, both men and women, including Paul Lawrence Dunbar, Mary McLeod Bethune, Roland Hayes, A. Philip Randolph and Paul Roberson. Indeed, the list of successful dark-skinned blacks was almost endless.

So despite the mocking that I received from time to time, I began to conclude that success rewarded individuals who had the zeal and determination to make something of themselves. And while I did not know who or what I might become, I began to inculcate a determination that I would "become somebody" despite my darker skin color.

To do so, I had to overcome an admonition given to my parents by my eleventh grade teacher, Mrs. Emma Chapman, who flatly told my parents "Walter is not college material." Mrs. Chapman was an uptight, humorless older woman I would have called a "biddy" back then. She might have disliked me because she was a neighbor of ours who knew I shook the pear tree of her mother, Mrs. Hillman, each year to knock down loose pears! I became determined to prove that Mrs. Chapman's conclusion was wrong, and that my darker skin would not hinder the life choices I would pursue.

SEPARATE AND UNEQUAL IN HAMLET

However, the difficulties I encountered over race were reinforced beyond my home and community. Hamlet had a thriving downtown, a public library, hotels, restaurants, all denominations of Christian churches, department stores, a YMCA, a hospital, a bakery, an ice cream factory, a Coca-Cola Bottling Company, a dairy, an opera house, banks, a jewelry store, and by 1940 a population of more than 5,000 people.

But blacks and whites functioned in separate societies. There were two Hamlets: the white Hamlet, with its all-white schools, churches, paved streets, sidewalks and many homes with indoor plumbing; and the black Hamlet, with all-black schools and church-es; mostly dirt roads; very little indoor plumbing and few viable business entities.

Railroad salaries for blacks and whites outstripped those of any other industry in the area — especially the low salaries paid to textile workers in the Rockingham mills, some six miles away. Unfortunate-ly, the town's leadership resisted the invitation of businesses desirous of locating their plant facilities near the railroad lines in Hamlet. In an amazing display of the short-sightedness racism produced, they feared the positive impact new business might have on local wages paid to black employees. No one at the time envisioned the effect those narrow-minded decisions would have on the town's economy once the railroad monopoly was weakened by the arrival of the Interstate Highway system and jet aircraft travel — a reality that hit Hamlet by the early 1960s.

Like most southern communities during the segregation era, Ham-let was not without hostile incidents involving racial transgressions. One

I remember vividly: one Sunday morning at our church a deacon rose and asked that "we all pray for the Lee boy" — a young man accused of rape and subsequently put to death in the electric chair. In stark contrast, his brother Kenneth later became the first black student to enter and successfully graduate from the University of North Carolina Law School.

The harsh racial environment of those years prompted my parents to maintain close vigil over my brother, my sister and me. We knew whites but generally kept our distance. Whites closest to our home were the Hicks family, who lived two blocks away. Their father was a police officer who eventually became Hamlet's Chief of Police. Billy Hicks — the younger of the two boys — and I grew up together. He and I played together many times as children; and, during my years in Hamlet, he and I always acknowledged each other in passing and maintained a cordial relationship toward each other. Years later, Billy was killed in a train accident while attempting to stop a runaway train from the roundhouse in Hamlet.

Yet, ways were found to accommodate special situations, such as the 1901 visit by Washington. Another such incident occurred while I was in high school. It involved a concert arranged to host the great opera singer Roland Hayes, who was to visit Hamlet and perform at the recently rebuilt Capitol Highway High School. (The older Rosenwald High School caught fire in August 1940, and burned to the ground because there was no fire hydrant close by. We all attended school in half-day shifts until the new high school was completed.)

Our neighbor, Mrs. Florence Smith, was a soloist who arranged for the visit of Hayes, an accomplished, world-renowned tenor who was probably that era's most revered black performer, next to Paul Robeson and Marian Anderson.

Many in Hamlet's white community appreciated his singing talent and wanted to attend his performance. But Jim Crow created a problem with venue and protocol. Whites and blacks could not, in the segregated 1940s south, simply attend a concert together.

The solution? A rope that divided the auditorium. Whites sat on one side of the rope and blacks sat on the other side — in this instance, separate but equal.

HOW MY FATHER HANDLED RACISM

In the midst of the racially tinged environment in which I grew up, my father enforced an abiding principle. He would not allow my brother Fred, my sister Shirley or me to work for white people, or outside our hone. I believe he wanted us to grow up without experiencing situations or incidents that could turn dangerous or abusive.

He certainly believed in us working; he demonstrated it by purchasing a farm where Fred Jr., and I toiled during summer vacations and after school. My father had other chores for us, as well. During the summers of 1945 and 1946, he rented a block-making machine and then charged my brother Fred and I with the task of hand-making the three thousand blocks necessary for the new home he was planning to build next door. By hand, we mixed the cement and sand to make the mortar — while simultaneously digging the basement of our potential new home. Years after, as I looked at the completed home, I always marveled at our effort to make the three thousand brick-emboss-faced cement blocks that created our new home. That endeavor taught me to appreciate the value of hard work, and the tangible rewards that one can enjoy as a result.

Work set the backdrop, however, for an encounter that my dad had with his boss — the white superintendent of Hamlet's school system. In those days, Hamlet's schools used coal to heat the buildings and purchased it by the rail carload. The carload was bought and placed on a side rail. The school district was then responsible for unloading the coal and transporting it, using their own truck to deliver the coal to the various schools.

The superintendent H. M. Kyzer asked my father if my brother and I could do the job of unloading the coal from the railroad car and delivering it to the local schools.

"No," my father said. "My sons are busy. They already have their own chores to do."

That we did. My dad had purchased the farm to occupy our summers, and we were making cement blocks — both alternatives to running the streets. We had meaningful work: chopping cotton and corn, plowing, taking care of livestock, slopping our hogs and doing other farm chores. I learned a lot about being a farmer and about handling livestock.

Besides the hogs we raised out in the field away from our home, we kept a horse and cow in a barn in back of our home, which was at the edge of town. After staking the cow where she could graze all day, on many mornings, I would ride the horse out to the farm — about two miles away, where the gentleman my father hired to plow the planted fields would meet me. My father then picked me up and drove me home so I could go to school. The reverse was true after school, where my father drove me to the farm so I could ride the horse back to our home. The system he devised worked, and it didn't provide any time for any of us to work for whites. Of course, this all occurred — in addition to the school bus route I drove — once I got my driver's license. I was approved for the license at age fifteen; I lied about my age — with my father's approval.

A Lesson on Assuming Responsibility

During my junior year in high school, my father taught me a valuable lesson about assuming responsibility for one's actions.

It was inspired by an incident in shop class one afternoon at my high school. Our shop instructor, Mr. R. L. Jones, had been excused by our school's principal, Mr. J. W. Mask, to handle a personal matter.

As would happen, the Hamlet Superintendent Kyzer visited our shop class and noted the class was unsupervised. What seemed to make the matter worse was a boisterous group of students who were playing cards. Kyzer asked where our shop instructor was. Someone responded that we did not know where he was. Kyzer immediately went to Mask's office and raised the issue of us playing cards and not being supervised.

Shortly, I was summoned to the principal's office. Mask and Kyzer asked me to sit down. They grilled me for the names of all the students in my shop class who were playing cards. At first, I was coy, but then began to list the names of the boys who were playing cards. I had not been playing cards; however, I had been an observer. Mr. Mask expelled all of us from school for two days.

Walter E. Douglas
Craft Club, 1,2,3
Crown & Scepter Club,3,4
Y-Teen, 4
Dramatics, 3
Math Club, 4

Figure 4. *From the Capitol Highway High School yearbook, 1950*

I was devastated, having never been involved in such an incident. I also felt rotten, having ratted on my classmates. No one said anything to me as school was dismissed. Upon arriving home, I said nothing to my parents.

The next morning when it was time to leave for school, my mother inquired, "Walter when are you leaving for school?"

"I don't have to go," I remarked, "I was expelled yesterday."

My father then intervened, revealing that he knew all about my expulsion, for he had been told by several students who rode the school bus to his school in East Hamlet, close to where many of them lived. "Walter has been expelled with several of his classmates for playing cards," they reported to my dad.

Incensed, my father visited both Superintendent Kyzer's office and principal Mask's home, which was near our home. His position was that since we were unsupervised, why were we being punished? Neither gave him an acceptable answer.

I listened to my father rant and rave, but he never criticized me. That surprised me, because I had feared I was in big trouble. Never uttering a harsh word, he told me that Mr. Mask was wrong to have expelled us and was only placating the white superintendent, rather than acknowledging his role in the incident. My father believed that Mask should have taken responsibility for the incident — because it was he who had allowed our teacher, Mr. Jones, to be away from his class — thereby permitting his class to be unsupervised.

We all served our two-day expulsion from school and returned, never hearing a word about the incident.

This situation was one of the proudest moments I ever had regarding my father's judgment. Moreover, it taught me an important lesson about accepting responsibility for one's actions, rather than blaming others. It became a lesson about integrity that I have never forgotten.

Even with my varied experiences, my high school years had not been the equal of my brother Freddy's. I was an average student and did not graduate valedictorian of my high school class as he had. I was just poking along, doing my thing at my pace. I was a day-dreamer, absorbed in my own private world. Perhaps Mrs. Emma Chapman's comments actually did me some good; for as I went off to college, I knew that I had to figure some things out for myself. The older I became, the more aware I was becoming of my innate strengths and abilities. But I had yet to discover my true identity. That still needed to happen.

CHAPTER 3

COLLEGE AND THE ARMY

A Kid Goes to College and Grows Up

I left home for North Carolina College at Durham (now North Carolina Central University) on the Sunday following Labor Day in 1950. Four of my high school classmates were headed to NCC along with me — my friend Calvin Adams, Gloria Ledbetter, Herdasine Duncan and Pearline Briley. Herdasine was driven to Durham by her older sister and her husband, Robert Edwards, who as a returning veteran was completing his degree at NCC. I do not know how Pearline got to Durham.

Calvin, Gloria and I left together from the Queen City Bus Terminal in Hamlet. I remember feeling somber but did not have the sickening feeling I had earlier in the summer when I left to spend the summer with Calvin and his folks in Lakeland, Md., where I worked for the summer. Calvin's family had relocated from Joe's Creek, a rural community just south of Hamlet, and Calvin had remained behind to complete high school. Thus, Calvin, who had become a friend, had invited me to accompany him to his new home for the summer.

The summer trip had been my first extended stay away from home and I became quite homesick. I had been excited to go, but hated my decision once I was in Maryland — and could hardly wait to return to Hamlet. Calvin and I returned from Maryland in late

August and he stayed with us until it was time to leave for college.

As I pondered my departure for college, I somehow felt different. I did not wonder much about it, nor did I feel fearful at all about leaving for college.

My father drove Calvin and me to the bus station where we met Gloria. I recall that I was thankful he had decided not to drive us to Durham, for that surely would have been an adventure, with all of us and our luggage in our 1940 two-door Ford. I also recall that my mother was crying when we left for the bus station. In addition, Mrs. Flora Mask — our neighbor across the street who had terminal cancer — was being driven to the hospital. She, the mother of our high school principal, always liked me and stopped to say goodbye to me. She had been my seventh grade teacher and taught me South American geography — where I first learned of the mighty Amazon River. I never saw her again, because she died just days later.

The bus left at two-thirty in the afternoon and put us in Durham around five o'clock. Gloria, Calvin and I had been instructed to hail a taxi once we arrived that would take us to the campus. We had been given a few dollars of spending change, but our tuition had not been entrusted with us. It had been given to my brother Freddy who would come to Durham a day later. He had all the tuition money for the three of us. Freddy was a senior at NCC and would graduate the following June.

We did as we had been instructed and asked the taxi driver to take us to North Carolina College. He loaded our luggage into the trunk of his taxi — all of it fitting inside — my footlocker, along with Gloria and Calvin's suitcases. I held my typewriter on my lap.

He seemed to know exactly where he was going. First, he took Gloria to Annie Day Shepard Dormitory — the freshmen dormitory for girls; then he took Calvin and me to McLean Hall — the men's dormitory. Calvin and I became roommates in room "311" where we were joined by Frederick Wilkins of Spring Hope and Thaddeus Beasley from Elizabeth City — both eastern North Carolina towns. Beasley was a football player, and had arrived days earlier to join the team's training regimen. Wilkins walked in after Calvin and I had arrived and settled in.

Figure 5. (L-R) My friend Calvin, my sister Shirley and me with my family's 1949 Ford, in front of our home in Hamlet

We were now ensconced and ready to begin freshmen orientation, which included taking placement tests for English and math. I passed both — as did Calvin and Gloria.

Freddy arrived late Monday and stopped by our room with one of his Omega Psi Phi fraternity brothers Preston Diggs, whom I knew all about from discussions that Freddy and I had had during his visits home.

As I observed, the two of them seemed on equal footing — neither seeming to have an upper hand on the other. I observed them closely. Preston, like my brother, was handsome and popular, as was Freddy. As I listened to them banter, both seemed to know all the right people; later, I noted that they were always surrounded by pretty girls, or connected classmates. Preston eventually married Thelma Gordet — one of the most beautiful women I ever knew — and settled in Washington, D.C..

Thus, as a college freshman, I made it my goal to emulate Freddy and his fraternity brothers. My goal was to become my brother's equal in the minds of those I would eventually meet — especially those who would get to know me as they knew Freddy. I started with a fierce determination to equal or excel beyond his achievements at NCC. Interestingly, I had never thought to compare myself to Freddy while in high school; but here at NCC, I was starting to measure myself against his putative reputation.

North Carolina College at Durham — founded by Dr. James E. Shepard in 1910 — was touted as a liberal arts college and ranked high among historical black institutions. Dr. Shepard passed away in 1947 and had been replaced by Dr. Alfonso Elder. Beginning in January 1948, Dr. Elder, a graying statesman and the institution's second president, served until September 1963, nearly a decade after my graduation.

While addressing our incoming class during freshmen orientation, Dr. Elder made a point of making sure we knew about the large number of PhDs on NCC's faculty — a fact that made him quite proud. He pointed out to us that no matter our choice of major, we could be assured that highly educated faculty would teach us. We students learned early to be proud of NCC's academic ranking amongst historical black institutions. In fact, NCCU is still at or near the top: it ranked number one among state-supported historically black institutions in the nation, according to the 2010 "Best Colleges" list of *U. S. News and World Report* rankings. We also learned that NCC was the first historically black college to receive state funding in the nation.

Our perennially victorious basketball team was coached for years by the legendary John B. McClendon, a student of Dr. James Naismith, the founder of the game. Our football team competed annually for the CIAA (Collegiate Intramural Athletic Association) championship. Our college mascot symbol was an eagle. We described it by asserting that "the eagle is no ordinary barnyard fowl." Back then (as now) we were determined to distinguish NCC from other comparable schools.

My freshman class included Ivan Dixon and Jacquelyn Barnes, actors who became stage and screen performers after graduation; and Charles "Tex" Harrison of Harlem Globe Trotter fame. Many other famous athletes attended NCC during my matriculation, including Earnest Warlick, who became an offensive end for the NFL's Buffalo

Bills; Sam Jones, who starred as a Boston Celtic; and the multiple gold medal-winning Olympic track star Lee Calhoun.

I settled into college life pretty easily, and made lots of friends. Several individuals I met became lifelong friends. They include Nathan Simms of Winston Salem, North Carolina; Hebrew Dixon of Enfield, North Carolina; and Raymond Bell of Evanston, Illinois. We all graduated and remained in close touch for most of our professional careers. For years we continued to see each other from time to time, especially during class reunions. Nathan eventually earned his PhD from Lehigh University in Bethlehem, Pennsylvania, and worked at several universities, including A & T University in Greensboro, North Carolina, before joining the University of North Carolina Higher Education System. Ray Bell became an engineer, while Hebrew became a computer programmer at Wright Patterson Air Force Base in Dayton, Ohio. Hebrew, a relentless smoker, died in the early 1990s of lung cancer.

NCC seemed to lack the cliquish social circles and biased admission policies reported and rumored to plague many other historic black colleges and universities.

Perhaps because NCC was a state supported institution, enrollment appeared open to all who could afford to attend and work-study arrangements were made to assist others. My freshman class numbered just over 300, including a rich mixture of students from the many small cities and towns within the state, like Hamlet. Others came from New York City, Chicago, Washington, D.C., and Philadelphia; and from many small towns in Florida, Georgia, Indiana, New Jersey, South Carolina, Tennessee and Virginia.

The 1950s were a watershed era that followed the end of World War II. It produced prosperity that began to improve the economic conditions among blacks, making it possible for many more youngsters to attend college. In addition, the GI Bill helped by providing benefits to returning veterans. As a result, my freshman class became NCC's largest incoming class to that point in its history. And the composition of our class showcased a wider age-range and richer hue of colors.

This larger and more diverse freshman class would eventually affect some of the standing traditions at NCC, which not unlike those at other black college institutions tended to favor light-skinned individuals. Some of these traditions were especially pervasive among the membership of the more elite Greek organizations. Happily, during my tenure at NCC, all of the Greek organizations began to represent the diversity of our growing student body. In short, it became rare that any student at NCC ever felt left out of activities he or she desired to participate in during the years I attended. Indeed, our class elected Gail Mack, a dark-skinned, beautiful girl as Miss Homecoming during our sophomore year — breaking a longstanding tradition that had preferred light-skinned homecoming queens.

Before arriving at NCC, I had decided to major in business administration. The notion of becoming a business major began to intrigue me one day following a conversation between my father and a farm laborer.

"Fess," the man asked, "do you know what Walter is going to do when he grows up?"

My dad answered, "Oh, I don't know. He's probably going to major in business or something like that."

That conversation stuck in my mind and seemed to resonate with my innate thoughts, which were suggesting to me that I should consider something different from the careers my parents had chosen. Growing up, I never wanted to become a teacher. While I was in high school I learned to type and became a proficient typist, easily able to type 100 words a minute.

Having decided on a business major, and determined to match my brother's accomplishments, I began to settle into college life pretty easily. Following his lead, I pledged the Omega Psi Phi fraternity during my sophomore year in February 1952, becoming its youngest member at the time. Also, I did well in my classes, worked in the dining hall as a dish washer and busboy, and eventually obtained a job in the college bookstore. My parents had not insisted that I work and continued to pay my college expenses; however, working was my own choice, and provided extra spending money.

In general, I enjoyed college life, and felt protected as a student from the harsh race relations that troubled the broader society outside the college campus.

During my college years, racial segregation remained widespread throughout the South. Segregation permeated every aspect of life. It was especially manifest in the condescending demeanor that whites tended to inflict upon blacks in every imaginable circumstance. For example, whites intentionally demeaned adult blacks by referring to them as *boy* or *girl;* and occasionally used the "N" word — nigger. This reinforced the clear determination of most whites to "keep us in our place" — a never-ending effort we blacks knew all too well.

My first experience of integration followed my sophomore year, when I boarded a Greyhound bus at the New York City Port Authority. The bus was transporting a group of black college students to Waymont, Penn., where we were to assume summer positions at a Jewish camp called Camp With-A-Wind. We had been brought up from North Carolina and hired as dishwashers and kitchen helpers by the Camp With-A-Wind chef, a black man named Eddie from Long Island, New York.

The bus was fully integrated and I sat near the back alongside two young white women, who chatted with me from time to time. I found their conversations amusing; it was a first for me, as I had not ever conversed with two white females on any subject. Now, on my way to Camp With-A-Wind, I did not know what to expect, but began to assume that I would have many more such conversations during my summer experience. I became intrigued as I anticipated the interracial experiences I might encounter.

This summer job opportunity was typical of the practice by black college-age youngsters who went north in search of summer employment. My father, knowing the black chef for whom I would be working, had encouraged me to pursue this job opportunity.

Riding in the integrated bus was totally new for me, since passengers were segregated on my train ride from North Carolina to New York — and I sat in the "colored" section. Moving from South to North, blacks had to sit in the colored section on trains or buses, even though one could sit in any seat once the Mason-Dixon line was crossed — a creation of surveyors to delineate North from South during slavery. When travel was reversed, moving from North to South, blacks could sit anywhere on public transportation vehicles until the Mason-Dixon Line was reached, then segregation laws and customs were again enforced.

This practice remained in effect until shortly after 1954, when the Warren Court ruled in *Brown vs. the Topeka Kansas Board of Education* that segregation was inherently illegal. This ruling started the slow process "of change," further instigated by the Montgomery Bus Boycott of 1955-56, courageously initiated by Rosa Parks. That boycott preceded the sit-in phenomenon led by black students at A & T University at a lunch counter in Greensboro, NC.

But in 1952, during my summer employment experience in Pennsylvania, integration was limited. While we worked hidden in the kitchen at Camp With-A-Wind, local white youngsters worked as waiters and bus boys and interfaced with the Jewish campers.

However, at this sub-rosa venue away from the institutionalized glare of segregation, relationships formed between us and the local white youngsters. We ate together, played basketball, volleyball and cards, and generally got to know each other fairly well.

And since we were in Pennsylvania, I just assumed the relationships we formed were reflective of the local mores, which were totally different from any experiences I had ever encountered. On one occasion, several of us ventured into town to obtain haircuts administered by the local white barber. We were never sure that he had ever before cut the hair of black individuals; yet, we did not ask. We returned to the camp without incident. I couldn't help but believe that Pennsylvania was quite different from North Carolina. With my summer sojourn to Camp With-A-Wind, I had experienced my first interracial encounters of any note. (At NCC, my music appreciation instructor was white — a Mr. Johns; however, the class was quite large and I had limited contact with him.)

PATRICIA

In the spring of 1951, my roommate, Fred Wilkins, whose home was in Spring Hope, a small town about 20 miles east of Raleigh, North Carolina, invited me and a fellow classmate, Ted Massey, home with him for a weekend. The three of us were to attend the junior/senior prom at his former high school. Fred had even arranged blind dates for Ted and me. Little did I know how my life would change because of the events of that weekend. At one pivotal point in the evening, my blind date and I sneaked out of the dance.

In January of 1952 I received a call from a schoolteacher that I'd met during that weekend in Spring Hope. She said that she wanted to get in touch with my parents for some kind of a survey project. I gave her my father's name, address and telephone number. I found the conversation strange, yet I dismissed the call, hung up the phone and went back upstairs to my dorm room. I reported the telephone call to my roommate, who remarked, "I bet you done gone down there and knocked some girl up."

I paused to reflect on his comment, and then dismissed it. It would be several weeks before I would hear anything else.

I knew nothing further until my mother wrote a letter to me that said, "The baby's fine." I learned later this was a second letter that followed a more detailed letter I never received — one that explained everything that had happened. I never knew whether or not my mother mailed the first letter, as it more than likely included a dressing-down of me for my actions.

I later learned that the Spring Hope teacher had called my father to explain that my blind date, a young lady named Ersell Burgess, had given birth. Hearing of the child, he immediately drove to Spring Home, met the Burgess family and first saw the baby girl.

Before his arrival, Ersell, the baby's mother, had decided to allow a family selected by her aunt Margaret, with whom she resided, to adopt the child. Yet, when my father arrived, he was granted permission to adopt her instead. Somehow, after what I am sure was a lengthy but convincing discussion, the Burgess' gave their consent for my father to take the child with him back to Hamlet. He and my mother immediately assumed total responsibility for raising the newborn. I would later hear from my mother about the appeal that he made: promising to love and care for the newborn and make her a full member of his family. My parents named the child "Patricia Diane," legally adopted her and began raising her in their home, treating her as a sibling to my brother, sister and me.

When I received that "second" letter saying the baby was fine, I didn't know any of the facts that had transpired. I called home and found out in retrospect all that had occurred. Ersell's child was born January 18, 1952. (Coincidentally, January 18th is the birthday of Retha, the woman I was to later marry). Not only was I dumbfounded, I was embarrassed, remorseful and truly regretful of my actions. My father never said anything; however, my mother admonished me about my episode; and, in no uncertain terms lectured me each time I returned home — for the better part of a year. I acknowledged my dalliance and promised that it would never happen again! But it was years before I could outwardly acknowledge or openly discuss my deed with others, and remained sensitive when similar situations were experienced by others as I observed their reactions. However, many years passed before I could discuss my feelings openly.

My parents raised Pat as my little sister, and they took care of everything for her. As soon as she was old enough to understand, she was told I wasn't really her brother, but her biological father. However, because of the parental oversight given by my parents, neither Pat nor I viewed our relationship as anything but brother and sister, for during that period, I was away at school. My father, affectionately called "Fess" by all became her dad and Inez became her mother, parents to her just as they were to Fred, Jr., Shirley and me. Growing up, Pat recognized and loved them as her parents.

Neither Patricia nor I had much of a recurring relationship with Ersell. Ersell graduated high school and completed her college training, later earning a graduate degree in sociology. In the early years, my mother took Patricia to visit the Burgesses, who by then were living in Richmond, Virginia. On occasion, Ersell visited with Patricia and my parents in Hamlet.

Ersell later married, but had no other children. She maintained a relationship with Patricia, continuing to visit her from time to time as she grew up — sometimes while I was present. On those visits when I was present, neither Ersell nor I ever discussed our chance encounter.

As I observed their relationship, Patricia and Ersell never seemed to form a mother-daughter relationship; yet, they were both respectful of each other. Ersell seemed to understand that Patricia always considered her parents to be "Fred and Inez." Ersell passed away in 2008.

In recent years, especially since the death of my parents, Patricia and I have formed a father-daughter relationship. Her two children, Morgan and John Tyler, call me "Granddad." Also, Pat's husband, Arnold, and I get along quite well.

FATHERHOOD INSPIRES PERSONAL CHANGE

Recognizing that one reckless night had changed my life forever, I began to focus more intently on my lifestyle — how and what I did — and began to make life choices much more carefully. I became determined that reckless encounters would never again be a part of my lifestyle.

During this time I began to understand I would have to keep on the straight and narrow if I planned on building a successful life. It is here, I think, that I began to exercise leadership. I stepped forward and was elected vice-president of my junior class. I later held an elective office in my fraternity. I also exhibited leadership is other ways as well, particularly with my academic performance. I set a standard in accounting at the business school at North Carolina College, thereby encouraging competition among my classmates and me while establishing a high performance curve for us all.

As a student, I always felt that college was about academic learning, which I considered the most important prerequisite for leadership. Beyond the elective offices I mentioned above, I focused on academics and gave little thought to other forms of campus leadership.

I never considered myself a person who was eager to speak publicly, or one anxious to pursue campus leadership roles. Yet, I instinctively knew that public speaking was a prerequisite skill that I needed to develop to succeed in life. Often, though, I felt the ability to speak in public was not an indication of leadership, even though our society seems to value it so highly. Knowing this, I became determined to overcome my introverted nature and at least develop the fundamentals needed to make cogent statements in public or in group discussions.

I began to develop my premises about speaking ability and formed a number of conclusions. I concluded that the ability to speak articulately in public was an enviable trait that reaped rewards to those possessing such skills. Then, I observed that exceptional verbal skills often afforded leadership opportunities to anyone who possessed them.

But my over-arching conclusion was that content was more important than delivery style. Therefore, to increase my level of confidence, I learned to write out the content of comments I anticipated making, therefore giving me more confidence when I needed to speak in group settings.

As I applied these premises to my daily life and campus experiences, I began to build more confidence in my speaking ability. As a result, my class and campus experiences began to reflect this greater level of self-assuredness.

By my junior year, I had taken most of the required "core-curriculum" courses at NCC, which included English composition and literature; general biology; French; psychology; art and music appreciation. These courses made me a better-rounded individual. I was beginning to feel more prepared for the course work I would have to take in the business curriculum.

At NCC, business administration was referred to as "Commerce," which consisted of typing, shorthand, business law and an introductory course in accounting. NCC's business curriculum had been designed to prepare students for the limited employment opportunities that existed for them in the business world during the 1950s. At the time, most students majoring in commerce eventually wound up relocating to Washington, D.C. where they pursued employment with the federal government or U. S. Postal Service. Few opportunities existed for black business students to gain employment entry into the private sector.

But as I pondered my future prior to graduation, I was determined not to wind up as had many NCC graduates before me, becoming government clerks, postal workers, or, worst of all — using their business curriculum skills to teach high school courses.

I wanted to do something more. Indeed, some of my earliest visions of careers were of me sitting *behind* a desk, performing important duties, rather than sitting *in front of* a desk, taking directions from a superior. As I matured, these visions seemed to preordain my future.

Once I began the business portion of my college curriculum, which included courses in principles of business, business law, and introductory accounting, vistas began opening to me. They provided me a greater understanding of mundane business jargon, familiarizing me with terms like debits and credits and the purposes they served in measuring business performance. Before, I had often wondered how businesses made money, particularly banks. How did they earn profits? How did they pay interest on savings accounts? It just seemed impossible that banks could ever generate enough interest to be profitable. At the time, I knew nothing of the Federal Reserve System and had not begun to understand the scale of banking or the American economy. Once I began to sense the scale of the American economy, I was hooked on business and commerce.

During library visits, I read *Fortune* magazine and other business publications. These articles fascinated me and gave me a broader understanding of the world of business. One *Fortune* article I read dealt with the Ford Motor Company and its turnaround following the introduction of the 1949 Ford. It detailed the efforts of Henry Ford II and Ernie Breech, Ford's Executive Vice President and General Manager, to cut costs and return the company to profitability. In a twist of fate or providence, I later had the privilege of serving on the Henry Ford Hospital's holding company board. In January 1987, at my first meeting of the board, I had the honor of actually hearing this story first-hand from Henry Ford II himself — with Ernie Breech's son, Bill, in attendance — during a private dinner in Palm Beach, Florida.

North Carolina College did not offer an accounting major when I arrived, but upon my urging and the encouragement of some of my classmates, an accounting major was introduced at the start of our senior year. This required those of us interested in an accounting major to double our course load if we were to graduate with our class the following June.

Working with Dr. Lincoln J. Harrison, our class advisor, the curriculum was established. My classmates and I completed the additional coursework and graduated on time. Dr. Harrison was the first Certified Public Accountant (CPA) of any race that I had ever met. His being black made a profound impact on my classmates and me and created in us the desire to become certified. He believed in us and guided us through the difficult task of mastering the additional course work, nearly doubling our senior year class load. We all did very well, and I became the "poster boy" of our class, mastering the challenging curriculum with proficiency and flair.

Dr. Harrison was quite proud of this first class, and of me in particular. He said as much to my mother during graduation and years later, gave me high recommendations as I was considered for teaching positions at Edward Waters College in Jacksonville, Florida, and Tuskegee Institute in Alabama.

Upon my graduation in June 1954, and with the encouragement of my father, I returned to NCC to pursue a graduate degree in business administration. My brother Freddy had also returned to graduate school after his graduation in 1951; however, before completing his work, he was drafted into the U. S. Army and sent to Korea.

I chose NCC because the practice of segregation precluded me from enrolling at the University of North Carolina at Chapel Hill; Duke University, which was just across town from NCC; or any of the other North Carolina universities at the time. Though I could enroll in any one of several northern universities where blacks were more readily accepted, and receive reimbursement from the North Carolina Department of Education, I chose not to pursue that option for my graduate studies. One reason, perhaps, was that I was not quite sure I could compete with what I assumed were better educated students I would encounter at the prestigious northern schools. Another may have been my ingrained attitudes about race and feelings of inadequacy. Yet, I now know — considering how I have since faired when thrust into such unfamiliar settings — my success as a graduate student at a northern university would not have been in question.

As a graduate student at NCC, I learned that in order to provide the depth of expertise in the various graduate course offerings, the graduate faculty at NCC was supplemented with faculty from UNC Chapel Hill. For example, my economics and tax professors were both from UNC Chapel Hill, and they were excellent instructors. As we reviewed examples of current business trends, I enjoyed our many class discussions and through them felt more connected to the world of commerce.

I recall presenting a report to my graduate class on the 1954 revisions to the U.S. Tax Code, which Congress had just passed. I sensed at the time that my report was well received by my professor. I was to hear years later from Dr. Stuart Fulbright, my graduate faculty advisor that the "imported instructors" often asked about me, as they had been impressed with the breadth of my understanding of business principles and their applications.

In June 1955, I graduated with honors, having completed all of my course work, including the writing of my thesis. Though I was not allowed to attend Duke University, I was granted permission to utilize the Duke library to complete the work on my thesis, entitled "A Comparison Study of State Income Tax Systems in the United States." I chose the subject because of my interest in taxes, not knowing at the time that I would eventually work for the IRS.

DATING

I dated a number of girls during college. I never considered myself a playboy. However, I looked and chose from the variety of attractive ladies who stood out on campus. During our freshman year, my high school friend Calvin and I dated roommates for a short time. The young lady I dated was named Evelyn Mason and Calvin dated Luticia Thompson. An incident quickly terminated these relationships. Somehow, the two of them agreed to do Calvin's and my laundry. We brought over our shirts, which they laundered, ironed and folded neatly. However, once their laundering tasks were discovered by girls who observed them in their dormitory, they were told in no uncertain terms that "doing your fellow's laundry" was totally unacceptable. Calvin and I moved on.

As a sophomore, I dated an attractive girl from Wagram, North Carolina, who had attended Mary Potter, a boarding high school near Henderson, North Carolina. We dated for some time and saw a lot of each other. I began to sense that Delores seemed a lot more interested in me than I was in her, and that she was more serious about a future together than I was. Eventually, she asked if we could get married. I was floored and initially responded with a weak "yes" — knowing full well that I had no intentions of getting married. It seemed that Delores was a lot more interested in snagging a man than securing an education.

As matters turned out, at year's end, Delores fell ill and had to skip the fall semester. She did not return until the following January. By then, I had decided to move on, yet Delores continued to target me. Upon her return, she no longer lived in the dormitory, but off-campus with her grandmother. She called constantly, attempting to inveigle me into coming over, particularly during times when her grandmother was away on shopping trips. Having learned my lesson earlier, I refused her invitations. At the end of that semester, Delores left NCC and I was never to see her again.

Another classmate I enjoyed dating for an extended period was Bernice Jordan, from Seaboard, North Carolina. Bern was popular, attractive, and an active member of the Alpha Kappa Alpha (AKA) Sorority. One highlight of our time together was meeting in New York during the summer between our junior and senior years to attend my fraternity's annual boat ride. This popular annual event attracted college students from up and down the East Coast. Being seen at the "Q's" boat ride in Harlem gave one bragging rights upon returning to college in the fall. We had fun and continued to date during our senior year, but for whatever reason, our relationship did not fully blossom.

Retha

I began to date my beloved wife, Retha, in the fall of 1954. She and I had met earlier when she was a sophomore and I was a senior working part time in the college bookstore. She was very attractive, thin and shapely — named *"Miss Fine-Brown-Frame"* in high school. She seemed to have a business head, as she worked for the Campus Echo, the student newspaper. I liked her right away. However, we didn't date until after I returned to graduate school the following year. As I entered graduate school, Retha was beginning her junior year. She was popular with her classmates and that year joined the Delta Sigma Theta Sorority.

Our first date took place at a Halloween party in the basement of her dormitory — Rush Hall. Nothing had been prearranged. I was there with several of my male friends. I just asked her to dance, and as they say, the rest is history.

At first, my parents didn't seem to understand my seriousness about Retha, even though I had invited her to Hamlet during Easter break of my graduate year. Later in June, she stayed beyond the end of the school year to attend my graduation. My parents seemed not to consider her staying over for my graduation to be a significant event; or if they did, they discounted the strong interest Retha and I showed for each other.

After graduation, my parents decided to give me a party at home in Hamlet. I went to Fayetteville to pick Retha up and when we arrived in Hamlet, I learned that my parents had invited a former hometown girlfriend whom I had dated for several years. When Retha and I arrived, there was Ethel Mae James, my high school girlfriend, standing in the living room, waiting for me. What an awkward moment! However, it helped my parents finally understand how special Retha was to me.

Before I left NCC at the completion of my graduate studies, Retha and I had agreed to marry. However, we did not announce our intentions at that time. I told her all about Patricia. She was very understanding.

EDWARD WATERS AME JUNIOR COLLEGE

After graduate school, and upon the recommendation of my accounting professor, Dr. Harrison, I accepted a position at Edward Waters African Methodist Episcopal (AME) Junior College in

Jacksonville, Florida. While teaching was not a profession in which I had ever expressed a strong interest, I accepted the position as needing something to do. Rightfully so, considering I was unemployed. The position paid $2,900 for the school year.

In early September 1955, my brother Freddy, his "current" girlfriend Evelyn, my sister Shirley and Retha drove me to Jacksonville. We left late one evening, drove all night and arrived early the next morning. I was deposited at Edward Waters and they returned immediately to North Carolina — without rest or sleep — leaving me to begin my life as a college instructor. Such travel arrangements were typical during the 1950s; there were few accommodations throughout the South where blacks could stay.

Edward Waters provided housing for several of its employees close to the campus in homes owned by the college. The homes were not in great repair, yet they were adequate — and cheap. I lived next door to two women employed by the college: Betty Stewart, the president's secretary, who had a young child named David; and Ethel Richardson, the college's nurse who also taught health subjects. I shared a two-bedroom house with another faculty member, Paul Driver, the science teacher at the college. Paul was from Butte, Montana, and annually drove across country from Jacksonville to his home in Butte.

Over time, I became close friends with the ladies next door, sharing meals with them and watching their TV, as Paul and I did not own one — and TV ownership was somewhat rare at the time. While visiting next door, I soon met Albert Dunmore, a friend of Betty Stewart and the Florida Editor of *The Pittsburgh Courier*, a popular black newspaper at the time. Al and I would later reconnect once I moved to Detroit. I recall helping Al complete his tax return once he found out I was an accounting major and familiar with federal income taxes.

On my first day at Edward Waters, I was assigned non-teaching duties about which I knew little, if anything. It began when Dr. James Espy, the academic dean, looked at me and said, "Walter, I want you to handle our public relations work." I had gone there to teach business courses and knew absolutely nothing about public relations. I took a deep breath and decided that if Dr. Espy thinks I can handle such responsibilities, then I can! I accepted the challenge.

The daily newspaper in Jacksonville was *The Jacksonville Times*. In back of its headquarters building was an office about a third of the size of a standard office. The office contained three desks — all pressed in together — and it was through this small office that blacks in Jacksonville gained entry to the *Jacksonville Times* for news stories pertinent to African Americans. One page of *The Jacksonville Times* was devoted to "black" news. In order to get an item published, it was necessary to meet the paper's black editor there in that little office, who would then decide whether or not your story was newsworthy.

I quickly learned his preference was to have stories presented that were ready for publication. Armed with that knowledge, I was equipped to function as Public Relations Director for the college. I also took on the role of announcer at school sporting events, and helped build the parade floats for the homecoming parade.

Shortly after receiving my first paycheck from Edward Waters, I began prowling the used car lots in downtown Jacksonville. With no established credit, I purchased a blue, 1950 two-door Plymouth Coupe for $300, which I financed with a loan from the used car dealer. I soon learned why the vehicle was so cheap: its engine was completely shot. The proprietor then sold me a "rebuilt" engine and added its cost to the balance I owed. I now had reliable transportation, but then discovered that like most cars in Florida back then, the car had no heater — something I definitely felt I would need when I drove back north. I decided to have a heater installed, which I purchased from a local junk yard. Later, my Plymouth's heater would inspire many stories from passengers who endured its discharge directly on their legs because it was mounted under the dash board, quite close to the passenger seat.

Next, I went shopping for an engagement ring, having earlier proposed to Retha. I found a suitable ring (close to a carat), laid it away (a common practice at the time) and made monthly payments to satisfy the balance owed. I planned to complete the purchase in time to present it to Retha upon her graduation the following June.

As I reflect on these early challenges during my first professional position, I conclude that fear of failure was most likely my principal motivation. That early career crucible taught me an important life lesson, which follows me to this day: I never shirked from responsibility because I never wanted to be known as a quitter.

I also learned that, because of my introverted nature, leadership didn't come naturally for me. Being "front and center" was not a natural calling or a comfortable position. But I also learned that few knew me better than I knew myself, and however I chose to present myself was more important than any natural instinct. I was learning how to maximize my innate skills and how to gain favor and results.

In April of my first year at Edward Waters, just as I was getting settled into my first professional position, Dr. Harrison, my accounting professor at NCC, recommended me for a position at Tuskegee Institute in Alabama. The offer was for $3,800 and I would be named head of the college's Business Studies curriculum. I had enjoyed the year at Edward Waters, but was excited to be moving on with a 30 percent raise! When that first year was up, I paid off the balance due on Retha's ring, packed my belongings in back of my blue 1950 Plymouth Coupe, said my good-byes and headed not to Tuskegee, but north to Hamlet.

Once home, I returned to NCC to attend Retha's graduation and present her with the engagement ring I had purchased. I gave her the ring and told her of my new position at Tuskegee. Having made plans of her own, she informed me that she was moving to New York where she would share accommodations with her girlfriend Madelyn.

In New York, she secured a position as the secretary to the manager of the comparison shopping department at Macy's Department Store, earning roughly fifty-five dollars a week. Out of those meager wages, she was able to save a surprisingly large sum of money. I was to find out how thrifty Retha was once we were married. Although we were not able to see each other often, we exchanged love letters. Later that summer, one particular letter I sent her announced a big adjustment in our plans for the future.

My Tuskegee Institute Adventure

Following Retha's graduation and after spending a short stint with my parents in Hamlet, I loaded up my Plymouth Coupe and drove non-stop to Tuskegee to begin my new career as head of the Business Studies curriculum. Upon arriving, I received a standard introduction to my position from Dr. Joseph Fuller, dean of the General Studies Department, who oversaw the Business Studies curriculum. He arranged for me to lunch with Tuskegee's president, Dr. Luther H. Foster, Jr. — a fine gentleman who was both charming and well prepared to lead the institution. The faculty and staff at Tuskegee always spoke glowingly of Dr. Foster and lauded his work ethic, his generosity and his spirit. I did not disagree with their description of him.

(In 2002, Foster was honored by Tuskegee's president Benjamin F. Payton and the Board of Trustees for his foresight, wisdom and service with a dedication and naming of the engineering building launched during his tenure as "Luther H. Foster Hall.")

I then began to teach summer school classes in business law, economics and typing. Little did I know that within weeks I would receive "greetings" from Uncle Sam for my U. S. Army induction.

One of the highlights of my two-months stay at Tuskegee was learning to play chess, a game I quickly mastered and played daily with several professors in Thrasher Hall, where I resided. We played frequently, and surprisingly, I became quite good. Years later, when challenged to a game by my erstwhile idol, Larry Doss, I whipped him soundly — and he never offered to play me again. There was not much else to do in Tuskegee except attend the black-owned local drive-in movie — frequented by blacks and whites alike, but separated by a center divider — maintaining the South's strict policy on segregation.

Tuskegee, a dry county, did not have a liquor store. To purchase beverages, we drove to Opelika, about fifteen miles away. Opelika is the home of Auburn University, which we passed on our way to and from the liquor store. In my mind's eye, I can still see the large banner hanging from one of the men's dormitories, which read "Heartbreak Hotel," reflecting a popular Elvis Presley recording of the time.

I stayed busy in my new position while reorganizing the business studies curriculum. In 1956, it contained modest offerings consisting of typing, shorthand, a course in business law, and a beginning accounting course. Working with the institute's librarian, new books were ordered and a section of research and periodical offerings was established to give business students access to timely materials reflecting current trends in business. The Tuskegee library had contained few business books or reference materials prior to my arrival. I also developed course syllabi for each course offering, as I taught summer school classes. Dr. Fuller seemed quite pleased with my performance and the changes I was making.

Finally, as it neared time for me to report for duty, I began to wrap matters up. I invited my mother and Patricia to visit Tuskegee and accompany me on my trip back to North Carolina. They arrived by train from Hamlet and stayed in Dorothy Hall, an on-campus residence maintained by the college. They enjoyed their stay of several days before we headed back to Hamlet.

As I said my good-byes to all, including Dr. Fuller, I could sense that he was upset that I was departing, having been unable to gain a deferment for me from my impending draft. He gave me his blessings and wished me well, and seemed genuinely sorry to see me leave. He assured me that my position would be available upon the completion of my armed services stint. However, at the time of my discharge, I decided not to return to Tuskegee.

THE UNITED STATES ARMY

Upon returning to Hamlet with my mother and Pat, I sat in idle contemplation for the day or so I had remaining before my induction into the Army. Not needing a car, I allowed my sister Shirley to trade in my 1950 Plymouth for a 1953 Chevrolet Bel-Air that she purchased. On a Tuesday morning in August, I reported to the Army Recruitment Station in Rockingham, North Carolina — the county seat of Richmond County. I left home with other black and white inductees on a segregated bus; ate at a segregated lunch counter en route; then joined an integrated basic training Army unit in Columbia, South Carolina.

We arrived at Fort Jackson, South Carolina. We would begin our basic training on the infamous Tank Hill, where the 3rd U. S. Army trained infantry recruits at that time. However, with Providence prevailing, I was spared the rigors of basic training, except for a few required training exercises.

On my first day after induction, while standing in formation, the company commander asked if anybody could type. I didn't put my hand up, but I whispered to the soldier standing next to me that I could. He immediately shouted out, "Sir, here's a soldier who can type!" The commander called me out of the formation and informed me that I would become the company clerk. Becoming the company clerk allowed me to avoid field training like the other recruits — but I did have to pass the field test for using the M-1 rifle and be certified in Chemical, Biological and Radioactive Materials training — mandatory requirements for all recruits.

Both the barracks and the training cadre of officers were fully integrated. The company commander and first sergeant were both white and I worked directly for the two of them. Our field officer, Staff Sergeant Expose, was black; he was responsible for all field training activities.

I learned to do the morning reports, a daily requirement that had to be sent to Battalion Headquarters. Before my arrival, the reports had been poorly executed and were returned daily for correction. After my arrival, they were accurate and were no longer returned.

The company commander and I got along quite well; so well that he attempted to retain me once basic training concluded. While Fort Jackson was close to my hometown of Hamlet and close to Columbia, South Carolina, where my brother Freddy lived with his wife, Estelle, I declined his offer because I was ready to move on. I envisioned that the U. S. Army would be my ticket to "see the world."

After basic training at Fort Jackson, I was assigned to Fort Belvoir, Virginia, just outside Washington, D.C., receiving a Class-Two assignment for my Military Occupational Specialty (MOS). Because of my college training and advanced degree, the Army had given me a special classification called "Scientific and Professional."

I again became the Company Clerk for my unit at Fort Belvoir, which made liquid oxygen for the Redstone Missile Rocket being deployed in Germany. The plan was for my unit to be deployed there in order to provide the liquid oxygen necessary to fuel the Redstone Rockets. However, after being stationed at Fort Belvoir for ten months, I was given a Class-One assignment for my MOS and transferred to Walter Reed Army Medical Center in Washington, D.C., just fifteen miles away. My notion of "seeing the world" never materialized.

Once I was stationed at Fort Belvoir, Virginia, Retha and I made plans to see each other more often. She came to Washington for a weekend in November of 1956 and I traveled to New York that Christmas. I invited my high school friend, Halbert Jackson, to accompany me as I drove from Hamlet to New York. We arrived early in the morning the day after Christmas. To my surprise, Halbert and Retha's roommate Madelyn hit it off; the visit to New York proved fruitful as all four of us did the town.

I enjoyed Retha's visits to D.C.; we both knew many people from our college days who had moved there after college. On the other hand, I did not like going to New York. As we discussed our future, we agreed that she would move to Washington. After moving in July of 1957, Retha was immediately hired by the National Bureau of Standards and found a room to rent on Franklin Street in Northeast D.C.

CHAPTER 4

WONDERFUL WASHINGTON

FINDING OUR FIRST APARTMENT

Our first home was a third floor furnished apartment at the residence of Dr. Arthur Carr and his wife, Lelia, at 913 S Street N.W. After Retha and I set the date for our October 1957 marriage, I began looking for a place for us to stay. At the time, I was living in the barracks at Walter Reed Army Medical Center. We had no furniture, so I looked for a furnished apartment.

I soon found a listing in *The Washington Post* classified ads for a furnished apartment on "S" Street in Northwest D.C. — an area with which I was familiar. One Saturday in late September, I drove by, surveyed the surrounding neighborhood and decided to make an inquiry. I rang the doorbell and soon heard someone approaching the door and asking who was there. I responded that I was inquiring about the furnished apartment I had seen in *The Washington Post* classified ads. After some further exchanges, Dr. Carr opened the door and invited me in. His movements seemed strange; I soon realized that he was blind and alone in the house.

I found out later that Dr. Carr had been blinded years earlier by glaucoma. Quite familiar with the house, he immediately took me upstairs to the third floor and showed me the apartment. He explained the renovations they had made — informing me that we would be only the second couple to reside there. The first occupants had been a medical student attending Howard University and his wife.

I liked the apartment from the start. The apartment had a kitchen, a small but comfortable bedroom and a huge living room with a king-size sofa bed. It had elegant but modest furnishings. There was a full bath off the hall between the living room and bedroom.

As we conversed, we seemed to hit it off and when Mrs. Carr arrived home from her bridge outing, we had already struck a deal. He and I had agreed to a price of eighty dollars a month, which I knew to be the going rate for unfurnished apartments at the time. That meant that Dr. Carr's furnished apartment was a great deal for us.

After further chatting with the Carrs, I arranged a time with them to bring Retha over so she could see the apartment. I knew she would like it just as much as I did. They agreed and the next day, a Sunday, I brought Retha over. Indeed, she loved the apartment as much as I had. We spent an hour or so with the Carrs talking about our wedding plans, how we had met, plus when and where the wedding would take place.

We related that once we decided we were going to get married, we had called Retha's mother and father and her favorite aunt Bertha Wilcox to inform them of our plans. Retha's aunt immediately insisted that we get married at her home in Raleigh, North Carolina. Having not yet set a date, we discussed possible alternatives with her and agreed on Saturday, October fifth.

We informed the Carrs of our wedding date, noting that it was just a week away. We explained that our decision to get married had been somewhat impromptu, following Retha's move to Washington in July. Retha mentioned that just days before, she had purchased her wedding gown at a dress shop on Seventh Street; she shared that our wedding would not be an elaborate affair, but rather, one with only close family and friends in attendance. The Carrs congratulated us, remarked how pleased they were that we would be occupying their apartment and commented on us being a lovely couple. We were both a little giddy — not knowing the Carrs very well, but accepting their warm comments with appreciation.

I paid Dr. Carr the first month's rent, received keys to our apartment and the front door of their home and departed. We returned the next day with Retha's belongings, along with my own from the barracks at Walter Reed.

Now, being all set with a place to stay, we departed from Washington, D.C. on Tuesday, October 1 for our wedding that upcoming Saturday.

North Carolina Wedding

During the 1950s, it was almost impossible to do anything or go anywhere without encountering some incident that was racially tinged. Our trip to North Carolina was no exception. En route, we decided to stop in Richmond, Virginia, to get something to eat. After looking for a place we thought would serve blacks, we entered a corner restaurant and ordered two breakfast sandwiches. A white gentleman took our order, and just as I was indicating to him we wanted the sandwiches "to-go" from the kitchen, the female black cook commented: "Well, they will have to be to-go, because this place is strictly all-white."

Astonishingly, here was the black cook — not the white counterman who took our order — reinforcing the policy of segregation. While it was amusing to Retha and me, we did not miss the irony — and felt it somewhat sad.

We continued on to Raleigh, where the wedding would take place. After a short visit with Aunt Bertha, we drove sixty miles to Fayetteville where I dropped off Retha at her parent's home. I then traveled to my parents' home in Hamlet, again some sixty miles away.

On Saturday, our wedding day, I drove from Hamlet to Raleigh while listening to the radio, as the New York Yankees played the Milwaukee Braves in the World Series. I was particularly interested in the performance of Hank Aaron, whose sister Gloria I had taught while at Edward Waters College. I also listened to reports on the launching of Sputnik, the first man-made object to orbit the Earth, sent into space on the preceding day by the USSR.

Our wedding was a small and intimate affair, held in the home of Thomas and Bertha Wilcox, whom we affectionately called "Uncle Tommy" and "Auntie." The wedding came off without a hitch. My brother Freddy was my best man; Retha's sister, Esmeralda, affectionately known as "Boot," was Retha's maid of honor; her uncle Henderson Hughes, the senior pastor at Bethel AME Church in Harlem, N.Y., officiated. Also in attendance were my parents; my sister Shirley; Patricia; Freddy's wife, Estelle; plus my friend Halbert Jackson. Our long-time neighbor from across the street, Edith Mask-Breeden, was a wonderful soloist who sang "Ah, Sweet Mysteries of Life, at Last I've Found You."

Present with Retha's parents were her older brother Jimmie and his wife Ida; Retha's younger brother Eddie; "Auntie" and her husband, Tommy Wilcox. Several other local friends of Auntie joined in the celebration. Uncle Henderson immediately left for the airport, as he had to be back in New York to deliver his regular Sunday morning sermon.

Retha and I left following the ceremony, not even taking time to eat. My friend Halbert and my brother Freddy chased us out of town, honking their car horns, having painted Bon-Ami all over my freshly polished Plymouth, complete with cans dangling behind. We later stopped en route to the motel room I had reserved in Fayetteville, where I ordered greasy hamburgers at a popular restaurant called "V-Point."

Feeling somewhat sheepish, we showed up Sunday morning at Retha's parents' home for breakfast. I guess that this is a natural feeling for newlyweds early on. Later that day, we drove to Hamlet where a brunch had been planned by my parents. Having had no time (or money) to plan a honeymoon, we headed back to D.C. later that Sunday to begin our married life. What a whirlwind week it had been.

MARRIED LIFE IN WASHINGTON

Upon returning to D.C., we spent Monday getting Retha's credentials in order as a new Army wife. Her credentials provided for her health care and access to base facilities, including the Commissary where we purchased all our food and housekeeping needs. We unpacked our wedding gifts that included a set of china from my parents and a number of other items from Retha's parents and Auntie, including towels, bed linens and kitchen utensils. After shopping for groceries and other incidentals, we were all set.

Figure 6.   Wedding Party: The newlyweds with my brother, Freddy, and Retha's sister, Boot

Figure 7.   Wedding Day: Retha's parents on the left; mine on the right

We found our new home to be just perfect. The Carrs treated us warmly. They were very nice, and always wanted to converse with us as we passed on the stairs going to and from our third-floor apartment. On occasion, when we were in a hurry, we would sneak past their bedrooms on the second floor to avoid the sometimes long conversations that Dr. or Mrs. Carr enjoyed having with us. They were both engaging, especially Dr. Carr, who was an avid Republican eager to engage in political discussions. He had been born and raised in Ohio and used to recite many reflections about his Republican roots. He also discussed with me the misdiagnosis that caused his blindness, done by a fellow physician and friend. He once said, "Mr. Douglas, I started to get my gun and kill that son of a bitch."

With that line in mind, I could never forget his story about a friend's misdiagnosis. And I marveled that even though Dr. Carr was blind, he continued to see patients daily in his office on the second floor of their home. We remained on "S" Street for a year while we saved money to purchase furniture for the first unfurnished apartment we planned to rent. We enjoyed the Carrs, had regrets when it was time to leave, but knew that we should move on.

WALTER REED WORK

My job assignment at Walter Reed Army Medical Center was in the purchasing department, where three other inductees with advanced degrees were also assigned. The group included: Joe Burger, a University of Pittsburgh and Penn State graduate; Ken Ackerman, a graduate of Harvard Business School; and Don Gray, a law student at Valparaiso University in Indiana.

I was the last to arrive in the office and became an analyst, performing mostly clerical functions. Interestingly, when I arrived, I outranked Joe, Ken and Don. Major Andrew Cappy, the assigned commanding officer who ran the office, immediately sought to have the three of them promoted to my rank of Specialist Third Class — not being tolerant of me as a black soldier outranking the three white soldiers assigned to his command. The promotions were quickly approved.

Joe and Ken were product buyers for the hospital from the General Services Administration Catalogue; Don was the in-house legal counsel. While I am sure more prominent duties had been planned for the newly arriving Specialist Third Class before I arrived, once I was assigned, I was handed mostly clerical and messenger-type duties. That included handling copying machines, which during the 1950s consisted of stencil copying and smelly mimeographing machines.

Once Major Cappy accused me of drinking — confusing the stench of mimeo ink on my hands with the smell of liquor on my breath. I disagreed with his assertion and we had a heated argument that ended badly. He directed me to salute him while he sat at his desk and reminded me that he could court martial me. I saluted him and left. As I fumed, I thought to myself that he should have been confronting Lofton, his civilian co-director of the purchasing office. Lofton was a rotund individual with a red and veined nose that reflected his excessive drinking. I thought to myself that Lofton's demeanor should suggest a problem with alcohol a lot more than any odor coming from me, which Major Cappy had mistakenly assumed to be that of alcohol.

For months we did not speak — even on the Saturdays when I was assigned to come in and answer phones while sitting directly across from him for four or more hours. I was determined not to take lightly his unfair accusation of my office behavior. We never reconciled our disagreement; however, when I was discharged, he wrote me a glowing letter of recommendation about my performance and character. I was surprised that he wrote the letter; however, I never thanked him for it.

Joe, Ken, Don and I all lunched together with Dick Spangler, also a Harvard Business School graduate who was assigned to another office at Walter Reed. At first, I was in awe of these gentlemen, especially because of the education and training they had all received from the prestigious universities they had attended. Yet, I did not allow it to show; nor did I feel intimidated by their race. By then I had adjusted to the integrated army and had gotten used to interfacing with whites. Indeed, prior to my arrival at Walter Reed, I had been an authority figure over most of the enlisted men assigned to my training unit at Fort Jackson and the Redstone Missile Company I had been assigned to at Fort Belvoir, Virginia.

Yet, I was cautious, listened closely to the conversations we had and learned a great deal from the four of them while we lunched and engaged in wide-ranging discussions about the world of business. As we neared the end of our enlistment terms, when we all would be discharged within days of each other, I became somewhat embarrassed as they each had definite plans for their futures, while I had no clear vision of what I might do. I was left alone to ponder what career opportunities I might pursue in my job search. All of them were quite sure of their plans and pondered any number of opportunities they might consider. Indeed, Spangler, who had attended UNC Chapel Hill as an undergraduate, would later return to North Carolina and aggregate banking in Charlotte, making it one of the major banking centers in America. After leaving banking, he would become President of the North Carolina University Higher Education System.

[Dick Spangler and I reconnected during his tenure as President of the UNC system. We saw each other somewhat infrequently and reminisced about our Walter Reed experiences and marriages, which occurred at about the same time. I subsequently met his son-in-law, a senior executive with Marsh McLennan, a Fortune 500 insurance company, during a luncheon held at the Double Eagle Club in Galena, Ohio, a suburb of Columbus. At the time, Marsh McLennan was the title sponsor of the PGA tournament at the Muirfield Village country club in Dublin, Ohio, and was hosting their senior executives in town for the event. That luncheon occurred in May of 2001. Sadly, many of the executives at that luncheon perished on Sept. 11, 2001, at the World Trade Center in New York City. Thankfully, Dick's son-in-law was not among the victims.]

I began my job search by writing dozens of letters of inquiry to prominent D.C.-area firms and to others with which the Walter Reed purchasing office was doing business. However, I received only one response. This one response was the return of my letter of inquiry that prominently displayed handwritten notations, where my letter had been circulated to various company departments. The last entry was a conspicuously written "Not Interested." Incredibly, Becton Dickinson & Company, a prominent drug company with whom Walter Reed did business had returned my letter with a hand-written notation, rather than sending me a proper written response! I was learning quickly the difficulty I would face in landing a professional position of any kind. Yet, I was also learning the ways of business and gaining confidence that I would survive, once I gained entry.

Many memorable experiences occurred while I was stationed at Walter Reed. One was the occasion on which I was chosen to accompany the body of a black twenty-one year-old soldier home to Sapulpa, Oklahoma, for burial. The First Sergeant of our barracks picked me from among several other black soldiers for this detail, which occurred in February 1958, shortly after Retha and I were married. It would be the first time we were separated since our October marriage. I was away for nearly a week, traveling to Oklahoma both ways by train, where I had my first Pullman car experience, which I considered a real treat. The whole experience has remained memorable to me, mostly because it taught me something about death and the respect that the U. S. Army shows for fallen soldiers — even though this twenty-one year-old enlisted man had died of natural causes.

Being at Walter Reed also allowed those of us who were stationed there to encounter prominent Washingtonians in passing, including retired generals and other officers of the U. S. Military Services. One personal encounter was with General George C. Marshall, the American General and statesman. On another occasion, I was given duty to keep a walkway clear of snow until Mrs. Dwight D. Eisenhower arrived for a medical appointment. These were all mind-expanding events and experiences for a kid from Hamlet, North Carolina.

Retha and I also developed friendships with two wonderful black couples while at Walter Reed. One couple, Carlton and Jocelyn Hodgson, were already married when we met. The other, James and Lucy Sparks, were married within weeks of our marriage. We all became close friends. Both Carlton and James were interested in becoming physicians and went on to complete their medical training after their U. S. Army discharges: James at Howard University and Carlton at a medical institution in Sweden. While at Walter Reed, the six of us spent lots of time together and through Carlton and James, met a number of medical students from Howard University.

Most weekends became times to party and kick back. The Kenyon Grill near the Howard University campus became our favorite meeting place after work and during evening outings. Once we had a birthday party for both Retha and Jocelyn, whose birthdays fell in January. The pre-party, at the Hodgson's apartment, started at about two on a Saturday afternoon and lasted well past midnight. Carlton supplied the alcohol, which came from the "stock of 200 proof" alcohol at the Walter Reed Army Institute for Research, which we diluted with orange soda. Our guests arrived around seven in the evening; by then the four of us were well into the party and slowly "wasting away." The following Sunday was an "aching head" day.

Once while eating crabs at our apartment, Carlton, Jocelyn, Retha and I decided to take a weekend trip to celebrate the July Fourth weekend that was approaching. I suggested that we visit Mark Haven Beach, about eighty miles away, just south of Fredericksburg, Virginia. I remembered the place because my cousin Fannie Brown and her husband, Lawrence, had honeymooned there years earlier. Of course, Mark Haven Beach was a black resort sporting a hotel with several cottages strewn around the perimeter of the property. Arriving there the next day, we rented one of the two-bedroom cottages, swam in the Tappahannock River and again ate crabs, cooked by a gentleman we hired on the beach. What a weekend blast we had! We traveled back to D.C. on Sunday afternoon, and upon our arrival at our apartment noticed a pungent and awful smell. We discovered we had forgotten to dispose of the shells from the crabs we enjoyed before our weekend departure. We learned a great lesson that weekend about crabs' waste. Nothing — and I mean nothing — smells worse!

Retha and I stayed in touch with James Sparks and his wife, Lucy, as well as with Carlton and Jocelyn Hodgson for several years, but lost touch when we moved to Detroit.

In addition to my work and social life while at Walter Reed, I began to envision my professional future. To better prepare for my dream of becoming a CPA, I enrolled in graduate accounting courses at George Washington University. Unfortunately, even with the additional course work and numerous attempts at seeking employment, I was never able to receive any consideration from local accounting firms. I needed on-the-job experience to sit for the CPA exam. This early dream of mine would never materialize.

YOUNG, HAPPY CIVILIAN

In the midst of a growing recession, I was honorably discharged from the Army in August of 1958. As I began my job search, George Romney, CEO of American Motors, was giving the small car movement new momentum by marketing the popular 1958 Rambler American — an updated version of the Nash Rambler, which debuted in 1950. America was singing the popular song "Beep Beep" by a group called the Playmates — about a Nash Rambler racing at high speeds to overtake a Cadillac on the road.

Meanwhile, I tooled around DC in my 1948 two-door Chrysler Plymouth looking for an entry-level job. It was frustrating for me as a jobless college graduate with a master's degree, plus the added value of graduate accounting coursework taken at George Washington University. So while I searched for a professional position, I began selling Kirby vacuum cleaners door-to-door. I was cold calling on homeowners, trying to get into their homes and sell vacuum cleaners that many probably did not need. But it taught me how to persevere, and I actually did well: at one point, my rate of sales would have earned me $10,000 if I had kept it up for a full year. Ten thousand dollars was a very high annual salary in 1958.

The following January, I finally did get a job as a GS-3 clerk with the IRS. My job was to file tax returns for the IRS' International Operations Division, which handled tax returns from American citizens living abroad. I recall viewing the tax returns of movie stars, names I recognized, and seeing how much money they were making: $350,000 or more — quite significant sums for that time, and quite impressive to me. Even my clerical position was introducing me to a world I had not ever seen.

The following November, three months after my discharge from the military, Retha and I found a two-bedroom apartment at 1610 K Street N.E. that was two or three years old. The rent was eighty-two dollars a month, an amount that fit our budget. We had saved enough money to purchase a king-size bedroom suite, which we still own; furniture for a second bedroom; and a living room sofa, chair, coffee table, end tables and lamps. This all went well with the black and white Muntz TV we had purchased while we resided in the Carrs apartment. Our furniture was very nice and all paid for! We also traded in my 1948 Plymouth. I had purchased it a year earlier when I arrived at Walter Reed for $150 from a soldier, who was returning to Pittsburgh. We were now taking possession of our first new Ford car, a 1958 Mercury Monterey.

Retha and I had agreed that her younger brother Eddie could come and live with us, as he had just graduated from high school. He had spent the summer in upstate New York and returned home in the fall, flush with earnings from his summer work. He had led us to believe he would reimburse us for the furniture in the second bedroom. Once he arrived, however, we learned there was no money; but Eddie quickly went to work and began earning his keep. Eddie lived with us for about a year and then found his own place.

Our years in D.C. were idyllic, and that first year after my military discharge was one of the best. We were a young couple, both working that first year. We had lots of friends, most of whom we had met in college at North Carolina Central. For fun we'd go downtown to Haines Pointe, a park just across from Washington National Airport (now Reagan National). On early Friday evenings, we sat on the grass, drank beer and ate fish sandwiches — all at a cost of about five dollars. We watched the airplanes take off and land, flying directly over our heads so low we could read all the wing markings. We'd have people over, couples we had known from college who lived in D.C. We'd get together, get a couple of beers and eat popcorn because nobody had any money. We would entertain ourselves playing cards. Everybody was broke. I didn't play golf or anything. Back in those days, our small group or friends planned numerous picnics and cookouts in area parks, or we'd visit each other. We'd just get in the car and go by and knock on a friend's door. You didn't even have to call first. If they were home, they'd let you in and we would makeshift the food and entertainment that we would enjoy.

We joined Asbury Methodist Church — a downtown black church, founded in 1836 that remains at its original location at the intersection of Eleventh and K Streets, NW.

YOUNG, BLACK PROFESSIONAL:
COMPUTER PROGRAMMING AT THE IRS

In April of 1959, I took the Federal Service Entrance Examination and passed it. I was quite pleased with this accomplishment, for many of my colleagues from NCC took the exam but failed it. Passing the Federal Service Entrance Exam lifted my spirits and set me on a course to seek a professional position. Passing the exam was the first step in establishing eligibility for a wide variety of entry-level analyst positions at the GS-5-GS-7 levels, the first professional grade steps in the Federal Service.

Passing the test also put me on the professional jobs register. Since I was already employed by the IRS at the time, I was eligible to apply for professional jobs that were posted by the IRS Personnel Office. One day, I read a posting for a job titled "Digital Computer Programmer GS 5/7" and it seemed I was qualified for that position. I visited the personnel office and talked to a personnel officer, a white lady who looked at me, scanned my credentials, and immediately said, "No, you are not eligible."

I knew I was eligible and qualified for the position, so I decided to wait until she went to lunch. I then went back and talked to another personnel officer. The second lady reviewed my credentials and confirmed that I was eligible. She immediately referred me to the Statistics Division of the IRS, where I was interviewed the same day. Following my interview, it was only a matter of weeks before I was transferred from my clerical post to the position of Digital Computer Programmer GS-05, the entry level for computer programmers. Thus began my professional career at the IRS — a year after my U. S. Army discharge.

Within a short time, I became a competent computer programmer. Computer programming just clicked for me. It was something I liked and I quickly mastered. I was now working in the Statistics of Income (SOI) Division with the responsibility of processing tax returns and producing annual statistics, a requirement of the IRS statute amended by Congress in 1916. That statute required that "Statistics of Income will be produced annually from tax returns that are filed." In my section, we were responsible for tabulating data from individual, partnership and corporate tax returns. We tabulated data from a randomized statistical sample of returns — except the very large returns were not sampled, as all of them were included for processing. For example, we tabulated all of the returns of individuals with an annual income of $1 million dollars or more, and believe it or not, that number amounted to fewer than 200 American taxpayers in the late 1950s.

At the same time, there were also fewer than 100 name-controlled corporate returns, which represented those with assets of $250 million or more — a scant dollar amount when measured against the asset size of today's corporations. My specialty became partnership and corporate tax returns, including both regular Corporate Returns (Forms 1120) and Small Business Returns (Forms 1120S).

The IRS was several years behind in producing statistics of income, as the processing was being done with very slow punch-card accounting machines. It would take the SOI Division five to six years to produce reports for any given year's tax data. However, shortly before my arrival, the IRS had hired a progressive Director of SOI by the name of Ernie Enquist, PhD. Dr. Enquist was not only a progressive thinker with regard to applying technology to problem solving, but also with regard to racial and gender diversity in the workplace. It was because of his progressive thinking that several other black professionals in addition to me had been hired. The SOI Division became more inclusive of professional women and minorities than any of the other National Office IRS divisions.

Dr. Enquist introduced electronic data processing to the IRS by renting computer time from the Bureau of the Census, which had purchased a UNIVAC 1 computer system to process the 1950 decennial census. UNIVAC 1, Serial number 1 was the first electronic computer system developed in the U.S. By 1959, when I joined the SOI Division, the Bureau of Census owned two UNIVAC 1 computers (Serial numbers 1 and 13). At the time, SOI was about two years into processing statistics of income at the Census Bureau. The SOI Division was well along in hiring and training computer programmers. The Census Bureau only allowed us access to their computers during the afternoon and midnight shifts. The Bureau did however, agree to provide a limited amount of time during the day for us to test and debug our programs.

Part of my initial orientation to the SOI Division was to learn about the Division's charge, and as such, my orientation sessions included several other new hires employed to handle the analytical side of the division's work. We received special treatment and had several opportunities to meet with Dr. Enquist. He encouraged and challenged us to be vigilant and take advantage of the developing technology to provide timelier processing and produce accurate SOI data for publication. This was my first professional experience where I felt part of a peer group charged with a challenging task and important vision, and a personal opportunity for growth. It was unfortunate that Dr. Enquist died suddenly of a heart attack a year or so after I joined the SOI Division.

STARTING OUR FAMILY

Retha worked at the National Bureau of Standards for about a year, and then moved to the Agency for International Development (USAID) at the State Department. Her duties were quite avant-garde, as she was part of an initiative started by the Kennedy Administration that brought young men from African nations and taught them English, if necessary, before placing them in prep schools or universities throughout America.

Interestingly, President Barack Obama's father was probably part of that contingency of young African men who passed through the USAID agency. Obama's father came to America during that period and undoubtedly was processed through the USAID office; however,

Retha does not recall his name, which was indeed a tongue twister for many Americans who first tried to enunciate it when the president began his 2008 campaign. Retha remembers only a name or two, one of whom was a young man whose first name was "Sumbie"; he was most interested in adopting the cultural ways and dress of black Americans. However, during his initial transition, he did not quite get the dress, expressions or mannerisms just right — though he was a most amusing and charming individual to be around.

The number of individuals entering this program was small, with groups of fewer than ten being processed at a time as they made their way into various study arrangements. Once their training was completed, they had to return to their native countries. Nonetheless, Retha recalls that all of them were quite proud of their nationalities and confident in their abilities. She would come home and relate stories about the characters among the young Africans — especially those who were desirous of adopting American culture and styles of dress.

Retha would also tell me about her experiences at cocktail functions sponsored by the State Department to welcome incoming students. On occasions, those attending would include the Secretary of State and the Director of USAID, other agency officials and Washington icons. On one occasion, guests included U.S. Air Force General Curtis Lemay. This was quite fascinating for me to hear and for her to experience, since we had recently moved to Washington, and we had both come from modest and segregated life experiences in North Carolina.

Retha became pregnant in early 1960 and I felt really proud. Our daughter, Petra, was born October 17, 1960, at the Freedman's Hospital on the campus of Howard University. While Retha was in the hospital, I painted our apartment. She never knew I had such skills, but I have always been handy around the house, having learned those skills from my father and in high school shop classes. I never will forget the look on her face when she came home and saw the apartment had been totally painted. She was really pleased and complimented me for my effort.

This was the first time, but not the only time, I demonstrated my many talents as a handy man. Retha would later learn that I could do just about anything around the house, which I really demonstrated in our Detroit home by installing a Kitchen Aid dishwasher, finishing off our basement and later building on a sunroom complete with hot tub!

I remember how strange, but happy I felt the first time I saw Petra in the hospital. Lying in an incubator, Petra had a very large pair of scissors clamped to her navel. I asked the nurse why this was so and why she was in the incubator. She informed me that they had left them there after delivery because Petra had been in the birth canal for quite some time and she was "a little blue" at birth. That alarmed me somewhat but she turned out to be completely normal, with no after effects of her lengthy birth.

Petra was beautiful and she grew just fine. Like many new working parents, the first challenge we faced was babysitting, or childcare, as it is now called. We arranged for Mrs. Ford, our next door neighbor and a stay-at-home mom, to babysit Petra. This was great, for we only had to knock on her door, hand Petra to her and be on our way to work. On the downside, I remember going over there one day and Mrs. Ford had fallen asleep (leaving the door ajar), holding Petra tightly and almost smothering her. I didn't like that at all.

I quickly became leery of babysitters and not at all happy about entrusting our daughter with one! Thankfully, the situation was soon to change — permanently.

OUR FIRST HOME

We remained on K Street until 1961. Once I was satisfied that my career was progressing, we began to look for a home to purchase. Our preference was to locate in the Riggs Park section of Northeast Washington close to Silver Spring, Maryland.

In early spring, we looked for our first home and selected a semi-detached residence on Jefferson Street near South Dakota Avenue in Northeast Washington. Nearly all the homes were similar — all brick, semi-detached, with a common adjoining wall and approximately 2,000 square feet in size.

Our purchase offer of $16,500 was accepted and with the approval of our FHA loan, we closed and moved into our new home on Labor Day weekend of 1961.

We were now owners of our first home at 427 Jefferson Street, N.E. We loved it — a two-story house with a finished lower level, which walked out into our back yard. We lived on Jefferson Street until we moved to Detroit in 1966. We enjoyed great relationships with our immediate neighbors and with friends in the neighborhood — most of whom were young black couples or single professionals employed by the federal government or former classmates of ours from NCC.

Moving into our new home required us to get a new babysitter. By this time, Retha's brother Eddie had gotten married to Barbara, a stay-at-home mom of three boys. Barbara agreed to babysit Petra and it seemed a good fit, since they lived on Sherman Avenue, which was on our way to work in downtown Washington. We began to take Petra there every morning, but before long the arrangement just didn't feel right. It was okay but it wasn't okay.

The last straw was one day we brought Petra home and noticed that she was limping. We took off her shoes and discovered there was a hair barrette inside one shoe. That was the last straw. We just got mad and concluded, "This is not working." We confronted Barbara, and afterward remained skeptical of her babysitting, but were not in a position to make a change immediately.

STAY-AT-HOME MOM

However, one day in the weeks that followed, Retha and I had a talk. She said that she felt it would be best for her to resign from her State Department position and become a "stay-at-home" mother to take care of Petra. I quickly agreed.

Retha quit work in February of 1962, five months after we moved into our Riggs Park home. It was not long after that Petra had a crisis, being allergic to food products we were not aware of. The allergic reaction produced a quick and potentially deadly swelling of her face and neck. Retha immediately took her to nearby Providence Hospital, where Petra received an injection that reduced the swelling. We both wondered how a babysitter would have handled such a crisis!

Retha seemed to flourish in her new role as a stay-at-home mom. We were both happy with this new arrangement, even though we had a limited amount of money. We never regretted our decision and I always enjoyed the fact that she would be home with our kids. One of the things I missed as a child growing up was that my mother always worked and was not at home. I believe this was the underlying rationale that guided me in quickly agreeing with Retha that she not work.

To make up for Retha's lost income, I used to work all the available overtime I could get. Overtime was available if we worked the midnight shift at the Bureau of Census, where we processed tax return data. Mostly I chose to get paid for the extra time rather than receiving compensatory time off. I used to work nights and go directly from the Bureau of the Census to the IRS's offices in downtown D.C., where I would work all day before coming home to crash.

The extra income helped us avoid financial problems and really started us on our way. Except for those first few months after Retha quit work, we have never experienced financial difficulty. We were good stewards of what we had. We never overextended ourselves, and seemed to always make modest progress in saving and managing our finances.

Our children appreciated that Retha was there. She used her time by volunteering at the local school and became an outstanding seamstress, making many of our children's clothes.

We settled into our new home and our life in Washington was good. I had a great job and had been promoted to GS11, which was very rewarding.

WASHINGTON POLITICS

Working in a high-level civil service position in the nation's capital was a heady experience at that time, especially for a young African American like me who had promising career prospects. The growing number of black professionals in Washington, combined with the burgeoning Civil Rights Movement, filled us with pride and hope. Yet, the political situation in the District of Columbia itself reminded us of the injustice and lack of power that confronted us in other areas of our lives.

The interesting thing about Washington, D.C, in the 1960s is that there was little local control of government and the city had no locally elected officials. The entire governance of the District was the responsibility of the U.S. Congress' District of Columbia Committee. The city had no mayor, no city council. Of three appointed commissioners, one was black. D.C. residents didn't vote at all in any elections, national or local. (The vote was finally extended to Washingtonians just before we left for Detroit in 1966. Retha and I voted for the first time while living there.)

Even though there was no elected mayor or city council, many neighborhood civic associations played a key role in managing neighborhood issues. Up until the purchase of our home in Riggs Park, neither Retha nor I had ever been involved in local civic community work

Despite working long hours, I volunteered with the Lamond-Riggs Community Association, which encompassed our neighborhood. Lamond-Riggs concerned itself mostly with matters involving our community's schools and public transportation. Transportation was a hot issue in D.C. at the time, as planning was underway to begin construction of the Washington Metro Rail Transportation System. The Metro Rail System was supposed to come through our community, and the question was whether or not it would destroy part of the Riggs Park community as it snaked its way toward Silver Spring, Md. As it turned out, the Metro design incorporated the use of the railroad right-of-way that passed through northeast Washington, so our neighborhood was not adversely affected at all.

THE CAMELOT ERA BEGINS

We were living and working in Washington at a time of historic change. As interesting and unique as the local political scene was, the national scene was epic. President John F. Kennedy's Administration inspired and embodied the optimism Americans felt about the new decade of the 1960s. When President Kennedy took the oath of office on Jan. 20, 1961, I was an employee of the IRS and Retha was still employed by the State Department. But the day before his inauguration, a huge snowstorm shut down all government operations. Employees were released at about 2:30 p.m. The snow was so bad that it took Retha and me, who both worked downtown, about three hours to get home; where it usually took less than a half hour. Eight to ten inches of snow fell.

Amazingly, the next morning, not a speck of snow dotted the parade route down Pennsylvania Avenue between the U. S. Capitol and the White House. On that bitterly cold day in January, all the snow had been removed from the parade route for Kennedy's Inauguration. Retha and her girlfriend Sarah viewed the Inaugural along the parade route along Pennsylvania Avenue while I remained home with Petra.

I remember President Kennedy standing outside the nation's Capitol, dressed in tails — but without an overcoat — making his inaugural speech. "He's going to catch pneumonia and die!" I worried. But he survived and the Camelot era was born.

It was an exciting time in Washington and we all kind of grooved with it. We had a new young president with a young wife, and they were having children at the same time we were having children. A general feeling of renewal and promise was everywhere. Petra was born about a month before the birth of President Kennedy's son, John Jr., who arrived approximately three weeks after his father's election.

THE MARCH ON WASHINGTON

No small part of the optimism African Americans felt was due to the growing momentum across the country for social equality and equal rights under the law. Black people, especially those my age and younger, were actively resisting segregation laws that were at least sixty years old and racial injustice that had become status quo since the end of Reconstruction. The nascent Civil Rights Movement was encouraged by President Harry Truman's integration of the armed forces in 1948 and achieved a great victory when the U.S. Supreme Court ruled in 1954 that racially segregated schools were unconstitutional in the *Brown vs.*

the Topeka Kansas Board of Education case. The movement picked up steam with President Dwight Eisenhower's 1957 decision to send federal forces to protect black students integrating Central High School in Little Rock, Ark., and the Montgomery, Alabama, bus boycott which launched Dr. Martin Luther King's career as a civil rights leader followed in 1957-58.

Lunch counter sit-ins and the Freedom Rides that integrated interstate buses kicked off the 1960s, followed by nonviolent — yet tense and confrontational — demonstrations against segregation throughout the South. The stage was set for one of the greatest triumphs in the history of the Civil Rights Movement — the March on Washington. It was at this epic event in August 1963 that Martin Luther King, Jr., made his famous "I Have a Dream" speech on the steps of the Lincoln Memorial before the great reflecting pool of the National Mall.

Although Retha didn't go because our son Edmond was an infant, her uncle Henderson Hughes, who had married us, came down from New York with his wife, Ruth, and their daughter, Hendrean. Together we went downtown and joined the throng of supporters who meandered down Constitution Avenue to join the gathering crowd at the foot of the Lincoln Memorial.

For me, this was the largest crowd that I had ever been a part of. It was a peaceful gathering whose participants included blacks, whites, actors, union leaders and several hundred congressional representatives. I was particularly struck by the long line of buses from Detroit that had brought hundreds of UAW workers.

The District of Columbia police force and reinforcements from neighboring cities were omnipresent. None was needed, except to handle traffic congestion. Indeed, as I proudly read in newspapers the following day, the march had been carefully planned to send the right message to America — a message of peaceful protest, but with a call to action.

I was amazed at how easily one gets caught up in events such as this. Prior to that day, I had only observed the Civil Rights Movement — beginning with the Montgomery Bus Boycott, the sit-ins by A & T University students in Greensboro, N Car. and other occurrences;

however, I was simply a government employee living in Washington, D.C. who went to work every day to take care of his family. Before the March on Washington, I had felt mostly helpless to do anything more than sympathize with the victims of the civil rights struggle, although I supported their many efforts. However, the March on Washington was close and I had become an active participant. This imbued in me an unprecedented sense of belonging. It remains an experience I still reflect upon as a mind-altering event that introduced me to the Civil Rights Movement — inculcating in me a sense of wanting to belong in some way to the movement.

Later, I began to pay more attention and kept myself abreast of the happenings in the South: the marches and demonstration; re-calling the drive-by shooting of a Washingtonian on a rural Alabama road; the lynching of three Congress of Racial Equality workers, Michael Schwerner and Andrew Goodman of New York and James Chaney of Meridian, Mississippi in June 1964 and the shooting of Viola Liuzzo — a Detroiter — near Selma, Alabama in March 1965.

A few years later, after I learned I would be transferring to De-troit, the fact that Martin had first made his "I Have a Dream" speech in Detroit before delivering it to the thousands on the Na-tional Mall made me proud I was moving my family and career to the Motor City.

THE KENNEDY ASSASSINATION

President Kennedy's assassination was a very traumatic experience for every individual American, for the city of Washington, for our nation and the world. Retha and I were no exceptions.

From the time of its occurrence that Friday afternoon, November 22, 1963 all of us just sat and watched our TV sets. The next day, Retha's aunt Bertha Wilcox drove up to D.C. from Raleigh. Then on the following Sunday, we all went downtown to see the caisson pass as it went from the White House to the Capitol, where President Kenne-dy would lie in state until his funeral the following day. I vividly remember the processional passing with the rider less horse — boots turned backwards in the stirrups to connote the death of a fallen leader.

As Retha, Auntie and I watched this profoundly sad event, we had no idea that Jack Ruby had shot and killed Lee Harvey Oswald in the basement of the Dallas, Texas jailhouse. Our friend Bill Beckham witnessed the shooting, as did many other Americans, while watching the events of the weekend non-stop on television. Later that Sunday Bill Beckham — laid up with a broken leg from a touch football accident — gave us a "blow-by-blow" account of the shooting, as he had observed it live on TV.

The funeral took place on Monday. Our nation halted all commerce and activity during this three-day period. We all just sat and watched the television. Perhaps the most touching moment was when little John Kennedy, Jr., saluted his father's casket during the recessional in front of the Cathedral of Saint Matthew the Apostle on New York Avenue in northwest Washington.

I was so personally affected that the following Monday in my first management training session (Management Development I), I snubbed a fellow IRS employee attending from Dallas, Texas, feeling he somehow bore some responsibility simply because he was from Dallas. I believe many other Americans would have reacted similarly.

THE JOHNSON YEARS

When Lyndon Johnson got off the airplane at Andrews Air Force Base after Kennedy's death, he said, "Ladies and Gentlemen, this is a sad time for all Americans." His long, southern drawl made me think, "My God, now we've got to listen to this guy?"

His manner of talking was different from the snappy, "hard-A" New England accent that John Kennedy had gotten us all used to. But with President Johnson, we quickly began to listen past his drawl to the words he was speaking. The media were kind to him and focused on his past ability as Senate Majority Leader to manage the U.S. Congress and get legislation passed.

In actuality, Kennedy hadn't gotten a great deal through the Congress. But early on, President Johnson was able gain passage of the Civil Rights Act of 1964. Because he was effective in managing the Congress, he received positive media coverage.

In 1964, Johnson had to defend his presidency against Senator Barry Goldwater of Arizona. Goldwater, a right-wing Republican, made shocking statements as a candidate. I recall one such statement declaring, "What we need to do is just saw America in half and let the East Coast float out to sea."

Responding to Goldwater's assertion, Johnson's campaign created a response ad featuring a saw cutting America in half while the voice-over remarked, "This is what our opposition wants to do. He wants to saw off the eastern half of our country and let it float out to sea." Goldwater didn't make a very good showing, and Johnson trounced him in the 1964 presidential election.

The Republican Convention preceding Goldwater's defeat was the first time I remember Ronald Reagan playing an active role in national politics. Earlier, Reagan had been a Democrat but had changed his party affiliation and was making his first appearance as a Republican. He appeared on the platform during the convention at the Cow Palace in San Francisco. Although I don't remember the content of his speech, I do recall how he delivered his remarks in a somewhat firebrand manner. At the time, Reagan was a well-known movie actor and often appeared on national TV as the spokesperson for the General Electric Company.

That convention also produced an unsettling event involving a black Republican delegate. While sitting in the audience in nonchalant fashion, a "fellow" delegate lit a fire under his chair. He jumped up out of his seat. National TV broadcast the incident; it troubled me greatly. I concluded that blacks still had a way to go in terms of respect and dignity, regardless of the venue or situation.

I began to recall the discussions my parents engaged in during my growing-up years. My father's views seemed to lean toward giving support to the Republican Party, while my mother's seemed to favor the Democratic Party. Their views coupled with my knowledge of the support blacks gave the Republican Party, the party of Lincoln, left me with mixed views. And, during the Nixon-Kennedy election in 1960 — living in D.C. did not afford us the opportunity to vote. Had I been able to cast a ballot, I am not sure which candidate I would have supported.

However, my choice became crystal clear following the election of Richard Nixon in 1968, when he defeated Hubert Humphrey by employing his "Southern Strategy." Nixon's Southern Strategy sent clear messages to Southern Democrats regarding the Civil Rights Movement and caused nearly all of them to support him and change their party affiliation. Nixon's Southern Strategy firmly fixed my view of the 20th century Republican Party. While some may continue to link Republicanism to the era of Lincoln, any linkage I still had to the Republican Party ended conclusively in 1968.

THE VIETNAM ERA

Elected now in his own right, Johnson's major challenge became the Vietnam War. The nation was badly divided over the war, and protests against it occurred daily. Johnson maintained his strong support for the war, severely damaging his personal credibility and that of his Administration. Of course, support for his presidency waned so severely that he did not seek a second term.

As I later reflected upon the Vietnam era, I began to more fully understand Martin Luther King, Jr.'s opposition to the Vietnam War. While Dr. King was fighting on behalf of blacks in the 1950s and 1960s, he reflected upon the world order — remarking along the way that preference had traditionally been shown to fair-skinned people, while people with swarthy or darker skins were constantly demeaned and shown little or no preference on the world stage. Dr. King's vehement opposition to such treatment inspired him to speak out against what our government was doing in Vietnam.

During the era of Kennedy, Johnson, King and Vietnam, when I lived in the city where the most critical national and international decisions were being made, my firm focus was on my family and career. Not recognizing any role I could play in the national debate, I sat on the sidelines. My rude awakening regarding political involvement would come with the rebellion in Detroit, when social upheaval would be thrust in my face and I would recognize the need to respond.

A Detroiter in Washington

Detroit, my future home, rarely crossed my mind while we lived in the District. But the city was introduced to me by one man and his influential family in the fall of 1962. One evening Retha mentioned that her friend and work associate, Sarah Speed had met a wonderful young man from Detroit and they were dating. His name was William "Bill" Beckham, Jr., and he worked on "the Hill" (as all Washingtonians referred to Capitol Hill) for Michigan's Senator Phil Hart. Retha suggested we invite Sarah and Bill to dinner the next Sunday. When Sarah and Bill arrived, I was watching the NFL on TV. Bill was quite interested and while Sarah joined Retha in the kitchen to put the final touches on our dinner, Bill and I watched the Redskins game. We conversed and immediately seemed to develop an affinity for each other.

By the time we sat down to dinner, Bill and I were freely conversing as he updated us on his experiences in Detroit as well as his many experiences in politics. Because of his strong interest in politics, Bill had dropped out of Wayne State University to work for Senator Hart in Washington and was now enrolled part time at American University.

Bill also shared that his family had only been in Detroit for a short time. They had relocated from Cincinnati, Ohio, following a promotion his father received to become Special Assistant to Walter Reuther, President of the UAW. Later I learned that Bill's father was born in Georgia and worked for General Motors in Cincinnati as a senior plant representative for the UAW, before he began working for Reuther. That Sunday dinner was the first of many get-togethers for the four of us. Bill and Sarah were married six weeks later!

Retha and I attended the wedding reception, where we met Bill's parents. Like Bill, his dad was quite friendly and a great fan of the NFL. He predicted the Packers would defeat the Lions in the upcoming Thanksgiving Day game and repeat a last-minute win over the Lions in the closing seconds that occurred at their earlier meeting. I disagreed and was proven correct when the Lions resoundingly defeated the Packers on Thanksgiving Day, sacking Bart Starr numerous times in a one-sided affair.

Meeting William Beckham, Sr., and his wife, Gertrude, was a harbinger of relationships that Retha and I would form after our subsequent move to Detroit. Indeed, our friendship with both generations of Beckhams established a relationship between our families that would endure for decades; gave us our first personal connection to Detroit, our future hometown; and contributed to a smooth transition to the Motor City once we made the move.

Following their wedding, Bill, Sarah, Retha and I visited often and developed a close couple's relationship. We enjoyed music and spent hours listening to our favorite recordings by Motown artists, while discussing politics and other subjects of mutual interest.

For all we knew, the Beckhams were simply part of a comfortable network we would enjoy in Washington for many years. Retha and I were happy in our home, and with the birth of our son Edmond — at Providence Hospital on May 22, 1963 — we felt quite settled. We lived in a wonderful neighborhood, had great neighbors and lots of friends all over D.C. We were reasonably close to our roots in North Carolina and had no thoughts or interest in moving to Detroit or anyplace else. But things change, and the most significant change for us began on my job.

PROGRESS AND CHANGE AT THE IRS

I was very good at data processing and I advanced rapidly at the IRS. I could say without exaggeration or arrogance that I was the best programmer in the SOI Division. My accomplishments included introducing many innovative and technological advances to our data processing systems. Paul Howard, a middle-aged black man who commuted to D.C. from Baltimore, was my boss. A GS-13, Paul had progressed faster and to a higher-ranking grade than most blacks at the time, yet he was cautious and unwilling to take many chances at changing our proven processes. I was not sure he appreciated many of the innovations I suggested, for he turned many of them down.

However, he did not stop me from finding newer and better ways of doing things, and at times he acknowledged my abilities. For instance, as we were transitioning to the newer and faster UNIVAC

1105 computers, Paul selected me to spend two months at the Bureau of the Census to learn the programming methodology and lead our transition team. I was quite proud of this selection. I completed my assignment without issue, developing the needed programs to complete the transition.

It was sometime in 1964 that we first began to hear rumors that the SOI Division would probably consolidate its data processing operations with other similar activities within the IRS. The agency had developed a strategic plan in the early 1960s that required the deployment of regional service centers throughout the nation. Each would have the capacity to process income tax returns. The goal was to streamline tax processing and better serve individual taxpayers and American businesses.

This was an enormous project anticipated to take several years to complete. It would require millions of dollars of funding that needed the approval of the U.S. Congress. At the time, Senator Patrick McNamara (D-Michigan) was chairman of the Senate Appropriations Committee, which meant that the IRS had to seek his committee's approval of the funds to establish the network of nine regional centers. The proposed network would include centers in Lawrence, Massachusetts, (now moved to Andover); Philadelphia; Atlanta; Memphis; Austin, Texas; Ogden, Utah; Kansas City, Missouri; Cincinnati; and Fresno, California. As the budget proposal was being floated, McNamara, who was from Detroit, inquired of IRS officials: "Well, what about Michigan? What about my state? Perhaps you should come back when your expansion plans show some dollars for my state."

The IRS appeased Sen. McNamara; a data center would be established in Michigan. Two sites were considered: Port Huron and Detroit, with Detroit finally selected. The IRS would consolidate some of its data processing needs, including Statistics of Income (SOI), Taxpayer Compliance Measurement (TCMP), and payroll processing at a new Detroit IRS Data Center. The Service gave in to Sen. McNamara's *quid pro quo* in order to build the other service centers they wanted to establish nationwide. The Detroit Data Center became operational in an old warehouse on Detroit's near east side in July of 1965. Years later, I would find it an interesting coincidence that Henry Ford established one of his very first manufacturing operations at nearly the identical location, on Piquette Avenue, between Brush and John R streets.

Early in 1965, as the center was being formed, I was approached by a former SOI colleague, Chuck Copeland, the newly named chief of the Systems Division of the IRS Data Center, which was still operating in Washington before being deployed to Detroit. Chuck knew my reputation and ability from my work at SOI. One day, he invited me to his office and asked that I consider joining his team in Detroit. Genuinely excited to move to Michigan, he described the opportunity and growth potential he foresaw for me at the new data center. He then mentioned the position he had in mind for me: Team Leader of the Corporate Tax Section, a GS-13 level position. At the time, I was a GS-12.

"In fact," Chuck said, "we could promote you to GS-13 right away if you're willing to join our team." Chuck affirmed that the center would become operational in July 1965, with my move following a year later. I told him I would think about it very seriously.

The promotion would require my family to leave our beloved D.C. and move northwest to Detroit. But, after talking to Retha, we agreed that it was a great opportunity and she encouraged me to accept the new position. Days later, I informed Chuck that my answer to his offer was "Yes."

CHAPTER 5

REBELLION IN DETROIT

Once the decision was made, Retha and I spent the intervening year in great anticipation. I was pleased with my immediate promotion and excited by the new opportunity. But I was also apprehensive, as it would require Retha and me to relocate our family — lock, stock and barrel. We first had to sell our D.C. home, and then purchase one in Detroit. At the time, we knew very little about Detroit, having visited only once with our friends Bill and Sarah Beckham during the summer of 1964. We knew it was the fabled "arsenal of democracy" during World War II, and had a stellar reputation for producing domestic cars and trucks. Of course, it had an emerging reputation as the venue for a new phenomenon in music that would be dubbed "The Motown Sound."

We also knew Detroit had earned a national reputation as the city of home ownership. It was reported that more Detroit residences were owned by their residents than in any other city in America. We assumed the housing patterns were similar to those of Washington, where 80 percent of African Americans in the metropolitan area lived within the city limits, and very few lived west of Rock Creek Park, according to a 1962 report by the U.S. Commission on Civil Rights. In other words, in the nation's capital, which by 1962 had become the only major city in the U.S. with a majority black population, housing segregation was real. Yet, many black families lived in some of Washington's most attractive neighborhoods, such as ours. Nevertheless, a rude awakening awaited us in Detroit! We never imagined the deeply entrenched patterns of segregated housing and off-limits neighborhoods we were about to encounter there.

During the one-year transitioning process, I learned that several other SOI employees agreed to make the move to Detroit as well. Vince Finelli signed on to become the SOI Branch Manager and would become my boss. Prior to his promotion, Vince had been the Team Leader for the IRS Form 1040 Personal Tax Return section, just as Paul Howard had been responsible for the IRS 1120 Corporate Tax Return section. Others involved with corporation and partnership return processing included Barbara Vatran and Lil Dorsey — both senior analysts who were also black. However, like Paul Howard, they were unwilling to relocate — leaving me as the only senior analyst on our team willing to make the move to Detroit. However, one junior analyst, Alan Schrier, and a recently hired black female from the Department of Defense, Mary Reed, did accompany our team to Detroit.

Vince then recruited several of his existing team members to ac-company him, including two black professionals — Charles Harvey and Ann Mundy — along with Collette Bowden, Dick Keiffer and Tom Neitzey. Like me, everyone who agreed to move to Detroit received a promotion. Also, Ken Wheeler and Cliff Johnson, two black computer specialists responsible for monitoring our programs while they processed data at the Census Bureau, joined us as well. Later during the year, I was to recruit Tom Diggs, who had been introduced to me by my neighbor York Campbell. Tom, a U.S. Air Force veteran, was a computer programmer employed by Andrews Air Force Base. After relocating to Detroit, he and his wife, Sarah, became great friends — and remain so. Those who accompanied me to Detroit became the core group that formed the corporate/partnership SOI team.

THE MOVE TO DETROIT

Our home sold quickly and in July 1966 the moving process began. We didn't have a place to live right away, so I arrived alone. I rented a room in a duplex on Euclid Street just east of Woodward Avenue for a few weeks, while Retha, Petra and Edmond went to stay with my parents in North Carolina. Our furniture had been packed and transported by North American Van Lines to Detroit and was in storage, awaiting the processing of our FHA loan and eventual closing on our house in the Motor City.

The first home that we settled on was owned by Berry Gordy of Motown fame. Mr. Gordy and his wife were divorcing and selling their home in northwest Detroit on Washburn Street. Months prior to our move, in February of 1966, Gordy quickly accepted our offer to purchase. However, the deal was conditional upon us attaining a conventional mortgage. We learned this fact later and found out that Gordy would not agree to finance our purchase under the FHA loan program because of the "points" that he would be required to pay from the loan proceeds.

Yet the difference in cost to us for conventional financing was substantial — a whopping 1.5 percent, which was a huge amount in our minds. We did not want to pay the going conventional rate of 6.75 percent for a mortgage when the FHA rate was 5.25 percent. Refusing the conventional financing, we made a special trip to Detroit in mid-June and found an even better home — one more suited to our liking on Lichfield Street, in an attractive northwest Detroit neighborhood. We made an offer that was quickly accepted; however, the timing of the purchase would delay our move-in date.

Nonetheless, we began our due diligence and hired an attorney to review our paperwork, including the property abstract. We were concerned about language we discovered embedded in the abstract that cited a "Caucasians Only" restriction on ownership. We assumed this restriction would govern the potential transfer of the property we were attempting to purchase in a nearly all-white neighborhood. Retha and I later learned from our attorney that this provision had been commonplace in Detroit and other American cities but had been declared illegal by the U.S. Supreme Court back in 1948. At the time, however, we were not aware of the court's ruling. Interestingly, years later when we sold our home to our son, Mark, he asked, "Dad, do you know what is in my abstract?"

"Yes, it was there when we purchased the home 30 years ago," I said. He was astonished — and experienced a lesson in American history. The "racial covenant" restrictions were in real estate contracts nationwide, and did not just affect blacks — the language spoke to "Caucasians Only" — obviously excluding *all* other racial groups.

Our friend Bill Beckham helped us process the paperwork for our new home. Bill had returned to Detroit in May of 1966 to manage the Detroit office for Senator Phil Hart and literally walked the paperwork through the FHA office in the Federal Building, a few floors below his office. Finally the paperwork was approved, allowing us to close on our home and prompting me to send for my family. An airline strike that summer affected travel on Northwest Airlines and several other air carriers. The only way my family could get from North Carolina to Detroit was for my parents to drive them from Hamlet to Columbia, South Carolina, about 110 miles away. There they would fly a Delta flight to Atlanta, where they would board a connecting flight from Atlanta to Detroit.

While working out these travel arrangements, I discovered that only first-class fare was available. I submitted my reimbursement request to the IRS's Washington office, where I surprisingly learned that they had already issued coach tickets for my family to fly directly from D.C. to Detroit. However, my arguments were persuasive, and I received full reimbursement for their first class travel I had arranged.

HELLO, DETROIT

In early August, we closed the FHA loan on our home for which we had paid $24,500 — requiring a monthly mortgage payment of $90. We immediately arranged to have North American Van Lines deliver our furniture from storage. Days later, when the truck arrived and our furniture was being unloaded, we observed several of our neighbors congregated across the street from our new home. However, not one of them approached us or acknowledged our move-in. Nonetheless, we completed the move and began to settle into our new home — which we immediately enjoyed and where we would remain for the next 28 years.

Figure 8. Our Lichfield Street home in Northwest Detroit's Green Acres subdivision

Our Detroit home was a three-bedroom, brick colonial with a wood face on the upper front, typical of many Detroit homes. It was part of the Green Acres subdivision of northwest Detroit, an area bounded by Eight Mile Road on the north, Pembroke Avenue on the south, Livernois Avenue on the west, and Woodlawn Cemetery on the east, which abutted Lichfield.

Our home had 2,500 square-feet of interior space, and had been built in 1955, which made it just over 10 years old. The master bedroom on the upper level had its own bathroom with shower, an attractive feature to us. The two other bedrooms shared a bath, which we referred to as the pink bathroom. There was a nice sized living room with a fireplace, a kitchen with built-in range and a pleasant dining area where our table and chairs from D.C. fit nicely. Nearby, a formal dining room led to a lovely den that looked out on our back yard. We had no garage. Instead, a paved side drive led to a gate to our backyard. There, a five-foot high stone fence separated us from our back neighbor on Briarwood, the street parallel to Lichfield.

We simply loved our new home. Soon after moving in, I painted the wood trim exterior and replaced the worn-out carpeting throughout the house.

Our street was pleasant and typical of most streets in Detroit. Detroit streets were much wider than the streets in D.C. and other eastern American cities. We loved how huge elm trees on both sides of the street arched to create a green canopy over the street. Unfortunately, Dutch-Elm disease killed those beautiful elms, as it tragically claimed thousands of trees throughout metropolitan Detroit. Few elms remain in southeast Michigan today. Those that survived stand out in stately fashion. Fortunately, the city initiated an aggressive replanting program and in a few years foliage was restored throughout the city.

What we loved most about our new neighborhood was that the terrain was flat and our kids could ride their bikes around the block. They could not do this in our D.C. neighborhood, where our home rested at the crest of a hill that emptied into a main thoroughfare.

My enthusiasm for my work at the IRS Detroit Data Center and the city itself remained high as we settled in. I had no idea how future events outside of my control would soon alter the course of my life in my newly adopted home. In 1966 the city was busy; unemployment hovered near 3 percent. Housing was scarce — especially for blacks, who were beginning to move north and west of the Davison Freeway into northwest Detroit. That part of the city was transitioning from a predominately white and Jewish area to one that seemed welcoming to blacks — continuing the pattern whereby African Americans replaced Jews as they moved further north and west into the suburbs of Southfield and Oak Park.

I quickly grew accustomed to the peaceful neighborhoods with tree-lined streets and manicured lawns. Retha and I were amazed by the availability of shopping close to our Green Acres neighborhood, especially the "Avenue of Fashion" on Livernois Avenue, which offered a wide variety of items for purchase just blocks from our new home. We and our neighbors could purchase anything there, from a new car to home furnishings and accessories, and food and clothing as well. Plus, there was Northland Mall, America's first suburban shopping center — anchored by major department stores — just a few miles away in Southfield. All of this was new to us, as shopping with such variety had not been available close to the Washington, D.C. neighborhood we had left.

Yet, the comfort and convenience we enjoyed was part of a Detroit package that included conflict and controversy.

WELCOME TO THE NEIGHBORHOOD!

No African Americans lived on our street. Only a handful resided in the square-mile subdivision of Green Acres. Right after we moved in, we received two unsigned, derogatory letters. We assumed that our neighbors sent them, but this was never determined. We read the hurtful contents of those letters several times — absorbing the pain and hurtful tone they contained — then threw them away. Looking back, I wish we had kept them for posterity.

Figure 1. Wintertime on Lichfield Street

Disapproval tinged even gestures that appeared positive at first glance. For example, a day or so after our move-in, a white neighbor came to our door to enroll us in the Green Acres Neighborhood Association. Since we had been members of our neighborhood association in D.C., we were interested in joining. Yet, we demurred after listening to his sales pitch.

"I want to welcome you to the neighborhood," the man said in a demeaning tone. "And I want you to know that we checked you out. We know what you paid for the house and we know you can afford to be here."

He knew who we were because everybody in the community was aware of our arrival. In 1966, few blacks lived in the Green Acres, Sherwood Forest or Palmer Park neighborhoods — all considered high-end communities. He went on to say that we were one of twelve black families in the area and were certainly welcomed because we "could afford to live here."

His remarks stunned me — leaving me incredulous and outraged by his offensive sales pitch. I was mostly speechless that anyone would visit us with such a so-called welcome. And while we eventually joined the association, we never participated until years later when blacks (and young, friendly whites) populated our neighborhood.

The second unimaginable experience happened when our six-year-old daughter, Petra, met two sisters close to her age playing outside their home. Living two doors away on our street, they invited Petra to come over and play. She asked our permission, which she was always required to do. Permitted to go, she ran over and rang the doorbell. It was summertime and the two girls' mother could see Petra approaching through the screen. She came to the door and slammed it in Petra's face.

What hurt us most was that no one took the time to meet or get to know our family. The mean-spirited actions exhibited — plus two letters we received in the mail — crossed the line. Recalling the content of the letters, which admonished us for moving into their neighborhood "in the middle of the night" with a "large mixed family" and "strange foods." These cruel, stereotypical remarks intended to remind us we were neither wanted in their community nor highly regarded as individuals. To me, all of these actions crossed the line, for not only were they inaccurate and racially motivated, they lacked human decency — attributing characteristics about us in a stereotypical and racist fashion. Interestingly, the family that slammed the door in Petra's face moved away within the month.

Several of my IRS associates visited our new home. As each of us moved into our new homes, we would gather and offer celebratory toasts. So, I suspect the frequent visits to our home by our friends, all within the first week or so, troubled our neighbors. They had probably never seen so many black people in their neighborhood. Perhaps this prompted their assumptions about the number of persons living in our home.

Interestingly, all of this could have been avoided had our neighbors simply introduced themselves and said hello. We were from the South and had lived in D.C., but we had never experienced the kind of racial ostracism we experienced during our first weeks in our Detroit home. Here we were experiencing a lack of common decency that all human beings naturally expect.

Ours was not the only negative experience a black family encountered during the summer of 1966. A black family moved into Grosse Pointe — an all-white suburb just east of Detroit, and received similar treatment. Like me, the father of the family was a bureaucrat moving to Detroit as a federal employee. His situation was reported in the local media, and it was not long before he was reassigned and left Michigan.

Other metropolitan Detroit communities had also excluded people of color. In addition to Grosse Pointe, Dearborn had a national reputation as a white enclave during the 1960s; Orville Hubbard, Dearborn's mayor from 1942 to 1978 was an outspoken segregationist widely admired among Southern municipal leaders during the height of the Civil Rights Movement. Other communities such as Warren maintained reputations as white enclaves for a number of years following our arrival.

Another incident that exemplified the initial harassment we endured involved our son Edmond's toy tractor, which he could sit in and "drive" by operating its foot pedals. We bought it for him for Christmas 1965, before moving to Detroit. During our first week on Lichfield, someone stole it out of our yard and took it several blocks away, hiding it in an alley. Petra, Edmond and I walked around the neighborhood, up and down every street. We finally found it and brought it back home.

We hoped this series of incidents that greeted our arrival was a rash of crude harassments that would never happen again. We often thought: here we are, way out here in Detroit, at least fourteen hours by car from our roots; basically alone. We knew very few people in our new city except for the Beckhams and a few IRS employees who moved to Detroit with us. It seemed we had stumbled into a hostile environment full of active racists. I was determined to protect my wife and family from whatever might happen — not knowing what to expect next.

THE DETROIT REBELLION

Retha became pregnant soon after our move to Detroit, and our son, Mark, was born in May of 1967. We purchased a new Ford Mercury Park Lane and a few months after he was born, I took my family with me on a short business trip to Washington. We left Detroit on a Thursday for meetings I had scheduled on Friday; stayed the weekend and visited with my brother Freddy and some of our D.C. friends. On Sunday morning, July 23, we began our return trip to Detroit.

As we approached Pittsburgh, I tuned in to WJR, the 50,000-watt station which carried the Detroit Tigers baseball games. As we listened to announcer Ernie Harwell calling the game's play-by-play, he remarked, "Maybe there're some problems in the street. I think I can see smoke in the distance."

Harwell said little else about the emerging problems in the Detroit streets, and I continued to listen to his call of the Tiger's game — not knowing that disruptive events were indeed occurring not far from Tiger Stadium on Detroit's near west side, about a mile from the central business district.

We continued listening to the baseball game, then switched to music before we arrived in Detroit. It was approaching midnight when we exited 1-75 onto Telegraph Road, then continued north toward Eight Mile Road.

We saw no evidence of the Detroit disturbances along the city's western and northern perimeter.

"Are you guys all right?" asked our next-door neighbors, Fran and Isadore Malin, when we arrived at home. "There's a riot going on."

"Yeah," I said, "but we haven't seen anything. We're OK." And we went to bed. Shortly thereafter, my mother called from North Carolina and asked, "Are you all right? Is everything all right?"

"Oh, yeah," I assured her; everything was fine. "There's something going on, but it does not seem to be close by," I said.

At six o'clock the next morning, my boss Vince Finelli called and said, "Walt, there is no work today. The office is closed."

I said to Retha, "Maybe we need to get up and see what's going on." We turned on our TV to learn that Detroit was national news!

We further learned that there had been a major fire right around the corner from our home! The Merchandise Mart, a home convenience store at 7 Mile and Livernois — just a mile away — had burned to the ground.

We loaded into our car and drove around. Burning buildings lined Livernois Avenue. Our good friends, Tom and Sarah Diggs, lived near Dexter Avenue on Buena Vista Street. As we drove toward their home, we were shocked that Dexter Avenue was decimated. We were stunned by the extent of the destruction around us.

According to a historical timeline prepared by *The Detroit News,* Governor George Romney sent in 360 Michigan State Police on Sunday, July 23, and added 3,000 federalized Michigan National Guard troops by Sunday evening. (More than 10,500 National Guardsmen were federalized between July 23 and August 2, according to the website GlobalSecurity.org.) At two a.m. Monday, Romney asked U.S. Attorney General Ramsey Clark for 5,000 federal troops. However, it took until noon for Romney and President Johnson to agree on the circumstances under which they could be sent. It is widely believed that politics played a big role in the decision-making, because Romney and Johnson were expected to be rivals for the presidency in 1968. By Monday afternoon, 4,700 U.S. Army paratroopers from the 82nd and 101st Airborne Divisions arrived in Detroit. About 1,800 of them hit Detroit's streets on Tuesday, July 25. With armed, uniformed troops and even tanks in the streets, things began to stabilize. The last of the fires was extinguished on Friday, July 28. Army troops pulled out of Detroit on July 29, and the National Guard left on Aug. 2.

As the details of the civil disturbance began to surface, we all learned of the Algiers Motel incident — which occurred inside a motel located at the intersection of Woodward Avenue and Virginia Park. Three young black men were killed, and two young white women and seven other black men were brutally beaten — either by Detroit police or members of the National Guard. As Pulitzer Prize-winning author John Hersey concluded in his 1968 book, *The Algiers Hotel Incident,* the killings took place for no reason, except for the inference by the authorities that the black men and white women were engaged in romantic or sexual relationships.

Along with most others, my office was closed for two days. When we did return to work, the conflict was still raging. Tom Diggs — a fellow IRS employee at the Data Center — was on his way home from our first day back at the IRS Data Center when a National Guard Army Reserve soldier stopped him. His offense? Simply being at the intersection of West Grand Boulevard and Twelfth Street — near the epicenter of the rebellion, which was a continuing hotspot during the early days following the conflagration. The National Guard soldier broke Tom's nose with the butt of his rifle.

"Get the hell out of here!" the soldier ordered.

What an ongoing introduction to the city of Detroit!

DETROIT'S SEARCH FOR THE ROOTS OF THE REBELLION

After the flames subsided, the gunfire ceased and the military tanks rolled out, forty-three people were dead. Hundreds more were injured. Property damage exceeded $250 million. Burned-out buildings scarred the city landscape. And Detroit's psyche seemed damaged beyond repair. Many had been confident that race relations in Detroit were progressing to the point that the city would not experience a repeat of America's largest racial disturbance — the 1964 Watts Riots in Los Angeles — or the subsequent rebellion in Newark, New Jersey, in June 1967. There was recognition that the racial climate in many eastern cities was ripe for unrest. But the prevailing view was that calm would prevail in Detroit, due to the general prosperity of the city and partnerships that existed between unions, business and government.

The common theme I heard during the pre-rebellion months was that African Americans were doing well, principally because of the efforts of the United Auto Workers. Earlier in the 1960s, the UAW and the Michigan Democratic Party had demonstrated a pronounced commitment to equal racial opportunities in Detroit. Blacks were seen as having made substantial progress, perhaps enough to avoid the kind of disruptions being experienced by other American cities.

I had taken an interest in the history of key issues affecting blacks in Detroit, particularly after the personal experiences we encountered upon moving into our new home. I learned that the March on Washington in August 1963 emanated from a massive march involving thousands of Detroiters that took place in June of 1963. During that march, Reverend C. L. Franklin, pastor of New Bethel Baptist Church (and father of singer Aretha Franklin, whose superstardom was still several years away), and UAW President Walter Reuther marched shoulder-to-shoulder down Woodward Avenue with Martin Luther King Jr. In addition, the city's NAACP was the nation's largest and most economically secure branch of the civil rights organization.

Finally, I learned that a variety of smaller groups had formed in Detroit to fight racial injustice. One called GOAL — Group for the Advancement of Leadership — challenged the dominant position of the Detroit NAACP. Another, founded by Wayne State University students, used the Swahili word "UHURU" (which means freedom). The Detroit chapter of SNCC (the Student Non-Violent Coordinating Committee) and RAM (Revolutionary Action Movement) were founded with agendas that were more strident and demanding than traditional black organizations. Indeed, Robert Williams of RAM advocated violence, if necessary, to insure that more blacks were in control of their lives.

I remember discussing the likelihood of a disturbance in Detroit with a white female passenger seated next to me on a Northwest Airlines flight to D.C. in June 1967. She thought the chances were remote. However, because of my initial experiences in Detroit, I was not so sure.

I reflected on the fact that the number of black professionals I had met in Detroit was quite small. I was aware that GM, Ford and Chrysler had only a handful of white-collar African American employees at the time. I had met Claude Reese, a Chrysler mid-level executive and neighbor in Green Acres, who had become a family friend. I befriended Claude and his wife, Pat, when one day, I followed their daughter Leslie home from school. I did this to find a playmate for our daughter, Petra, who did not have one in our neighborhood. Following this introduction, our children walked back and forth to school together. In addition to Leslie, the Reeses had a younger daughter, Tracy, and later a third daughter, Erin. Tracy Reese grew up to be a nationally acclaimed fashion designer based in New York City.

Chrysler also employed Lowell Perry, whom I didn't know at the time, along with Earl Lloyd, the former Pistons' coach. I also knew Jay Hollis, a GM attorney and a neighbor who lived in nearby Sherwood Forest. I had heard of Levy Jackson, employed by Ford after studying at Yale during the time Henry Ford II was a student there. I was later to meet Larry Washington, another Ford Motor Company employee, as well as Gus Callaway and Ed Hodges — both of whom worked for Michigan Bell. I had reacquainted myself with Bill Beckham's dad, William Beckham, Sr., executive assistant to Walter Reuther of the UAW. I also knew of other prominent, black UAW executives: Nelson Jack Edwards, Mark Stepp and Horace Sheffield. I had heard of Bill Patrick, a Michigan Bell assistant vice president who was a former Detroit City Councilman.

But aside from those individuals, it did not appear that private sector employment of blacks as executives and white-collar professionals was widespread in Detroit. If blacks were employed by

Detroit corporations, they languished at very low salary levels. The Detroit Public School's governance board was mostly white, and the superintendent was white. None of the hospitals had any African Americans serving on their boards in Metropolitan Detroit — except Detroit Receiving, the city-owned hospital where Horace Sheffield and Dr. Charles Vincent were trustees.

THE FORMATION OF NEW DETROIT INC. — AND FOCUS:HOPE

Such fundamental inequality in the economic and social structure of the prosperous city of Detroit became glaring in the aftermath of the July 1967 rebellion. Within days, Michigan Governor George Romney and Detroit Mayor Jerome Cavanaugh convened the business and labor communities, along with some of Detroit's prominent citizens, to discuss the catastrophic event. Born of those discussions was New Detroit, Inc. — the nation's first "urban coalition" formed to address the deeply rooted racial inequities that led to a major civil disturbance.

Joseph Hudson, the 33-year-old Chairman of the J. L. Hudson Company, was tapped as the new organization's first chair. His company owned and operated Hudson's, Detroit's flagship downtown department store, which would soon merge with Minnesota's Dayton Department Stores — becoming Dayton-Hudson. The company would later develop the Target discount retail chain — taking on the "Target" name as its corporate moniker. Prominent business leaders were asked to serve as members of New Detroit's Board of Trustees and to fund the organization. Among the first invited were: Henry Ford II of Ford Motor Company; James M. Roche, chairman of General Motors; Lynn Townsend, chairman of Chrysler; and Walter P. Reuther, president of the United Auto Workers.

Other union officials included Jack Woods, secretary-manager of Detroit Wayne County Building Trades Council; and Robert (Bobby) Holmes, senior vice president of the International Brotherhood of Teamsters.

New Detroit's original trustees also included: Max Fisher, a prominent Detroit financier; Hans Gehrke, Jr. of First Federal of

Michigan; Stanley Winkelman, CEO of Winkelman Stores; Richard Huegli of United Community Services; Walker Cisler, CEO of Detroit Edison (now a part of DTE Energy); Ralph McElvenny, chairman of Michigan Consolidated Gas Company (also now a part of DTE Energy); William (Bill) Day, CEO of Michigan Bell (now a part of AT&T Communications); attorney William T. Gossett (former General Counsel of Ford Motor and President-Elect of the American Bar Association); Father Malcolm Carron, president of University of Detroit University; William R. Keast, president of Wayne State University; Dr. Norman Drachler, general superintendent of the Detroit Public Schools; and many other business, community and union leaders.

Black community leadership included: Tom Turner, president of the AFL-CIO; Lena Bivens, a welfare mother; Arthur Johnson, a former NAACP executive director and deputy superintendent of the Detroit Public Schools; Lorenzo (Rennie) Freeman; Norvell Harrington; Damon J. Keith, U. S. District Court Judge; Robert Tindal, executive secretary of the Detroit NAACP; and Jean Washington of the Tenth Precinct Police Community Relations Committee.

For some reason still unclear to me, Francis Kornegay, executive director of the Detroit Urban League, was not included and never served on the New Detroit Board. Soon, however, other blacks were added, including Dr. Reginald Wilson, president of Wayne County Community College; Glenn E. Wash, owner of G. E. Wash Construction; Gerald Smith, a social worker; V. Lonnie Peek, Jr. –a community activist; Wardell Croft, president of the black-owned Wright Mutual Insurance Company; and Frank Ditto, an Eastside community leader.

Elected officials included: Mel Ravitz, chairman of the Wayne County Board of Supervisors; Delos Hamlin of the Oakland County Board of Supervisors; Norman Hill of Macomb County; and state Senate and House members Emil Lockwood and Bill Ryan. Those responsible for determining New Detroit's board composition made sure that a substantial number of "non-traditional" leaders were selected from the black community, advancing the notion that had the right leaders been involved prior to the disturbance, it might not have occurred.

New Detroit's organizers selected as its first president William T. (Bill) Patrick, the Michigan Bell executive who had served on City Council. This initiated the tradition of naming a white board chair and black president as leaders of New Detroit.

New Detroit, Inc., began with more than $3 million in cash and pledges for the first year's operation. Direct funding came primarily from the corporate community, with area Foundations and the UAW providing funding as well. And as New Detroit began to operate, employing an elaborate construct of board committees, funding was provided to existing and start-up community organizations for all sorts of novel problem-solving initiatives.

A process called Community Self-Determination became the chosen vehicle for change. It suggested that whites should demur to the ideas advanced by blacks, offering suggestions only when asked for, as initiatives were advanced. In effect, Community Self-Determination implied that whites were not generally welcomed to offer their thoughts and ideas to address community problems and needs.

New Detroit's' staff consisted of both paid professionals and loaned executives from local corporations who were charged with addressing the problems that had apparently sparked the conflagration. The Big Three auto companies were tapped and generally led the way in providing loaned staff.

New Detroit's immediate efforts to address needs identified by community residents established it as a powerful force in resolving community disputes. The new organization seemed involved in all of the major issues affecting the city; it promised hope that wounds gashed open by the disturbance would be examined and healed.

In response to the priorities set by community representatives, education and economic development were the two primary issues the new organization addressed, with police brutality a close third on the agenda. Examples of bold actions New Detroit took on each of the issues included:

★ Establishment of Wayne County Community College, with a plan to locate campuses throughout Wayne County;

★ Creation of the Economic Development Corporation, whose charge was to spur the development of black-owned businesses. However, a newly formed black entity called the Inner City Business Improvement Forum (ICBIF) demanded that it — rather than E.D.C. — fulfill that role. Consequently, E.D.C.'s responsibility changed to include becoming a "funds-flow-through" organization that provided funding support for ICBIF's work and initiatives.

★ Investigation of the New Bethel Incident — - which involved the mass arrest of 142 black citizens following the shooting death of a Detroit police officer and the wounding of another officer.

These examples of New Detroit's work prompted a positive response from the Detroit community, black and white, with a majority of citizens collectively endorsing the organization's work. As the media provided a daily chronicle of the New Detroit's actions and deliberations, I followed its progress with immense interest and concern, intrigued by the scope of its work and its accomplishments.

At the same time, another organization formed to solve urban problems that had contributed to the civil disturbance. Focus: HOPE — founded by Father William T. Cunningham and a parishioner, Eleanor Josaitis — aimed to unite blacks and whites across the fault line that had split the community during the rebellion. Supported by the Big Three, Focus: HOPE specialized in training inner-city men and women to become assembly-line workers. It also sponsored a program to feed poor families.

Meanwhile, churches and community groups flocked to New Detroit, Inc., to benefit from its mission of providing financial support for groups whose initiatives aimed to rebuild the city of Detroit. While I watched from the sidelines, my interest in all of these activities continued to grow.

ADJUSTMENT, 1967

Despite the July disturbances and the aftermath of the following weeks, Retha and I decided we would not change our plans to take our first vacation since moving to Detroit. It was planned for the last three weeks of August. We loaded Petra, Edmond and two-month old Mark into our new Mercury Parklane and drove to Massachusetts to visit my college buddy Ray Bell and his family. From there we vacationed briefly in Montréal and elsewhere in Québec before driving to Newport News, Virginia, where we visited several of my father's siblings and their families. After that, we headed to North Carolina to visit Retha's parents and mine.

Leaving North Carolina on our way back to Detroit, we stopped in Philadelphia, where Eddie, Retha's youngest brother, was to marry his second wife, Billie. After the wedding, we returned to Detroit, bringing Retha's mother with us, who at the time was recovering from surgery. Although the city had begun to settle down from the rebellion and the disturbances that followed, tension charged the air. Retha and I knew that Detroit had changed forever. Just in case, I had the shotgun my father had given me upon leaving North Carolina.

"Son," he said, handing over the weapon, "You be careful and take care of yourself." I still have that shotgun today. As an accomplished handler of rifles and pistols — learning as a child from my father how to handle weapons, and having been a U.S. Army marksman — I felt confident that I could handle any circumstance requiring the use of a firearm.

RETURN TO THE CITY

Upon returning to Detroit, we braced for what we knew would be a difficult period of adjustment for blacks as well as whites. The following months would be fraught with rumors and sporadic community flare-ups. Businesses burned overnight, or racially tinged encounters suggested that destructive behavior lurked just below the surface of everyday interactions.

The community was not sure whether businesses being burned were the result of nefarious activity or the consequence of disgruntled owners unhappy with the unpredictable business climate they foresaw if they kept their businesses in Detroit. There was widespread speculation that business owners were deliberately burning their establishments to collect insurance proceeds and head to the northern suburbs. Perhaps some of both occurred, but I remained convinced that many business owners deliberately burned their establishments so they could exit the city of Detroit.

Adding to the difficulties Detroit faced was a prolonged newspaper strike that began in the fall of 1967 and continued into the summer of 1968. Having no daily newspapers to keep the metropolitan community attuned to events that were happening prompted even more rumors and unease. And while local weekly newspapers like the *Michigan Chronicle* attempted to fill the gap, the lack of information from the city's well-regarded daily newspapers was unnerving for Detroiters.

This restiveness played out at Don's Drug, a favorite store on Seven Mile west of Livernois. It provided out-of-town papers daily, particularly *The New York Times* and *The Chicago Tribune*. On Sundays, residents would line up to purchase out-of-town papers. The line would be nearly a block long and would include many white and Jewish residents along with the handful of blacks who had begun to relocate into this mostly white and Jewish enclave. I noticed that whites in line constantly whispered inquiries of each other as to whether they planned on moving. Many did, indeed, move. The result over the following year was a dramatic change in the complexion of residents in Northwest Detroit.

However, some did not move; they remained in Detroit. Our neighbors the Malins, plus two couples who lived nearby in Green Acres became friends to Retha and me. They sent their kids to Louis Pasteur Elementary School with ours, and over the years helped to shape the city — with many others who stayed put. They included the Malins — Fran and Isadore; Barbara and Carl Levin; and their friends the Drikers — Elaine and Eugene. In the late Sixties, Carl was elected to the Detroit City Council, where he served two four-year terms, the last four as council president. He then successfully ran for the U.S. Senate, where he continues to make a difference for the citizens of Michigan and our nation. Eugene Driker continues to practice law in the city of Detroit; he is a long-serving member of the board of governors at Wayne State University and chairs the university's foundation board.

SELECTING OUR DETROIT CHURCH HOME

During this time of tense transition, our local church membership was an additional source of stability and civic connection.

On my first Sunday in Detroit, July 17, 1966, I decided I would attend church. Mrs. Atkins, my temporary landlady, said, "Oh, you're Methodist. You ought to attend this real big church downtown called Central Methodist Church. But, you have a choice; for there is a Methodist church much closer — just a couple of blocks north of our street, Euclid. They're both on Woodward."

So on that Sunday morning in July, I first stopped at Metropolitan Methodist Church near Euclid. I stood out front, not sure I should go in after observing that all who were attending were white. I didn't see any black people going into Metropolitan, and quite frankly felt a little uncomfortable attending service there. (Interestingly enough, years later I was to meet Metropolitan's pastor, Rev. Bill Quick. He had grown up in a small community called Gio just outside my hometown of Hamlet, N.C. and attended Duke University — across town from NCC.)

I decided to attend church at Central Methodist instead, which was closer to downtown, on Woodward Avenue at Grand Circus Park. In front of the church, I met a fine gentleman by the name of Estemore Wolf. He was a teacher with the Detroit Public Schools and sang in the church choir. A graduate of Jackson State, a historically black college located in Jackson, Mississippi, Estemore made me feel very comfortable as I entered the church.

When Retha arrived a few weeks later, I introduced her to the church and our family soon joined, just months after our arrival in Detroit. Joining required us to attend a mandatory orientation session that stretched over our first month of membership. Ned Dewire, the junior pastor, conducted the orientation sessions; Retha and I attended with several other new members. What a fortuitous orientation session we experienced. Perhaps, for the first time in my life, I began to understand what it meant to be a Methodist. We came away from our orientation sessions more accepting of the church doctrines. We became enthused with the church programs, which included an especially tailored Sunday school curriculum. Developed at Union Theological Seminary in New York, it targeted our children's age range. We enrolled Petra and Edmond in the Sunday school program, and later taught Sunday school ourselves; and when Mark was born, he too was enrolled.

Church became more meaningful to me, for with my membership at Central, I could combine my religious beliefs with a tolerance for human imperfection and with meaningful community initiatives. Some were pedagogic in nature and stretched beyond the church door.

Central, being an activist church, quickly adjusted its programming to reflect concerns brought on by the tensions that faced Detroit following the 1967 rebellion. As members, we were encouraged to participate. As I joined the various discussion groups, consisting of a cross section of Centralities, I noted that while Central enjoyed an integrated church body, its leadership was all-white. I sensed that little real dialogue had ever taken place between the church's members. My early exchanges with whites there reflected their desire to have blacks relate to them "everything they didn't know about blacks and until the recent disturbance had never thought to ask." I attended Thursday luncheon groups for the men at Central Methodist, taking along my friend Tom Diggs.

We learned that Central Methodist, the first Protestant church in the state of Michigan, was perhaps the most liberal and well-integrated church in Detroit. It had a rich history as a human rights and activist church. Central's senior minister when we joined was James Laird, who had followed Henry Hitt Crane, a renowned Detroit preacher who led Central for years. We learned early on that Crane's quotes on simple life choices and actions remained in vogue under Laird. Those maxims excited me, because they presented a more earthly exercise of religion; they imbued me with a more natural feeling of religion than one that required a rigid discharge of duty and practice of ritual.

But change was in the wind at Central. Shortly after our arrival, Laird departed to join the Religious Society of Friends (Quakers) in Philadelphia, taking Central's associate minister Ned Dewire with him. Dwight Large became our senior minister and William Mate joined as associate minister. And with pressure to integrate the ministry at Central, Jim Cochrane was assigned by the church hierarchy, becoming Central's first black associate minister.

As new members during the sixties, we quickly observed the mixture of individuals who attended from Grosse Pointe, Dearborn, Southfield and other surrounding suburbs — calling themselves liberals or supportive of liberal causes. We also met many individuals that would be considered committed liberals, individuals who remained active at Central for their entire church lives. Central's membership included interracial couples and activists who brought issues before the congregation regarding racial strife and world peace. The Vietnam War ranked high among many issues discussed. Indeed, Central's membership reflected the true makeup of America, openly welcoming individuals of all persuasions — including sexual orientation.

Additionally, Central's membership included others who belonged to what I would term religious cults. The Ecumenical Institute (EI) was one such movement that took hold and grew at Central, after having formed roots in Chicago. Many of Central's members became involved with the Ecumenical Institute, and when asked, Retha and I agreed to become active participants as well. This EI group met every Thursday evening. Indeed, it was during a Thursday evening meeting at our home on April 4, 1968, when we were interrupted by the news that Martin Luther King, Jr., had been assassinated. Two weeks earlier, King had spoken at the Maundy Thursday Mass at Central during Easter celebration — a testament to Central's national prominence as a progressive ministry. That evening Kim White, the wife of current Methodist Bishop Woody White (both of whom were then Central members) was a guest at our home. Kim became quite emotional over the assassination, for she always saw her husband, Woody, a black activist minister, as being like Dr. King. Kim remarked, "That's the same fate he's going to come to," and she seemed genuinely concerned for her husband's life.

We attended weekend sessions on "EI" at the Boulevard Temple Methodist Church at the intersection of West Grand Boulevard and Rosa Parks (formerly 12th Street) where my friend Tom Diggs had gotten his nose broken, and where the dialogue was all about being "intentional." It was very much like sensitivity training. All of us were encouraged to "be true to one's inner feelings and be real in one's expressions." They suggested, "Don't hold back."

Harrison Frazier was a black minister with the EI headquarters in Chicago, and whites who knew him encouraged us blacks to get to know him, remarking to us, "You've got to meet Harrison; he's an exceptional spiritual leader." Well, when I did meet him, he was indeed an impressive black man; his message was both different and profound. He was a great preacher and expressed his thoughts very clearly and "intentionally." Harrison spoke with the vernacular of many black preachers I had heard — and I sensed that his style and delivery had helped him win over white audiences. In our weekend training, Harrison and the other speakers encouraged us to make sure that the actions we took affected the lives and issues around us. I left my first weekend retreat all pumped up and ready to tackle the world. This carried over into my work and office leadership at the Data Center during the following week. The cult had indeed "hooked" me!

Sometimes our dialogue sessions were held at people's homes. Once I was invited to a white Central church member's home in Northwest Detroit where she had assembled a group of her neighbors to whom I could speak "intentionally." Meeting in her 1,000 square-foot frame house, I responded to questions about being black and what it was like. I answered with respect and restraint, knowing that those in attendance, like most other white Americans, already knew too well, or had observed with either little thought or sorrow to the plight of most black Americans. Interestingly, they avoided asking me any questions about my career or where I lived. It seemed in these sessions that the role of blacks was to relate what it was like to be black while the role of whites was to seem shocked that we were treated as such in America. Also, we blacks were expected to assure them that like their own, our children ran the gamut from being normal to exceptional and at times having special needs. We were to remind our audiences that while many of us were college graduates, our lot in life tended not to rise to their level.

Most of the whites with whom we dialogued worked in factories or in other blue-collar and non-executive white-collar jobs. They already knew more than a little about blacks, our educational backgrounds and the fact that many college-trained blacks wound up working in mediocre positions in the private sector or at the post office — because they couldn't get ordinary jobs at Hudson's department store, General Motors, Ford, Chrysler, Detroit-area banks or any other corporation. Whites knew all of this, but wanted us to tell it to them. Perhaps the beauty of these sessions is that for the first time, many whites and blacks were talking face-to-face about issues that had not been addressed in a safe and structured environment.

Retha and I were only beginning to make our way and gain an understanding of our new community. We loved Central, our children loved Central, and we were meeting new people — black and white who were new to us, but friendly and engaging. Mostly, we just went about our church-related duties and assumed that sooner or later, we would become even more fully engaged in the life of Central. We taught Sunday school, and a majority of our students were white. This made for interesting dialogue. They represented a broad spectrum, from the suburbs and the city. In 1969, the Central teenagers performed a rather unique Easter skit. In it, a teenage girl was selected to preach. During her sermon, another youngster in a trench coat approached the pulpit, pulled a gun and pretended to shoot her. The skit aimed to show women in non-traditional roles while reflecting the reality of the times. It also depicted the assassinations of John Kennedy, Martin Luther King, Jr., and Robert Kennedy, while again reflecting on the "happenings" that influenced teenage thinking during the late Sixties.

During that era, many songs were recorded by artists like Joan Baez, Stevie Wonder and others that depicted the traumatic events occurring, while offering hope, encouragement and inspiration. During my Sunday school sessions, I played many of these popular songs, which we then discussed. I encouraged my students to be "intentional," honest and open in sharing their feelings with each other. On several occasions, we visited other denominations, including traditional black churches and Jewish Synagogues. Once, we invited in the Hari Krishnas, an emerging religious sect that joined our class to demonstrate in song and ritual their religious beliefs. My intentions during my Sunday school classes were to broaden my students' minds with greater understanding about racial and religious differences.

Everything was about dialogue. Some of it was open; some of it was role-playing, and all of it made for a very interesting time. It seemed that our world was changing. America was becoming more inclusive and we sensed good times ahead!

During one dialogue session, the most extraordinary thing happened during an "EI" event at the Boulevard Temple on West Grand Boulevard. An elderly white gentleman was asked to conduct the opening prayer. During the prayer, I was kneeling beside Tom Diggs when this gentleman in his prayer remarked, "Lord, you have to understand that I'm being intentional and I'm being honest and I'm being open and I'm being myself. And I continue to be well-aware of the evening my wife opened our bedroom door to discover me with my 'member' in my hand and my male friend and me performing as lovers." He said it out loud! With my head bowed, I was shocked! But that was the way people came out in those days and I've never forgotten the event.

Afterwards, I concluded that "EI" wasn't where or who I wanted to be. It's all right to be honest and open and intentional and all of that, but I also felt a need to be *doing* something. We continued our membership and Sunday school teaching at Central. For a time, I served as a church trustee. Indeed, Central remains our church today. Our daughter, Petra, and son Edmond both took wedding vows there. But the extent of my *doing* something eventually extended beyond my association with Central. My *doings* would take on a broader scope and would continue to expand over the ensuing forty years and beyond. They would encompass many organizations in the Detroit community and beyond, all starting with my close association with Larry Doss.

CHAPTER 6

BLACK ECONOMIC DEVELOPMENT

MY EPIPHANY: MEETING LARRY DOSS

In life, we meet individuals and encounter experiences that alter our perspective and change our direction. Events or individuals such as these create landmarks to which we later point in acknowledging that a new beginning took place, or that our vision was changed or life's calling came into focus.

My epiphany occurred when Larry Doss and I started to work collaboratively on urban issues in the late 1960s. His involvement in the urban laboratory heightened my desire to get involved, and subsequently created an opportunity for me to enter the fray. Larry became my coach, so to speak, and put me in the game! Once I was in the game, we became linked like navigational stars — pulling each other along like a binary star system.

Larry Doss was a unique human being and certainly a unique black American. He was a gifted, no-nonsense type of individual. Larry exuded a divine and afflatus nature. His presence was accented by his blue-gray eyes, and in later years, his silver grey hair prompted some to refer to him as "the silver fox." His handsome face and athletic build drew stares. Women talked openly about him — and yes, rumors swirled.

Larry was a forerunner and mentor for me in business, politics, and an endless number of social settings. His influence was unintentional at first; later, quite purposeful. Larry was a forceful, game-changing kind of executive at the IRS; then at the Inner City Business Improvement Forum (ICBIF), an economic development nonprofit organization he co-founded; as president of New Detroit Inc., and finally as the leader of United Communications, an investor group formed to purchase radio stations across the nation. I would be deeply involved in each of these organizations once Larry's trailblazing efforts had had their effect.

Larry had a pleasing personality; yet, he could intimidate nearly any person he encountered. It took a while for many, including me, to relax and feel comfortable in his presence. He pursued issues with great energy and vigor. Yet, he had a giving nature and was very committed to fixing the problems that affected the lives of black and poor individuals. I concluded, soon after getting to know him that Larry Doss was the most committed individual I had ever met. Early on, I also learned that he was a great tennis player — beating opponents often and winning tournaments while vacationing on Martha's Vineyard and nearby resort communities. Larry was very competitive, never backing away from a challenge; once, after learning I played chess, he challenged me to a match. I won, and he never offered to play me again.

Larry and I first met while we both worked for the IRS in Washington. He and my boss Barbara Vatran, a black woman with extraordinary ability and character, had lunch one day and she introduced him to me upon their return to the office. I was pleased to meet Larry and appreciated Barbara's introduction; like everyone else, I knew he was the highest-ranking African American in the entire agency. Ironically, both Larry and I would later relocate to Detroit, arriving within months of each other. While I worked in the IRS Data Processing Center, he was assigned to the District Office in downtown Detroit. Later, when Larry was reassigned as Director of the Data Center, I would get to know him and we became friends.

Larry was a Cleveland native who joined the Navy as a teenager, as soon as age would permit. The Navy helped to develop his natural abilities to lead and be a "take charge" individual. After being discharged from the Navy, he ended up working for the Internal Revenue Service in its Cleveland office and advanced quickly — eventually being reassigned to Washington, D.C. On the IRS fast track, Larry soon completed the agency's Executive Development program, and advanced to the GS-16 grade — an exceptional level for blacks at the time. He became Assistant Director of the IRS's Detroit District office before he had even earned his college degree.

In 1969, Larry's boss at the IRS Detroit District office died suddenly. The assumption was that Larry would replace him, since he had served as his assistant, knew the functions of the District office well and was already in Detroit. Replacing the deceased director would make Larry the first black GS-17 at the IRS, the agency we all called The Service. But Larry was not selected. Incensed, Larry resigned shortly thereafter — and resisted the agency's attempts to woo him back, even several years later.

DPS DECENTRALIZATION

Shortly after leaving the IRS, Larry was recruited to lead the School Decentralization Study Committee, an initiative designed to study a proposed decentralization of the Detroit Public Schools. The issue of School Decentralization, whereby regional governing boards would take responsibility for assigned geographic areas of Detroit, had become a heated and controversial issue. Decentralization was favored by many citizens who saw greater community control as the key to better education and the general uplift of African Americans. Larry took on the task of completing the study, and did so in a little over a year.

State Senator Coleman A. Young sponsored decentralization legislation that passed the Michigan Legislature, but it was only the beginning of a long, contentious battle over the governance of Detroit Public Schools and desegregation of schools and housing in metro Detroit. In 1971, U.S. District Judge Stephen Roth ordered integration by way of school busing throughout the entire region, but the U.S. Supreme Court struck down that bold plan, ruling in 1974 that only DPS would be subject to desegregation by busing.

The bitter battle over busing and school desegregation launched the political careers of several individuals, including Oakland County Executive Brooks Patterson, who argued the case against regional desegregation before the U.S. Supreme Court in 1973 as Oakland County Prosecutor; and Barbara Rose Collins, who was first elected to the Detroit School Board, followed by successful campaigns for election to the Michigan State Legislature, the United States Congress and finally to the Detroit City Council. Collins was backed by the Shrine of the Black Madonna, a powerful religious organization in Detroit from the 1960s onward. The Shrine and its political arm, the Black Slate, Inc., were founded and led by Bishop Albert C. Cleage — also known by the African name Jaramogi Abebe Agyeman. Under Jaramogi's leadership, the Black Slate helped Coleman Young become the first black mayor of Detroit in 1973, and later was important in the careers of U.S. Rep. Carolyn Cheeks Kilpatrick and other blacks who ran for political office in Michigan.

THE INNER CITY BUSINESS IMPROVEMENT FORUM

Even before Larry Doss resigned his position as the director the IRS Data Center, I read a *Michigan Chronicle* article in late 1968 about the Inner City Business Improvement Forum, a new economic development nonprofit organization that had been set up with Larry as its president. The news story told how Congressman Charles Diggs, who was Larry's Lafayette Park neighbor, had initiated ICBIF and Larry had helped him get the organization started.

With offices on Fourteenth Street on Detroit's west side, ICBIF was physically identified with the epicenter of the rebellion's street disturbances. Its purpose was to improve the lot of existing minority businesses in Detroit and create new companies with the ability to enter the mainstream of American commerce. Those behind the ICBIF initiative had strong notions that it was now time for African Americans to become serious participants on the business side of the American marketplace. Their view was that in order to increase economic opportunities, black voices should agitate when necessary. Yet, they felt it was just as important to identify and nurture black individuals capable of building new companies. It was strongly felt that this effort should be a tireless one, with a goal of maximizing the success of all available opportunities.

Other organizations had historically attempted to fill this role, with the Booker T. Washington Business Association (BTWBA) being the most prominent in Detroit. Founded in 1930 and taking its name from perhaps the most prominent African American of the first half of the 20th century, the organization had fashioned itself as a black chamber of commerce, with an emphasis on self-help and mutual cooperation. Yet, some were eager for a more aggressive initiative to advance black business development, and the methodical approach of the BTWBA — combined with the compliant image of its namesake — seemed out of touch with the times. Indeed, some who later joined the ICBIF board had been involved at BTWBA. For instance, local florist Ed Brazelton had been a pillar at BTWBA. But seeing the more aggressive business agenda of ICBIF and the funding it was attracting, Ed joined the ICBIF board and became an avid supporter. Within a year or so of ICBIF's founding, most of the controversy between the two organizations had subsided; I could sense enthusiastic support for ICBIF's mission.

ICBIF's initial project was the establishment of First Independence National Bank, Detroit's first modern-era black-owned bank. (Home Federal Savings Bank was formed in 1947; and perhaps, there were attempts to form other financial institutions in previous times.) ICBIF led the effort to sell shares of stock, managed the process that gained the bank its federal charter and hired its initial president, David Harper. There had initially been opposition to the bank by local banking officials, who feared that a black bank would materially affect deposits by black citizens in their institutions. Nonetheless, with the help of Andrew F. Brimmer, the first black Board of Governors member of the Federal Reserve System, Larry, Congressman Diggs, Dr. Karl Gregory and others won approval for a federal charter for the bank. Once established, Detroit-area banks served as correspondent banks for First Independence.

ICBIF also started "Our Super Market," a grocery store on Linwood Street in Detroit where few food establishments existed following the rebellion of '67. In addition, ICBIF teamed with the Ford Motor Company in launching a stamping plant owned by Ford employees Bob Renfro and Mohamed (Mo) Muthleb; the firm was named Renmuth by combining their names. Apparently, the two had never met before being plucked from the ranks of Ford's black senior manufacturing supervisors and introduced into this business by Ford. Interesting!

Projects of this type piqued my interest, for they were the sort of endeavors I wanted to be involved with. They seemed to offer hope for aspiring blacks interested in business and economic development. From my days at Walter Reed Army Medical Center and my discussions with the white business professionals I met there, my interest in business development had continued to grow. I saw this newly created organization as a prime opportunity to explore that aspiration.

So, one day I approached Larry and asked him if I could become involved. Not only did he invite me to come to their next meeting, he arranged for me to be elected to the ICBIF board! Securing that position was perhaps the most significant harbinger of my future involvement in community and economic development in Detroit. Larry's trust of me and respect for my capabilities made it all possible. I joined the ICBIF board in 1969.

A PUSH FOR BLACK BUSINESS DEVELOPMENT

ICBIF had three primary objectives for achieving black business growth: (1) providing equity capital to start-up or fledgling minority businesses; (2) serving as an intermediary to assist businesses in establishing contact with majority firms capable of providing financing and/or business opportunities, and (3) providing consulting services to minority firms to help them develop and expand.

Individuals interested in starting their own businesses could come to ICBIF, get a hearing and find direct assistance in fully developing their thoughts and ideas. They then could receive help raising equity capital, in much the same way that venture capitalists have always assisted aspiring entrepreneurs. Also, through ICBIF business aspirants could receive assistance in meeting local bank or

Small Business Administration officials and gain access to the services they offered.

ICBIF served an important political role. Its visibility — through the media attention it attracted — encouraged better lending practices by Detroit banks and the SBA. ICBIF's role was to open doors to corporate America (especially the Big Three) and to encourage all Detroit area companies to utilize the services of black start-up firms, as well as existing black firms who wanted to expand or grow their businesses.

It is important to note that although ICBIF had a few prominent white members, it was almost a completely black institution. It may seem strange, in the polarized political climate of the early twenty-first century, that such a stridently Afrocentric organization would quickly earn the respect, cooperation and contributions of corporations and other major white institutions. But it must be remembered how desperate America was for answers to urban unrest in the late 1960s. Corporate leaders and politicians realized that the racial injustice and economic inequality of the past was unsustainable. Things needed to change fast, and white executives and elected officials were ready to work with black leaders who offered realistic, hopeful solutions.

BURNING MIDNIGHT OIL FOR ICBIF

Once I was elected an ICBIF board member, I quickly became involved, spending many evening hours on the organization after my regular IRS workday. Retha and I still recall those marathon days when I'd get up at six a.m. to start my IRS workday, which began at seven-thirty a.m. Following my IRS shift, I would come home, have dinner with Retha and the kids, then head off to an ICBIF meeting, which started at seven o'clock in the evening and ended around nine p.m. After the official meeting, some of us would invariably go to Bonaparte's, a local bar on Milwaukee Avenue in the New Center Area, to review the meeting. This meant that I often arrived home well after midnight. In those early days, we met often. Although I would be drained of energy by the time I arrived home, the stimulating discussions and new individuals I was meeting gave my life a new purpose. I began to rapidly change my focus and primary interests.

Sam Gardner, who was later to become a prominent Recorders Court Judge in Detroit, became general counsel for ICBIF. Founding officers of ICBIF were Dr. Charles Morton, chairman; Dr. Karl Gregory, vice chairman; Larry Doss, president; Nathaniel Smith, vice president; the Honorable Charles Diggs, secretary; Dorothy Quarker, assistant secretary; and Wardell C. Croft, treasurer.

According to original records kept by Dr. Gregory, there were at least 30 charter board members, including: Ed Brazelton of Brazelton Florists; future City Council members Clyde Cleveland and Kenneth Cockerel, Sr.; chemist and entrepreneur Dr. Austin W. Curtis, Jr.; and Edith Woodberry, a prominent community activist who had founded a downtown neighborhood organization called Woodward East that was focused on restoring homes in an area just north of Central Methodist Church, where Retha and I attended. Whites on the ICBIF board included Gabe Werba, the owner of a Detroit consulting firm; Esther Shapiro, a consumer advocate; and Dr. John Tower, a professor in the business school at Oakland University in Rochester, Michigan.

Howard Sims, a Detroit architect, joined the ICBIF board around the same time as I did. Later, attorney Claudia Morcom and Brenda Rayford, founder of Detroit Black United Fund, were added, and I was able to bring aboard my friend Claude Reese, a Chrysler executive.

Walter McMurtry was ICBIF's Executive Director, on loan from Bank of the Commonwealth. Attorney Willie Lipscomb and Phil Sims headed up the professional loan staff, while attorney Nancy Rowe, later to work for the Coleman Young administration, was ICBIF's in-house counsel. Before I arrived, Carthan Spencer had become ICBIF's chief financial officer.

As I became more involved, Larry assigned me specific duties and responsibilities. He put me in charge of fund raising and I quickly garnered a grant from the United Methodist Church. Later on, Larry and I went to New York to visit with Lyle Marshall, a program officer with the Ford Foundation, which resulted in a substantial grant to ICBIF.

It was through a personal relationship between Larry and Henry Ford II that the Ford Foundation connection was made. Larry had met Henry Ford II during a "Six on Six" dialogue session following the 1967 rebellion, where six representatives from the black community met with six representatives of Ford Motor Company and members of the Detroit business community to discuss important issues affecting blacks in Detroit — with a special emphasis on black economic development. Whites included in that session, in addition to Henry Ford II, were: philanthropist Max Fisher; Arjay Miller, president of Ford Motor, Lou Gillette — an influential individual known to Henry Ford; Bill Schoen, another Ford executive; Bill Day of Michigan Bell; and Joseph L. Hudson — New Detroit's founding chairman and CEO of the J. L. Hudson Company. Blacks included with Larry in the Six on Six meeting were Walter McMurtry; economist Dr. Karl Gregory; Dr. Charles Morton; Congressman Charles Diggs and Levi Jackson, a black executive at Ford Motor Company who had attended Yale University with Henry Ford II. While at Yale, Jackson had been an outstanding football player and was once featured on the cover of *Time* magazine.

I would learn that this intriguing dialogue helped set an over-arching agenda that was privately shared between the white business leaders and emerging black leaders at the time. The session subsequently led to the initial funding for ICBIF — hence, the Ford Foundation relationship — and the establishment of the Economic Development Corporation, a flow-through mechanism established to interface between New Detroit and ICBIF. This formal separation of entities was prompted by ICBIF's "self-determination" stance and the organization's refusal to interface directly with New Detroit. Therefore, although ICBIF did receive funding from New Detroit, it flowed through the EDC organization. Again, the more conservative political climate that has dominated America since President Ronald Reagan's election in 1980 makes ICBIF's power in the late sixties and early seventies almost unimaginable today. But the times, and the nation, were very different four decades ago.

A Business and Political Education Provided by the EDC

The Economic Development Corporation, whose board was populated with a large number of leading white executives, had been created to help soften the exclusionary attitudes of majority businesses toward black business owners; to push for more opportunities and more inclusive procurement practices by area firms; and to provide funding support to ICBIF. While EDC received funding from New Detroit, some of its resources came directly from the nearly sixty firms comprising its membership. A select list of individuals from those member firms formed its board of directors.

Meanwhile, Walter McMurtry, ICBIF's Executive Director, and I became good friends, as he and Larry were also quite close. The three of us became inseparable as it related to strategic issues involving ICBIF and economic development in Detroit.

Often, Larry, Walt McMurtry, Ed Brazelton, Karl Gregory, select other ICBIF board members and I met from time to time with EDC representatives in the back room of Topinka's restaurant on West Grand Boulevard near the Lodge Freeway to hammer out strategies and funding needs advanced by ICBIF. At these meetings, we also discussed the respective roles of the two organizations, proffering how each organization would interface with the emerging minority businesses in Detroit. It was at one of these meetings that I first met Joseph Hudson, New Detroit's founding chairman, who had attended to "listen and learn."

The representatives who attended these meetings comprised EDC's executive committee, which was led by its board chairman Fred Matthaei — a prominent Detroiter who cared a great deal about the city and had earlier led an effort with his father to bring the 1968 U. S. Olympics to Detroit. I would later get to know Matthaei much better, but at this time I simply marveled at his leadership ability and prominence in Detroit. Others in attendance included Larry Carino, vice president and general manager of WJBK-TV; Alan E. Schwartz, a prominent Detroit attorney; Bill Schoen of Ford; John Steward, owner of Fabristeel Products; Frank Colombo of the J. L. Hudson Company and EDC's first president,

Phil Meek. Meek got the organization started then left to join the *Pontiac Press* (now the *Oakland Press*), newspaper. Mike Foley, EDC's second president, was a loaned executive from the Chrysler Corporation and served for several years before returning to Chrysler in June of 1972. He was replaced by Mike Weston, the son of Norm Weston, a prominent local banker at the National Bank of Detroit.

Like ICBIF, EDC had a professional staff of six or more individuals that included a black vice president named Tepper Gill. The EDC staff was responsible for a wide array of tasks, which included the direct funding of programs and projects beyond ICBIF. At times these programs and projects became the focal point of discussion at our backroom meetings at Topinka's. EDC funded a number of community initiatives, one of which was somewhat controversial: the Interreligious Foundation for Community Organization, which sponsored a Black Economic Development Conference. The conference was planned down the hall in the same building that housed EDC — in a space occupied by Rennie Freeman, a firebrand militant and former New Detroit trustee. The Black Economic Development Conference produced demands that mirrored portions of the "Black Manifesto" authored by conference participant James Forman — a former executive director of the Student Nonviolent Coordinating Committee who had become even more radical than that forceful and influential civil rights organization. Forman advanced for the first time arguments that called for reparations for slavery from Protestant churches. It is interesting that an organization funded by white business executives allowed some of their dollars to be so used.

As detailed in the EDC's fourth annual report published in 1972, the EDC board was composed of a number of prominent Detroit business executives. In addition to those listed above, the board included Robert Backstrom, a vice president of procurement at General Motors; Norm Bolz, partner in charge of Coopers and Lybrand; Rinehart S. Bright, vice president of purchasing at Chrysler; Fred Campbell of the Campbell Group; Frank A. Columbo vice president of the J. L. Hudson Company; Max Fisher of the Fisher-New Center Company; Dwight B. Havens, president of the Greater Detroit Chamber of Commerce; Melvin Jefferson, CEO of Superior

Beauty & Barber Supply; William Leckie of Leckie and Associates; Stanley Marx, president of Industrial Smelting; Fred Secrest vice president Controller at Ford; C. Boyde Stockmeyer, president of Detroit Bank and Trust; Wiley V. Thompson of Lewis & Thompson Agency and William H. Weltyk, president of the Borg & Beck Division of Borg Warner. Jefferson and Thompson were black.

The dialogue during our meetings generally flowed through the designated spokesman for each respective organization. Other meeting participants were reluctant to speak, fearing that they might cross the party line or speak out of turn. Larry would always speak for ICBIF and either lay out our concerns, present demands — or simply express the organization's position on matters being discussed. Fred Matthaei, Chairman of EDC, would then respond on behalf of his organization.

Following these initial exchanges, the two groups would engage in dialogue, attempting to find common ground. Most times, the EDC would rarely and reluctantly budge from its party line positions, but sometimes it would offer counter proposals to ICBIF plans and demands. That made the EDC an advocate for the MESBIC (Minority Enterprise Small Business Investment Company) concept, a national program developed by the Nixon Administration, for instance. Larry would regularly ask for increases in ICBIF's budget, while EDC attempted to maintain the previous year's level of funding. The discussions would go back and forth. Observing the facial expressions and eye contact of the participants, I learned a lot about reading non-verbal communication during these sessions. It was easy to detect who was most responsible for calling the shots on the other side by watching the participants' expressions. I also learned a great deal about structuring responses and managing dialogue during intense discussions between adversarial groups. These were lessons I would later put to good use.

Our meetings usually ended with both sides coming to closure on the issues raised. At times, however, one side or the other would demur in responding to a particular issue — essentially tabling it by saying, "We will get back with you."

These meetings helped me define both the issues and difficulties the ICBIF faced as we pushed to create successful minority business entities and simultaneously pressure Detroit's majority corporations to be more receptive to the black community and issues affecting black-owned firms. We all knew we were dealing with a group of white males who were quite used to assuming a hegemony relationship when dealing with blacks.

ICBIF's Interface with Washington

During the late sixties and early seventies, Larry, Walter McMurtry and I traveled to Washington, D.C, on numerous occasions, seeking support for ICBIF programs. In 1969, we planned our trip to coincide with the first of what would become an annual event sponsored by the Democratic Select Committee of the U. S. Congress. This Committee, which later changed its name to the Congressional Black Caucus, was hosting its inaugural event at the Sheraton Hotel on Connecticut Avenue. The Caucus was celebrating its founding by the twelve black members of Congress (plus Washington, D.C. Delegate Walter Fauntroy). Michigan Congressman Charles Diggs had been named the organization's first chairman, prompting many supporters from Detroit to attend, including Larry, Walter and me — plus Howard Sims and Dr. Karl Gregory. Following an evening dinner celebration, a reception was hosted by ICBIF, partly to honor Congressman Diggs. As it turned out, the ICBIF reception was the largest and best attended of the events planned on that commemorative evening. We from ICBIF used the occasion to garner greater support for our cause and to meet many prominent Washingtonians.

My responsibility was to make contact with Abe Venable, Director of the Office of Minority Business Enterprise, a new government entity established by the Nixon Administration to demonstrate their support for minority business development. That department supervised the MESBIC program and was seeking local sponsors to establish MESBICS throughout America. At the time, ICBIF's board — prompted by EDC — had discussed the concept of MESBICS but had yet to endorse the concept. The ICBIF strategy was that I, rather than Larry, would meet with Abe to feel him out and learn the position of his Agency on items of interest to us. From my meeting with Venable, I learned that he and Secretary of Commerce Maurice Stans were planning a meeting in Detroit with corporate leaders to discuss the MESBIC program and desired to meet with the ICBIF board and staff. I did not disclose to Venable ICBIF's reluctance to endorse the MESBIC concept, but reported back to Larry and Walt the agency's planned visit to Detroit.

Upon returning to Detroit, the ICBIF board met and discussed the planned visit by Stans and Venable. The board's decision was not to meet with Abe and Stans on their visit to Detroit — causing a minor stir among Detroit's business leaders. Abe was incensed and surely embarrassed by the fact that he, the black Director of the Commerce Department's Office of Minority Business Enterprise, could not set a meeting with the most prominent black business group in Detroit. A year or so later, Venable left the Commerce Department and joined the staff of General Motors in Detroit as Director of Urban Affairs. By then, Larry and I had joined the staff at New Detroit and Abe's responsibilities at GM required him to interface with Larry and me. We all made faint attempts to work together; however Abe never forgot ICBIF's snub of Stans and himself.

Following his tenure at the Commerce Department, Venable published a book, which he titled *Building Black Business*. In it, he attempted to set out his thesis of important do's and don'ts for blacks to follow. He introduced his work at a banquet in Washington, D.C., which Howard Sims and I attended — purchasing tables for $1,000 a piece. Abe had invited baseball great Jackie Robinson to be the evening's speaker and gave away free copies of his work. I read my copy of Abe's book on the return trip to Detroit. In it, I found nothing that increased my knowledge above what I already knew regarding the issues affecting struggling black businesses, and generally panned his work. Venable retired from GM after a relatively undistinguished career with the company.

Meanwhile, in late 1969, Walt McMurtry, ICBIF's best asset, announced that he was leaving the organization to help develop an off-shore bank in the Caribbean. The bank was being developed with Donald Parsons, a well-known banker Walt knew from his days at the Bank of the Commonwealth. As executive director of ICBIF, Walt's salary was roughly $20,000, but Don had offered him a salary of $37,000. That was an amount well above the Detroit market at the time, especially among black executives. None of us involved with ICBIF at the time made salaries anywhere close to Walt's new salary. We gave Walt a nice going-away party, a gift of a new set of golf clubs, and wished him well.

The ICBIF board hired Charles Brown to replace McMurtry. Charles and his brother Russ Brown, both ICBIF board members, lived in the Lafayette Park area, near Larry. Brown, an attorney, ran the organization for awhile, but received mixed reviews on his performance, which prompted Larry to dismiss him. His dismissal took place during a regularly scheduled board meeting where Larry presented a letter of charges that he read to Brown in front of the entire board. Reflecting back on it, I was never sure that Larry's approach was the right way to terminate the executive director, but at the time, I just sat, watched and marveled.

At the time of the firing and fortunately for ICBIF, Walt McMurtry's Caribbean bank venture had unraveled. Parsons, an unpopular individual within the banking community, had been unable to gain approval for his off-shore bank from the Comptroller of the Currency. As a result, Walt came back to Detroit and was rehired as ICBIF's executive director, holding the position until the late eighties — when the organization ended its operations.

PRIME, THE ICBIF MESBIC

In late 1970, ICBIF decided to embrace the MESBIC concept and agreed to establish a MESBIC called PRIME. PRIME stood for Pooled Resources Investing in Minority Enterprise. As the ICBIF board discussed possible chairs for the newly formed organization, my name came up and I was selected by the ICBIF board to become PRIME's chairman, while remaining on the ICBIF Board. Howard Sims was also asked to serve and he, too, remained on the ICBIF board. I remember being quite excited about my new role as chair of PRIME. I viewed the position as one that afforded me the opportunity to learn more about the fundamentals of the venture capital business. In addition, my role as chairman would afford me the opportunity to get to know banking and corporate executives during the entity's formation and as deals were consummated.

PRIME, a separate legal entity from ICBIF, set up offices on West Grand Boulevard, just across the street from the Fisher Building. With the help of EDC, PRIME began contacting Detroit-area firms to provide seed capital, which would be matched three-to-one by the U.S. Department of Commerce's Small Business Administration. Ford Motor Company invested $300,000 to start PRIME, and offered their Assistant Treasurer Robert White as a board member. Others followed, including The Maccabees Life Insurance Company; American Motors Corporation; J. L. Hudson; Burroughs Corporation and the Marathon Oil Company. Each firm invested additional dollars and each offered one of its corporate officers to join the PRIME board. Both GM and Chrysler chose not to invest dollars in PRIME; however GM set up its own MESBIC and named it Motors Enterprise, Inc.

PRIME's first president was James Hill, a Chrysler employee on loan. His leadership became Chrysler's way of participating. He ran the day-to-day operations and directed our loan operation, whereby we made loans to several already established minority firms. In July of 1971, we hired Prentice Gary, a Harvard MBA who remained with us for two years. Larry Doss had invited Gary to Detroit during one of his first acts as president of New Detroit. Nine other graduating black Harvard MBAs had been invited as well. The idea was that they would join us in Detroit and assist us in efforts underway to invigorate the city and improve the performance of minority firms doing business in Detroit. Two stayed: Prentice Gary and Dyke Moses. Dyke joined the ICBIF staff and Prentice joined PRIME's staff. After two years, Gary left to join a venture capital firm in Minneapolis, Minnesota, then moved on to become a successful real estate developer in Dallas, Texas. Moses continues to live in Detroit. Others in the group of Harvard MBAs started their own businesses, with one, Frank Anderson, starting an injection molding firm in Durham, North Carolina, and growing it substantially before selling it and retiring. He and I continue to see each other and remain friends.

PRIME's initial investment was a recapitalization loan to Bob Renfro, owner of Renmuth Stamping. Initially, Ford had provided Renmuth with stamping machines and technical assistance. Earlier, ICBIF had provided initial equity funding. Renmuth's stamping operation did well initially, but eventually failed. This company showed us that stamping out metal parts alone added little to change the value of a product — resulting in not enough mark-up: added value to help turn a continuing profit. We learned that stamping out parts was not a business to pursue.

We made a six-figure loan to Gary White, owner of The White Association, a public relations firm. Gary was a smart and energetic executive, and his firm initially had significant success, with one of its projects being the publication of the 1972 Annual Report for EDC. However, the firm never received enough support from area firms to survive. The White Association folded after being in operation for about a year.

PRIME made a loan to SKYPAC, a black-owned Schlitz Beer distributing company owned by a group of Chrysler employees. The name SKYPAC was derived from the owner's last names — Joe Skaggs, Corky Kendall, Buddy Young (son of former NFL running back Buddy Young), Lowell Perry, Virgil Anderson and George Chamchickian, an Armenian. SKYPAC, which purchased its beer from the Schlitz Brewery in Milwaukee, had difficulty with transporting its beer product to Detroit. As they looked for an answer to their transportation problem, another Chrysler employee named John James decided to purchase an over-the-road truck to haul beer for SKYPAC. That was the beginning of OJ Trucking, which John James subsequently built into a massive transportation and logistics firm that still operates in Detroit today.

We also made loans to Sam Gorman, probably the first black Detroit business person I knew who routinely flew to Europe to transact business with a European firm. Sam was in the stamping business and manufactured several products. His business eventually went into Chapter 7 bankruptcy, but he was smart enough to go before the bankruptcy court and purchase his company's assets at pennies on the dollar — then go back in business.

PRIME helped to start the Gilreath Manufacturing Company, a firm that operates today in Howell, Michigan. While the company has gone through several iterations, it is successful now because Gilreath's first CEO, a retired GM executive, had the right business concept when he started the business and worked hard to accomplish it. In addition, the Gilreath Company epitomized the familiar phrase "right place, right time" — as it was started in the mid-seventies, just as the Big Three began to look more favorably upon doing business with emerging minority firms. With stronger commitment from the Big Three (due mainly to increased sales) and with more value being added during the manufacturing process, Gilreath continued to be a profitable concern, generating enough profits and free cash flow to grow and survive.

PRIME loaned Nathan Conyers, the brother of Congressman John Conyers and at the time a prominent Ford dealer in Detroit, the funds to purchase his facility on West Grand Boulevard. Conyers repaid his loan in full.

Eventually, Jim Hill returned to Chrysler and the PRIME board hired John Thomas as PRIME's second president. John was assisted by Charles Holmes, who left EDC to join the PRIME organization. Thomas was an MBA graduate from Indiana University. He was smart but not always focused; after a short tenure, Thomas resigned to start his own business.

PRIME operated successfully until the late seventies, when it began to exhaust the invested capital that had been provided by Detroit area firms. Subsequently, its charter was returned to the Small Business Administration, which took over the responsibility of managing the MESBIC's portfolio. Having large receivables, but limited return on its invested assets, it became increasingly difficult for PRIME to cover the cost for the necessary loan servicing activities and meet its own cash-flow needs. Such were the experiences of countless other MESBICS around the nation, for they too experienced similar difficulties — forcing many to return their charters to the Small Business Administration as well.

LESSONS LEARNED

Although the notion of black business development had begun to evolve, a limited number of success stories inspired hope. However, a fantastic learning laboratory had evolved and introduced sound business principles to many individuals, including myself. It taught us all a great deal about how to develop businesses. From my vantage point as an ICBIF board member and PRIME chairperson, I learned that throwing money at business problems does not automatically solve those problems. One cannot throw money on the ground, sprinkle it with water, and expect successful businesses to sprout.

We all learned the critical importance of the person running the business to its ultimate success. That individual must possess the vision for the business and he or she must know how to put the total package together and manage everyday activities. He or he needs to know and must be able to articulate the needs of the business — and be prepared to spend the time and energy to oversee its operations. Consultants help, but it is the entrepreneur who must have an innate understanding of business principles and of the capital formation processes that are necessary to guide business development.

I learned those lessons well from watching situations at both PRIME and ICBIF. I always promised myself that if I were to go into business, I would first analyze its potential and not proceed unless and until I was convinced of its likelihood for success. I promised myself that if I did not believe strongly in the potential success of a business idea, I would not proceed. I learned that luck can play a role; but I also learned that a business cannot depend on luck to be successful.

ICBIF — SUCCESS OR FAILURE?

It is hard to assess ICBIF's true success because there are few lasting businesses from our early attempts, except for First Independence Bank and Gilreath Manufacturing.

Yet, from my point of view, the lasting effects of the many ICBIF and PRIME efforts are the laboratory experiences I gained, along with so many others involved. We learned a great deal about how to develop, nurture and evaluate businesses. We gained insight about false premises and assumptions. We were schooled on how deals should be structured: what part equity must play in financing a deal; and the amount of loaned funds a business can borrow — essentially the amount of debt that can be successfully retired out of profits from operations.

Before ICBIF, few blacks had ever had the opportunity to participate meaningfully in business development and capital formation initiatives in Detroit. These experiences proved to be very important lessons that helped to prepare many black entrepreneurs and executives. ICBIF planted seeds that have taken root in Detroit.

I applied the practical lessons I learned in subsequent business opportunities I've had, including my own start-up of a school bus company that grew from a fleet of ten taxicabs. I learned that business assumptions must be sound and constantly revised to reflect the reality of a business' day-to-day experiences.

ICBIF's greatest failure might have been its practice of occasionally making loans to individuals when it sensed that there was little chance that those loans would ever be repaid, yet hoping against hope that the businesses would somehow survive. Yet, I am not so sure those practices were wrong — because our true mission was to stimulate black business ownership. In spite of the numerous business failures over time, the loan approvals that we made were not individual approvals. The ICBIF and PRIME boards and their loan committees made them, just as banks have always done. What ICBIF and PRIME were attempting to do — assessing the loan capacity of small fledgling black businesses that were trying to grow and develop — was a difficult task and remains challenging even today. Helping to position fledgling businesses for competition against established, well-financed business entities remains a most difficult chore.

In more recent times, while serving as a trustee of the Henry Ford Health System, I observed minority firms as they attempted to establish business relationships with the health system. Many of these firms simply wanted the opportunity to sell or rent medical equipment to the system, provide home health care products, or sell manufactured products such as rubber gloves and other medical and surgical products. In many instances, they offered these products at competitive prices. The problem they faced was that the hospital already had vendors with whom they had long-standing relationships and were good suppliers. In essence, companies like the Henry Ford Health System do not want to disrupt their current operation.

The argument is that since the playing field has not been level, these minority firms deserve a chance. I agree! While serving, I did everything possible to encourage the use of minority vendors — knowing full well that the aforementioned reality might slow their progress.

COMMENTARY ON BLACK/WHITE PARTNERSHIPS

Since the EDC/ICBIF/PRIME days of the 1960s and 1970s, an emerging practice involves the formation of black/white partnerships (or other diverse combinations of owners) that consist of established businesses that partner with minority firms. Many of these partnerships have proven successful, as one generally white-owned company with proven experience and capital resources works with a typically smaller and less experienced minority partner. Such partnerships are usually better positioned to compete than completely independent minority firms, especially against well-established "Tier-One" suppliers serving the automobile industry and other large firms. These (typically) black-white partnerships have to borrow fewer dollars and therefore have lower debt-to-equity ratios. That is indeed a distinct advantage, for it is a well-learned lesson that businesses cannot operate with excessive debt loads. As debt is paid down, even as a business remains profitable, cash is generally depleted.

Black-white partnerships remain controversial. Proponents of wholly owned black businesses argue or question the point at which a minority business should no longer be considered a minority firm in a partnership relationship. Currently, the Minority Business Development Council has established the mark of thirty-percent as the tipping point for minority firms.

Nonetheless, black-white partnerships have worked and proven successes have emerged. Herb Strather of Atwater Entertainment, the predecessor of Motor City Casino, is one example; the late Don Barden was yet another, as he — in partnership with a Canadian cable company — formed a joint venture and wired the city of Detroit for cable television.

My own experience forming a black/white partnership allowed me to purchase Avis Ford in Southfield, Michigan — a successful, full-service, franchised Ford dealership. When I first became an automobile dealer, a number of blacks remarked, "You don't need a white partner; you want to own your business 100 percent. Otherwise you cannot control your destiny."

But I have found that partners can be very helpful, especially when one is a new business owner. Having a partner helps by deleveraging business entities, and reduces both debt levels and leverage multiples. Partners also provide skills and experiences to help businesses grow and develop. However, having an effective "buy-sell" agreement between partners is vital before agreeing to partner in a business relationship. Furthermore, one must always keep in mind that while ownership is important, the real goal is to amass capital, which will give an entrepreneur greater freedom of choice and even more ownership opportunities.

As I look back now over the decisions we made at ICBIF and PRIME, the businesses started, the few successes and the unfortunate failures, I would not trade anything for those experiences. To this day, my personal business decisions are still grounded in experiences gained while working with Larry and the others who were so dedicated to stimulating Detroit's economy after it was ransacked by the 1967 rebellion.

Finally, I have also learned that not only minority businesses fail, but others do as well. In recent times, I have witnessed the near meltdown of many major American firms — some because of greed and nefarious inclinations, and others because of arrogant and inept decisions that clashed with changing times. These lessons have taught me that whether or not businesses are black or white, the rules for success, growth and survival are the same for all of them.

CHAPTER 7

POLITICAL LEADERSHIP

In the spring of 1971, New Detroit was seeking a new President, just as Larry Doss was strategizing his next career move. He had established himself as a well-known community-leader and advocate for change, having completed his task of leading the Detroit School Decentralization Study Committee. Those impressed by his leadership skills included both Max Fisher, the outgoing chair of New Detroit, and Stan Winkelman, the incoming chair. Both had gotten to know him from his work at ICBIF.

The two of them asked Larry to consider the Presidency of New Detroit, Inc. And they pledged their unwavering support to him. This occurred shortly after William Patrick, New Detroit's first president, announced his decision to step down.

"New Detroit's presidency," Max and Stan told Larry, "will put you in the driver's seat and offer a broader platform for your Self-Determination philosophy."

As alluring as this sounded, it presented a dilemma for Larry. He was the president of ICBIF, an organization that until then had been unwilling to converse directly with New Detroit. Still, this was an attractive offer. Larry contemplated the offer and discussed it with me and other key individuals at ICBIF. We all encouraged him to take the position. He accepted the offer and New Detroit's

127

board elected him as its second president in June of 1971.

Elated with his election as president, we celebrated, knowing with confidence that Larry would become an exceptional leader — one sensitive to ICBIF's pronounced vision and goals.

The summer of 1971 was filled with both anticipation and dialogue as Larry made his transition from his non-paid presidency of ICBIF to the salaried presidency of New Detroit. During this period, Larry intimated that he would like me to join his team at New Detroit. This gave me much to think about.

I first had to consider the new position to which I had recently been promoted: assistant director of the Data Center, a GS-15 level position. This plum ranking identified me as an up-and-coming executive within the Service. I discussed Larry's offer with my boss Ernie Shaw, the Data Center's director who had replaced Larry.

"Have you considered what you might do after New Detroit?" Ernie asked. As I pondered this question, I had no answer. But I interpreted his inquiry as an endorsement that the New Detroit position could open to a career in politics. Or, perhaps without knowing it, I was tying my future to whatever Larry's future might be.

Having no long-term interest in politics, I demurred for a short time, and then settled on what had always been my vision — a prominent position in the private sector. That vision had been set by my fellow U. S. Army comrades while I was at Walter Reed Medical Center. Their talk of private sector careers they planned to pursue had convinced me that that was where I most wanted to eventually wind up. Thus, I saw my potential move to New Detroit as a move toward my career goal; and, I surmised, I could survive with or without Larry. I accepted his offer, confident of success in my new role at New Detroit and at whatever opportunities might lie ahead. Retha's full support and enthusiasm of my decision further bolstered my confidence.

A SIT-DOWN WITH AN AUTO CEO

In mid December, Larry asked me to meet with Lynn Townsend, the in-coming chair of New Detroit, who would replace Stan Winkelman at New Detroit's annual meeting in January. Days earlier, I had accompanied Larry on a visit with Stan, who ostensibly granted his approval for me in the new position.

Larry said it was also important to impress the incoming chair. He gave me Lynn Townsend's office number and suggested that I call him to arrange a visit at Chrysler World Headquarters in Highland Park. I immediately called for an appointment. His office suggested I come over right away.

This would be my first occasion to visit the headquarters of a major corporation in Detroit. All of the meetings I had attended with corporate executives up to this point had taken place in public restaurants, at EDC or ICBIF. Quite nervous, I parked close to the front of the building and went inside. The receptionist on the first floor directed me to Townsend's office, which included an escalator ride to the fifth floor. The wide hallway and high ceiling on the fifth floor reflected the grand history of the automobile industry, past and present. I noted the vintage automobiles prominently displayed on tapestries along the walls as I walked the full length of the corridor. I observed these historic reflections, but I did not tarry, sensing I would see these and other reflections many times over in my new role with New Detroit. I was already beginning to make an adjustment to my new position.

I arrived at Townsend's office at the end of the hall, went inside and introduced myself to a stately female sitting at a desk. She immediately escorted me into Mr. Townsend's office, where he met me and introduced Harwood Rydholm, a Chrysler vice president who would sit in on my interview.

Townsend was tall and slender with graying curly hair, which later prompted Larry's assistant Susan Watson to refer to him as "Curly." He was friendly and engaging with me and seemed to be a consummate professional. I later learned Townsend had joined Chrysler from Touché Ross, one of the Big-Eight accounting firms at the time, and he was responsible for Chrysler's successes in the late sixties and early seventies.

I handed Townsend my resume; he reviewed it while chatting softly with me. After a brief discussion, in which both Lynn and Harwood raised questions, I was told that my interview was over. I stood, shook Mr. Townsend's hand and prepared to leave.

Rydholm offered to accompany me and instead of leading me out the way I had entered, directed me to a private elevator that led directly to the Chrysler executive garage below. At the end of our elevator journey, Rydholm indicated that on future trips I should use the executive garage for parking and the private elevator to reach Townsend's office. I said goodbye and walked to the front of the building where I had parked my Ford Capri.

As I left, I pondered my first experience of meeting privately with a Big Three CEO and his associate. I later heard from Larry that the interview had gone well and that I could anticipate the New Detroit board would approve my election as one of its Vice Presidents.

MY NEW DETROIT CAREER

We set a target date for my start with New Detroit: February 1, 1972. As planned, the New Detroit Board elected me an officer at their scheduled meeting in January. Larry had also recommended that Howard Sims join the New Detroit board, and he heard of my election as a corporate officer during his first meeting. Howard later called to congratulate me, but seemed a little surprised about the career move I had made.

For most of the 1970s and even into the eighties, New Detroit was literally the most important institution in metropolitan Detroit, and a model for urban coalition organizations across the nation. New Detroit was the center of public policy development and debate, and every issue of importance to the city and the region ran through this unusual organization. New Detroit tried to balance the competing interests of black community organizers, neighborhood activists, unions and nonprofits of all kinds with those of the region's leading corporations and leaders of business and government. All involved realized change, immediate change was necessary for Detroit to recover and rebuild in the aftermath of 1967. As indicated by the constant tug of war between the ICBIF and EDC, public attitudes and the interests of established institutions were not so quick to change. New Detroit was the meeting ground for dialogue and, in the best cases, resolution of some of the region's toughest problems.

As detailed above, black business development was one of the primary issues New Detroit and its affiliates tackled, as was public education. But the organization also took a leadership role in confronting police brutality and the organization and operation of the Detroit Police Department, along with fair housing and affirmative action in hiring.

It was into this fray that I launched my Detroit career as an "influence peddler" — having learned the ropes as an ICBIF volunteer, dealing with issues in hope of advancing economic opportunities for minority individuals — now working full time as an officer of New Detroit, where I was to assist in addressing a maddening, countless, peripatetic array of issues that affected the life of Detroit. It was during this period that I learned in crystal-clear fashion important lessons about the difficulties our city — and by extension our entire nation — faced as it attempted to bridge the racial divide between whites and all minority groups.

I rose through the ranks of New Detroit Inc., and with the endorsement of my mentor Larry Doss, I was elected president of New Detroit Inc. — taking office on Jan. 1, 1978. I held the office until December 1985, in the process working with nearly every prominent business, political and community leader in the region on viable solutions to big problems.

It was the education of a lifetime, and the story of my New Detroit adventure deserves to be told in detail elsewhere. I have already shared quite a bit about the first part of my urban coalition career: my work at ICBIF and PRIME. I feel recounting that largely forgotten aspect of Detroit's history sheds considerable light on steps society took to jump-start African American business growth (and institutions like Wayne County Community College) after decades of repression — from job discrimination that inhibited skills development to Urban Renewal policies that literally destroyed black business districts. One of the key benefits of the ICBIF / PRIME experiment — essentially funded by the leaders of New Detroit — was the training it gave a generation of black professionals who were groomed for business leadership at high levels.

Yet, the political intrigue of New Detroit alone — dominated by the towering presence of Mayor Coleman Young — would fill a separate book. The historical ramifications of what New Detroit did and did not accomplish are immense. However, for this memoir — an overview of an African American professional's development into a successful business owner during one of the most volatile and fast-changing periods in U.S. history — I can only attempt to *summarize* what my New Detroit experience was all about. I will do so now — as it concerns my leadership of the organization. Perhaps at some point, Shirley Stancato, New Detroit's president and CEO since January 2000, will pick up the gauntlet and complete the telling of the organization's history.

HOW I LED NEW DETROIT

Central to the style of leadership I developed was the approach where if possible, I shared ideas and thoughts with individual board members and community and corporate executives, to gain their feedback in advance of presenting my summations to committees and groups, or to our board. I learned how to gain acceptance of proposed ideas and initiatives before meetings were to take place. Interestingly, my approach was neither new nor novel, yet to this day, I marvel at breakdowns I observe among leaders where they do not follow this approach. They allow arrogance or possessiveness to dictate their strategies when developing ideas for board or public consideration. I learned that short cuts do not work and was always willing to allow others to assume credit for advancing issues and ideas — never feeling that I had to be the one that got the credit.

I also focused on giving clear assignments to staff members. I always kept our chairman apprised of important issues, continuing the process employed by Larry in which I and my senior staff held periodic Chairman Briefings.

I reviewed every letter that went out over my signature and paid close attention to the content of all board and committee agenda material. Not only did I want to know where we were on every issue, I wanted to maintain a standard for content, appearance and style for everything that New Detroit did.

Finally, I decided that I would not pander to the media or allow them to employ me as a news source unless I needed them. I would not become a "deep throat." I would not use the media against people by sharing any information that was not supposed to be shared. Many have effectively used the media in this fashion; but I resolved that I never would, and I never have.

NEW DETROIT'S INTERACTION WITH DETROIT RENAISSANCE

Detroit Renaissance was essentially a spin-off of New Detroit. I believe the business leaders who were on the New Detroit board regularly held their own off-line meetings, out of the public eye. I'm sure they decided that although some things could get done through New Detroit, but because of the loudness and rudeness of New Detroit's public meetings, another organization was needed where business leaders could talk off-line about important issues. Thus, they created the Detroit Renaissance.

The same business leaders involved with New Detroit — Max Fisher, Henry Ford II, the Big Three automakers, banks and utilities — got together in April 1971 and hired Robert McCabe as president. He and Larry Doss, my boss at New Detroit, became co-leaders on many issues. After I became president of New Detroit, Bob McCabe and I, along with Diane Edgecombe, who ran the CBDA — the Central Business District Association, and Ron Steffens, who ran the Metropolitan Detroit Business and Visitors Bureau — all talked off-line. At times, we included the head of the Greater Detroit Chamber of Commerce in our meetings. We were considered "The Big Four," and we would meet periodically to talk about issues — sometimes just the four of us; on occasion as a group with the mayor. Detroit's economically oriented civic organizations always got along well. We blacks said: "Well, you know, if white cats want to get together and do their thing, there's nothing wrong with it." In fact, there was nothing we could do to stop it. The important thing was positive action.

Of course, Detroit Renaissance — which changed its name to Business Leaders for Michigan and took on a statewide perspective in 2009 — is no longer a totally white organization. It currently has a few black business owners as members, including Dr. Bill Pickard, owner of Global Automotive Alliance. Several African Americans have previously belonged to the group. Jon Barfield was a member; Don Barden was a member; and there are women who are members. Florine Mark, who owns Weight Watchers, shared at Don Barden's funeral in May 2011 that Don took her under his wing when she joined the Renaissance board, because she was nervous to be there with all of those heavy hitters. But Mark's membership showed the diverse makeup of the organization approximately forty years after it was formed. In the beginning, we knew it was essentially "the white caucus" — the place for white executives of the late 1960s and early seventies to have safe discussions.

Detroit Renaissance used to invite me, as president of New Detroit, to come and make presentations to its board from time to time about various issues. If there was an important tax issue, an important social issue, something about the Detroit Public School System, they would invite me to bring them my perspective from New Detroit. Max Fisher extended that invitation frequently when he was Chairman of Detroit Renaissance. It was a productive relationship, even though the hard issues of the racial divide in the region simply were not cracked.

NEW DETROIT AS FORUM AND CATALYST

New Detroit filled an important niche back in the sixties and the early seventies because there was not a vehicle where blacks and whites regularly met on an even basis, more or less, and exchange views and talk about problems. Even though we had few solutions to the problems, at least we could talk about them in what I would term a safer environment than confrontation in the streets, or even in the media. We African Americans called the diverse collection of activists and concerned people who represented the black community "the coalition." There was some yelling and screaming involved. The community people would call business and political leaders various names — "honkies," and that kind of thing.

The "establishment" participants were more reserved in their responses. After a while, Henry Ford stopped coming to the meetings;

I suspected the unpleasant prospect of combative confrontation was probably one of the reasons. He didn't want to feel importuned by the assertions that were made from time to time, either about him personally, or his company, or whites in general; but that was pretty much the sound of the time.

Up until that time, there were few blacks who represented organizations. Some prominent leaders of the black community had access to whites, but their relationships were more of the "go 'hat in hand' and ask for a favor of some kind" variety. That was the nature of the relationship that existed between the black community and the white community.

New Detroit created a forum where issues were discussed involving race — or even critical issues regarding the role of government or programs and problems the city was facing that needed resolution. The community standoff against police at New Bethel Baptist Church and how that came to closure under the leadership of Max Fisher was a good example. After Judge George Crockett released the accused citizens under a writ of habeas corpus, an interracial group discussed it and determined that what Judge Crockett did was not wrong. Maybe another judge would not have done it, but he certainly was within the rule of law, the panel concluded. While the group didn't resolve the issue, at least it sent a message to the community that New Detroit could and would abate major concerns — even if its role was sometimes merely acting as a community release valve.

The positive results emanating from the work during my years at New Detroit produced results that could be observed in the social strata of the Detroit community. In one example, the nonexistence of black membership in area private clubs began to change — first prompted by Henry Ford II in 1977 when he established a private dining club in the newly constructed Renaissance Center and invited blacks to join. Soon, other area private dining clubs followed — increasing the opportunities for social intercourse between blacks and whites. Then, in 1986, the Detroit Golf Club invited Coleman Young to join, making him their first African-American member — albeit thirteen long years after he was elected mayor of Detroit! I witnessed considerable change in racial attitudes toward blacks, increased opportunities for white collar employment and board service, and changes in social practices. Efforts put forward by New Detroit and many others on this matter certainly helped to point America toward progress. Racial discrimination no longer plays the blocking role of earlier decades, allowing a handful of blacks to scale the ladder of opportunity all the way to the top and showing that it can be done.

Today, the pioneering role of a New Detroit is no longer needed to open racial doors at most institutions. I believe blacks are far more respected, far more integrated into our total society now. For instance, at this writing, Mike Finney, director of Michigan's Economic Development Agency under Michigan's Republican Governor Rick Snyder, is responsible for the most important policy issue on the governor's agenda: economic growth. Similarly, George Jackson has been an influential director of the quasi-governmental Detroit Economic Growth Corporation through three mayoral administrations. Before him, Bob Spencer, who had been with New Detroit, was in the job — one which grew in stature and emerged as a local leadership position in a fairly natural progression.

Figure 10. Emmett Moten, Detroit Development Director under Mayor Young; the late Secretary of Commerce Ron Brown and me during my New Detroit years

Of course, with the election of Barack Obama, we have a black President of the United States — who obviously has access to every power structure that exists. So the last *symbolic* barrier to African American achievement in the United States has been toppled forever.

Nevertheless, racism is still a significant issue in our society; there's no question about it. Because the starting point for blacks, other ethnic minorities and women was so low, it will take many years and more hard work and sensitivity before anything close to parity will exist. Indeed, this is not only true about Detroit, but about our nation; for in my view, more opportunities for progress by blacks and many others are sorely needed. Statistics that measure the progress of anywhere in America continue to show a disparity between us and all other measured groups — with blacks faring worst. Therefore, organizations like New Detroit still do important work, and I believe they must continue to be vocal about our leading issues — public education, for example. What our children are actually learning and who controls the curriculum and operation of our schools are critical issues facing Detroit or any community. Any organization devoted to change and greater equity in society must always be prepared to speak out and be a social irritant, if necessary. Leadership often has to occur from the front, not just working behind the scenes — although that is sometimes an effective strategy.

I have constantly asked myself what I could have done better and what we all collectively could have done better during my tenure at New Detroit. It is clear that each of us could have worked harder, given more, to achieve increased regional cooperation and progress toward finding solutions to regional problems and opportunities, notably race relations. By the end of my presidency, I realized that the operating paradigms that governed the practices of City and institutional operatives in metropolitan Detroit would have to change if racial division, public transportation or many other regional problems and issues confronting Detroit and southeast Michigan were to be effectively addressed. Few elected or titular heads of organizations, area companies or governmental bodies, including school districts, seemed willing to effectively address the many problems confronting the region and its citizens.

At the same time, those of us who fought for an equal voice and equal standing for African Americans also could have been braver about demanding higher standards and more accountability to the public in the city of Detroit, where it is evident black leadership took too lightly the critical importance of policies and procedures that produce strong public schools and safe, prosperous neighborhoods. Strengthening inner-city schools and neighborhoods are the toughest challenges of the early twenty-first century for Detroit, and the future of the city and the region depends squarely upon those two fundamental goals.

A Few Thoughts about Coleman Young

As I mentioned, a second book would have to be written to fully describe the political landscape of the 1970s and 1980s; the many accomplishments and failures of Mayor Coleman Young; and my complex relationship with him, which included my acceptance of his appointment as chief civilian at the Detroit Police Department, 1974-76. On loan from New Detroit, I oversaw formation of the city's first Board of Police Commissioners and essentially helped Mayor Young carry out the major police reforms he had promised as a candidate.

I'm proud of the work we did, and in general, I admire the record of Mayor Young — who was unfairly demonized by much of the southeast Michigan region throughout his two decades in office. His willingness to confront all challengers, with an intimidating stream of profane condemnations, if necessary, kept his critics in a constant state of agitation.

However, Young took on the issues that were his biggest challenges — land use management and urban flight — just as well. He countered the flight of the Detroit Lions and Detroit Pistons to the Pontiac Silverdome with the construction of Joe Louis Arena, which kept the Detroit Red Wings in town when it opened in 1979. Although the Renaissance Center was already under construction when Young became mayor, he fully participated in its expansion, when Towers 500 and 600 were added. He and I attended the groundbreaking with Henry Ford and David Rockefeller, who was an investor. Despite the loss of hundreds of businesses and thousands of jobs, Young lobbied successfully for construction of General Motors'

Detroit-Hamtramck "Poletown" assembly plant; Chrysler's Jefferson North Assembly plant; and the Ilitch family's move of their Little Caesar's pizza empire to downtown Detroit, combined with their refurbishment of the Fox Theatre and purchase of the Red Wings and Tigers. The development of Max Fisher and Al Taubman's Riverfront Towers apartment complex and the construction of Harbortown Apartments and the Victoria Park subdivision on the city's east side kept Detroit residency in the public conversation, at least. But throughout the Young administration, the city failed to attract enough economic activity to reverse the downward economic trends taking place: a loss of 250,000 jobs and one-fifth of the city's population during the 1970s alone, according to the book Detroit: Race and Uneven Development, by Joe Darden, June M. Thomas and Richard C. Hill. Undoubtedly, the availability of thousands of vacant acres north of Detroit and the economics of race played a role.

Figure 11. The Stroh's Advisory Committee (Standing, L-R: Ann Cook; Charles Allen; Earl Graves; James Lowry; S. Martin Taylor; Robert Holland; Maynard Jackson; Thomas Burrell; Arthur R. Velasquez. Seated, L-R: Joe Anderson; Peter Stroh; Roger Fridholm; and me)

What kind of executive, what kind of leader was the controversial Mayor Young? As a person who could respond to a situation and give you a quick and concise answer, Coleman Young possessed the greatest instincts of any person I have ever known. If asked what he thought about something today, then asked the same question ten years later, Coleman would likely give the same answer — as long as the underlying assumptions were the same. A logical thinker, Coleman had the innate and uncanny abilities to know just what the right position was on something and to know it quickly. He could generally operate with limited input from his staff, perhaps because he had always done it that way. I always admired Mayor Young's ability to formulate thought in a creative fashion. I doubt that he ever later regretted a public policy initiative that he put forward.

A visionary aptitude characterized his thinking. As a former Tuskegee airman, he wanted only progress and success for Detroit; all the while looking for ways to ensure that the African American community was a part of his dream for the city.

Growing up, he developed street-wise sensibilities, which he refined to the point of sophistication. He was intelligent, well-read and precise in his word selection to express himself. Coleman invariably used febrile and graphic street phrases; he was notorious for his spicy language. But he was rarely misunderstood. He probably always regretted that he never attended college, and as such developed a love/hate relationship with learned people. On one hand, he seemed to resent people who had had the opportunity to attend college, while he did not. On the other hand, he put them in another category. He was not quite as comfortable with them as he was with people who had grown up as he had, experiencing the hard knocks of the street. His friend Buddy Battle had grown up similarly to Coleman, and their closeness was apparent. Yet, Colman possessed many of the same human graces and instincts that one would associate with learned individuals. He had studied them well and made adjustments in his style and manner.

I'll conclude with an anecdote that typifies the Coleman Young I knew. Near the end of my tenure as president of New Detroit, when the Stroh Brewery Co. was still a major employer in the city of Detroit,

I encouraged owner Peter Stroh to form an advisory committee composed of prominent black business owners and professionals from across the nation. Stroh agreed, and he and company President Roger Fridholm formed the Stroh Brewery Advisory Committee, which included: Thomas Burrell of Burrell Advertising in Chicago; Earl Graves, CEO of Black Enterprise Magazine; Willie Davis, former Green Bay Packer and Los Angeles beer distributor; James Lowry of Lowry Associates in Chicago; S. Martin Taylor, president-elect, New Detroit; Arthur R. Velesquez, Azteca Corn Products; Maynard Jackson, former mayor of Atlanta; Robert Holland, a former partner in the consulting firm McKinsey and Co., and later president of Ben and Jerry's ice cream; Jewel S. LaFontant, a prominent attorney from Chicago; Ann Cook, also a prominent Chicago attorney, who later married super-lawyer and political strategist Vernon Jordan; Herman J. Russell, of the H. J. Russell Construction Co. of Atlanta; Charles Allen, then president of First Independence Bank in Detroit — and me. We served for several years and met often. During this period Stroh prepared his company for sale to Schlitz Brewery in Milwaukee. Stroh demonstrated a sincere interest in our governance advice to him and his management team as he responded to community pressures targeted at his wholly-owned firm.

But the work of the advisory committee attracted unwelcome attention from Mayor Young one afternoon, when I was asked to assist Peter Stroh in arranging a visit with the Rev. Jesse Jackson of Operation Push. The meeting was arranged, and I picked Jesse up from Detroit Metropolitan Airport. Shortly after our arrival at Stroh headquarters in Detroit, while we were awaiting the start of our meeting, Peter's secretary approached me and indicated that Mayor Young was on the phone and wanted to speak with me. Not knowing the reason for his call, I quickly answered — whereupon Coleman spoke to me in a curt and inquiring fashion:

"Walt, I understand Jesse is in town. Is this so?"

I responded, "Yes, Mr. Mayor, he is here to meet with Peter Stroh."

Young then responded, "That son of a bitch ain't supposed to be in my town unless I know about it!" Young and Jackson had sparred for years — since 1973, when Coleman asked for Jesse's in-person support during his first campaign. That was a time when the election of an African-American mayor in a major U.S. city was still a momentous achievement. Jackson indicated his willingness to come to Detroit, but only at a steep price that included the cost of first-class tickets for him and his entourage; all the while knowing that the upstart Young campaign was struggling mightily.

I went on to explain to the angry-sounding mayor on the line that Peter Stroh had requested a meeting with Rev. Jackson and had asked me to pick him up from the airport and sit in on the meeting. Coleman then asked to speak with Peter Stroh before hanging up.

Our meeting went well, and I never heard anymore about it from either Stroh or Young. Yet, the mayor was sending a clear message to all: he wanted to be in the loop when those he viewed as "outside trouble makers" were in his city.

Figure 12. Mayor Coleman Young anticipating the Detroit Grand Prix, which was run through the streets of downtown Detroit

CHAPTER 8

ENTREPRENEURSHIP

DHT TRANSPORTATION: FIRST STEP AS AN ENTREPRENEUR

On several occasions during my tenure at New Detroit, I discussed my desire to start a business with Paul Hubbard, who remains a very close friend. But neither Paul nor I knew what kind of business to get into. We thought once about purchasing an apartment building, but quickly concluded that we didn't want the responsibility for maintaining a building or for collecting rental income.

Then by happenstance, during the mid-seventies while on vacation in the Bahamas, I met Al Barnes, a gentleman who owned a fleet of taxicabs in Detroit. I learned from him that cab ownership could be quite lucrative. I shared this intriguing discussion with Paul and we followed up by letting our interest of taxicab ownership be known to those in the industry. Shortly thereafter, we were introduced to a taxi fleet owner interested in selling his ten taxicabs and the attendant bond plates. Paul and I negotiated a purchase price with him, after bringing in a partner — John Thomas, an Indiana University MBA graduate who agreed to join us. As Chairman of the MESBIC PRIME, I had hired John as PRIME's President; after finding his interest in business was similar to Paul's and mine, we invited him to join our investment group.

The three of us arranged a loan through Les Johnson, a loan officer at Manufacturers Bank. In 1976, we purchased the fleet of ten taxicabs — noting that all of our cab identification numbers ended in "45" — being the way the Checker Taxicab Association identified cab owners. We were henceforth known as "45" owners around town and amongst the other Checker fleet owners.

We didn't know much about the taxicab business, but we learned pretty quickly. We learned that there was a finite number of "bond plates" issued for taxis in Detroit. We learned that the Checker garage was on the east side of Trumbull Avenue, facing Tiger Stadium, offering a great perk for parking when attending Tiger baseball games. We also learned that operators at the Trumbull garage would manage a fleet for a percentage of the revenue generated. But as we learned the hard way, some operators looked out for their interests first.

However, even with the "skimming," we broke even most of the time and sometimes even profited by a few dollars. We replaced some of the older taxis by purchasing state-owned vehicles at the state auction, a practice we learned from other cab operators. We had one new vehicle; unfortunately, it was "totaled" in an accident. Thankfully, no one was injured. Nevertheless, we wondered: "Why the *new* vehicle?" we wondered. Like in any business, we endured growing pains.

After operating the taxi fleet for the better part of a year, we heard about something called a "school-run." That was an arrangement whereby a cab owner could contract with the Detroit Board of Education to pick up a child with special needs and take that child to and from school each day. School runs paid a route fee, generally based on miles. We inquired at Student Transportation and were assigned several school runs. This was an excellent way to profit as cab owners.

After about a year in business, we noticed privately owned school buses on the streets of Detroit. Two taxicab owners we met had diversified their businesses by purchasing school buses, which they used to handle routes under contract with the Detroit school system. Safeway Transportation was one of those taxi owners; Citywide Transportation was the other. After learning a Request for Proposal (RFP) had been issued for additional bus route operators, Paul, John and I completed and submitted an application for routes, and were quickly awarded ten routes. We did not own any buses, but had time to acquire them, as it was near the end of the school year and the routes were being awarded for the subsequent school year. That gave us time to purchase the eleven required vehicles: ten to cover assigned routes, plus one spare to cover a potential breakdown.

Our taxicab business had been named DHT and Associates. We sold the taxis but we retained the name DHT, dropped "Associates" and added "Transportation." We rolled the money from the sale of the taxi fleet into the school buses. But we needed additional capital to complete our purchase of buses, which cost $11,000 each. We applied for an SBA loan, but soon learned that Paul and I were not eligible because we were employed by a "quasi-public" entity, New Detroit. This policy had been adopted by the Detroit SBA following a loan default that reportedly occurred earlier when Coleman Young had unsuccessfully attempted to establish a restaurant called Young's Barbecue.

We then pursued a commercial loan with Manufacturers Bank. With the assistance of Jerry McDonald, who was the bank's commercial loan officer at the time, we received tentative approval. However, Paul and I were required to pledge our personal residences as collateral and sign personal guarantees. We agreed, closed the loan, purchased our fleet and began operating in December 1979, a few months later than we had hoped.

In the fall of 1980, we were offered ten additional routes, which would double the size of our fleet. However, a loan covenant with Manufacturers Bank prohibited our start-up firm, DHT, from taking on additional debt until the bank loan was paid in full. To take advantage of this opportunity, we set up a separate company called TDH — Thomas, Douglas and Hubbard — and secured a loan through Ed Tinsley, a loan officer at National Bank of Detroit. In need of additional funds, we borrowed $100,000 from a MESBIC named Vanguard, located in Greensboro, North Carolina. We now had twenty routes and twenty-two buses at the start of the 1980 school year.

Paul and I were proud that over our years of operation, our bus company never experienced a payless payday for our employees. All of our lenders thought well of us because we serviced our debt in a timely manner. I operated as CEO and John Thomas left PRIME to become our Terminal Manager. Retha became our administrative vice president — handling payroll, billing and accounts payable. Paul oversaw public relations and marketing and spent time generating charter income for our firm. We stored our fleet of buses, performed necessary maintenance and dispatched our fleet out of rented space on West Chicago in a facility owned by Willie Brandon, who also had his own fleet of taxi cabs. We had few glitches for a start-up and became highly regarded by the Detroit school system. We generally passed the required annual state bus inspections with a limited number of problems.

After our second year, John Thomas decided to exit our firm and sold his interest to Sam Thomas (no relation), who remained an investor for several years before Paul and I repurchased John's interest.

Over time we repaid all of our initial loans and established lines of credit with both Manufacturers Bank (which became Comerica in 1992) and NBD. We used these lines of credit to purchase our own terminal on Rosa Parks Boulevard — as well as additional buses, expanding our fleet to more than sixty vehicles before selling the company at the end of December 2002. What started out with initial investments of $4,000 from each of three individuals, resulted in a handsome payday when years later Paul and I sold the firm.

My Detroit Cable Bid Involvement

During the mid-eighties, events began to turn more of my energies toward business development opportunities. It started with the franchising of the Detroit Cable System. Before long, I was knee-deep in the competitive process among those seeking to secure the franchise to wire the city. For me, it began when I received a call from Percy Sutton of New York. Sutton, a well-known former New York alderman, had contacted me to discuss my assistance in helping him meet local Detroiters who might be interested in joining with him and his radio station partner Gene Jackson in forming a group to bid on the Detroit franchise.

I agreed to help and organized a group of prominent Detroiters, including Howard Sims, Arthur Johnson, Harold Varner, Nancy

Rowe, Dennis Silber and Dr. Karl Gregory. Most of the individuals in the group I formed were close associates with Mayor Young, although none were current members of his administration.

I also arranged for Sutton and Jackson to meet local radio station owner Dr. Wendell Cox — a New Detroit board member — who had also approached me about assisting him in forming a group to bid on the franchise. I arranged a meeting between the two principals, who quickly agreed to bid jointly for the Detroit franchise — and, with my assistance, agreed to ownership percentages for the participants that both Cox and I had brought to the group. However, soon after, on the eve of the deadline to submit bids to the Detroit Cable Commission, Cox aborted his relationship with Sutton and Jackson — ostensibly because two investors, the Lopatins in Cox's group, did not want to do business with Dennis Silber in the group I had formed. I have often wondered why, and can only surmise that the Lopatins were indirectly driving the Cox deal and for whatever reason did not want Silber involved.

However, once this Cox/Sutton deal was blown, it was arranged for my team of investors to join Don Barden — a dark horse bidder, who was the current franchise holder in the nearby city of Inkster. And while Cox had already won the right to build the cable system in Highland Park, Michigan — a city surrounded by Detroit — he would not be selected to build the system in Detroit. Neither would Sutton's group, which now did not include the prominent list of Detroiters I had selected.

The franchise would go to the Barden group, which now included the individuals I had selected earlier — plus a few others that Barden had personally selected. In the end, Young selected Barden over the others, despite having earlier referred to him as a "suede shoe" operator.

Other groups who bid unsuccessfully included one formed by local attorney Ed Bell and another by the law firm, Charfoos and Charfoos. In all, five groups had bid on the much sought-after Detroit franchise, which would cost millions to build. Once built and successfully operating, it would be sold by Don Barden and his Canadian partner for hundreds of millions of dollars. Reported estimates were that Barden walked away with nearly $100 million for his efforts. Yet, according to several of his investors, he did not treat his investor group fairly and most of them were out of the deal before he selected his Canadian partner and built the cable system. Since I was not a part of the investor group — believing it to have been a conflict of interest for me — I cannot speak to what transpired between them and Barden as they worked their deal. If the reports I heard were accurate, I found it unfortunate that key investors might not have enjoyed the return on investment that Barden apparently did.

FM RADIO BANDS

In 1984, while attending the Congressional Black Caucus's annual weekend in Washington D.C., Larry Doss assembled a group of prominent individuals to meet with Early Monroe, an acquaintance of his. In this meeting, Monroe apprised the group of a potential business opportunity — prompted by a recent action taken by the Federal Communications Commission, which would allow interested individuals to gain access to additional FM radio bands that would be competitively awarded.

A former FCC employee, Early explained the process that would be followed to compete for the new bands. He informed us that minorities would be given preference in the process; and if selected, they could then build FM radio transmission facilities in the various markets where the bands were being awarded.

The group that Larry had assembled included Paul Hubbard; Dutch Morial, former Mayor of New Orleans; Dr. Robert Greene, a dean at Michigan State University; Dr. Gil Maddox, a Detroit TV personality; Howard Sims; Doctors James Freemont and Charles Vincent, gynecologists from Atlanta and Detroit, respectively; Johnnie Cochran and Clarence Daniels from Los Angeles; Glen and C.C. Haydel from New Orleans; Greg and Bruce Syphax from Washington D.C. and me. With the exception of Cochran, all attended the first meeting.

Early Monroe explained the FCC's process for bidding and filing applications. He presented the list of cities where bands were being offered. He then explained that FM bands would be granted to bidders following a lottery in which each applicant received one "ball" in the lottery and two if the applicant was a minority entity. The FCC, he said, would allow applicants to negotiate settlements among the competing entities before lotteries were conducted, hoping that likely partners would emerge through consolidations.

The group Larry had assembled was quite interested in filing licensing applications and agreed to form a corporation, thus providing an investment opportunity for those in attendance. Larry offered that he would be pleased to become president and suggested that I serve as the chairman of the board. Dutch Morial agreed to become vice president-treasurer and Gil Maddox opted to serve as secretary. The group approved the selected leadership and United Communications was subsequently set up with its headquarters in Washington, D.C., where Larry then resided.

The group eventually filed applications for FM bands in Jacksonville, Florida; New Orleans, Louisiana; Nashville, Tennessee; and Portland, Oregon. Little happened until Morial approached the group regarding a new TV opportunity in New Orleans, where Loyola University was secretly pursuing an application (not a part of the FM offerings) and lied to Morial about their involvement. Our group threatened to sue, causing Loyola to agree to an out-of-court settlement for a six-figure sum. That nest egg helped us to cover expenses for the recently formed United Communications.

With our minority preference, we negotiated with various parties through our legal counsel, David Hornig, a Washington-based FCC attorney. David helped us establish contact with local partners in cities where we had filed applications. Having local participation also gave preference to applicants — resulting in stronger potential for our sites in Nashville and Jacksonville, where strong partners joined with us.

After pursuing our several interests for a time, which included one where we competed with others to build a station in Portland, Oregon, we agreed to move ahead to develop FM radio stations in Jacksonville and Nashville. At about this time, Morial passed away. However, his interest was assumed by his sons Mark and Jacques.

We eventually sold our Nashville site to a Toledo, Ohio-based radio operating group identified to us by Paul Hubbard. That left us with Portland and Jacksonville.

Fred and Anna Matthews became our Jacksonville partners and operators as we built and launched the station. Unfortunately, the station did not prosper, primarily as the result of generating below-budget advertising revenues and producing unacceptable on-air programming. In general, the Matthews ran the station poorly. Communication broke down between Larry and the Matthews, resulting in a toxic relationship that led Larry to file legal action on behalf of United Communication. The suit resulted in a trial before the Jacksonville District Court, where both Larry and I testified — with the court finding in favor of United Communication. The Matthews were returned their modest investment and removed from the operation, giving United Communication full ownership and sole responsibility for operating the station. However, United Communication's attempt to operate the station was also unsuccessful — and after a short time, the station shut down and was mothballed.

Meanwhile, United Communication sold its interest in the Portland market and redeployed the capital generated to retire a bank note and support other corporate operations. We began to look for a buyer for the Jacksonville station. In 2000, a minority radio station group operating out of Tampa, Florida, agreed to purchase the station. Larry and I negotiated the final sale via conference call from his Martha's Vineyard home. But with delays, the final closing did not take place until January 2002.

Unfortunately, Larry did not live to witness the final closing; it occurred shortly after his death from prostate cancer in October of 2001. This was a devastating blow to our group and to me personally. Larry had not only put the group together, but had worked tirelessly with me and others to keep the corporation afloat — only to pass away just months before the conclusion of the sale. After Larry's death, his widow, Judith, replaced him as president and successfully help me complete the profitable sale of the corporation's final asset, the Jacksonville FM station.

Figure 13. With (L-R) Detroit icon Dr. Arthur Johnson, Paul Hubbard and Dr. Johnson's wife, Chacona.

THE EMERGENCE OF CELLULAR TELEPHONE TECHNOLOGY

During the preliminary work for the Detroit Cable bidding process and while conversing with Percy Sutton, I first learned of the forthcoming cellular telephone technology. Percy explained it as a technology that worked like tossing a pebble into a pond, then watching the ripples start forming. The ripples that formed could be likened to cells that would have the capacity to transmit messages wirelessly from hand-held devices located within the cell confines.

Sutton explained that cells would be built throughout a local geographic area and would contain the capacity to both transmit and capture information from cellular devices within a given range. The cells would wirelessly transmit the information to land-line telephones or to cellular devices in any areas where cells were located. This new technology would replace the current "in-car" telephones that were clumsy and unreliable.

Through an FCC licensing lottery that would be held for each city in America, Sutton explained, lottery winners would be allowed to build wireless cellular telephone systems, which would compete with the wired land-line systems currently offered by local and national telephone operators. Interested, I queried Percy Sutton about the process by which one might invest in the cellular telephone industry. He responded that the process was already underway and that if I was interested, he could put me in contact with lawyers familiar with the process. They would, on behalf of any client, file applications in selected markets.

I immediately convened a group consisting of Paul Hubbard and Sam Thomas, my school bus partners; architect Howard Sims; and Dr. Rudy Wyatt, a local physician. We agreed to apply in three markets — Columbia, South Carolina; Lancaster, Pennsylvania and Tallahassee, Florida. After our license applications were filed, I learned two things. First, the $35,000 we paid for filing our applications was too much; and second, our chance of winning was close to nil, considering the number of license applications filed in the three markets.

I then learned that the FCC allowed for settlement groups, where any number of licensees could band together and agree to share the license award if anyone of the members in the group won the lottery. Of course, the natural winner would receive a larger percentage. We joined three settlement groups. Fortunately, the Lancaster, Pennsylvania, group won us the right to build the cell site.

Subsequently, we sold our share of the award to a venture capital group specializing in the purchase of cellular licenses, which then packaged deals with firms having the capacity to build out the cellular sites. For example, Post-Newsweek Stations of Washington, D.C., which also owned other major markets, including Washington, D.C., Boston, Miami and Seattle, won the cellular rights for Detroit. Early Monroe, a friend to me and Larry, was part of the Post-Newsweek group called Cellular One, along with Gene Jackson (Percy Sutton's cable TV partner). Monroe and Jackson emerged wealthy, when a few years later Post-Newsweek sold Cellular One for $350 million to the Pacific Telephone Company!

By comparison, our small settlement was peanuts. However, we played in the process and walked away with a substantial gain on our initial investment of a few thousand dollars.

These varying technology experiences I have mentioned — coupled with my years with ICBIF and PRIME — taught me many valuable lessons that piqued my interests about business ownership. Despite many successes at New Detroit, the prestige of the position and the many privileges extended to me and my family, I began to hear the call of the private sector. I knew it was for me. I was becoming convinced that I was a businessperson at heart.

CHAPTER 9

TRANSITION

THE APPEAL OF VOLUNTEER WORK

While my interest in business grew, I had also begun to develop a strong interest in becoming a volunteer where I could apply my experiences and skills to support important not-for-profit organizations. I could envision doing volunteer work while pursuing my love of entrepreneurship. Both were top-of-mind interests of mine. I also knew that time was of the essence, with my advancing years. I had been at New Detroit since 1972 — some thirteen years — and the organization's president for eight years. I felt for a number of reasons that it was time for me to move on.

Earlier, I had joined the foundation board of my alma mater, NCCU, following a visit from Dr. Leroy Walker, who had been elevated to chancellor following a long and successful career as the university's track coach. He had visited Detroit to thank our local chapter for making a six-figure gift to the university, and also to visit several Detroit corporations, hoping to interest them in supporting NCCU. I enjoyed this work and also joined the institution's Board of Visitors. I later became president of the foundation and remained for more than a decade, through the terms of two successive chancellors to Walker: Tyrone Richmond and Julius Chambers. Richmond's short tenure was unspectacular; however, Chambers had returned to our alma mater at the behest of Dick Spangler, my old army friend who at the time was president of the North Carolina University Higher Education System. Spangler recruited Chambers from his position as legal counsel of the NAACP Legal Defense Fund, following a stellar law career in Charlotte, North Carolina.

I enjoyed the work I did to support NCCU and visited often — once during graduation ceremonies, where The Most Reverend Desmond Tutu Archbishop of the Anglican Church of South Africa was the commencement speaker. Retha and I enjoyed this spectacular weekend with Dr. Walker and Tutu, plus our friends the Sims, who accompanied us from Detroit.

The diversity of experiences gained by my work with NCCU, plus my work with the Detroit Symphony Board, the Health Alliance Plan Board, and the board of Channel 56 was convincing me that I would enjoy being more involved as a board volunteer.

FORMATION OF THE COMMUNITY
FOUNDATION FOR SOUTHEAST MICHIGAN

It was early in 1984 when Joseph L. Hudson briefed me on an initiative that he had gotten underway. Joe reported that he and other community minded corporate leaders had completed the preliminary work to establish a new organization in the city — the "Community Foundation for Southeast Michigan."

Joe explained that community foundations were vehicles established solely to facilitate the spirit of philanthropically minded citizens. He said these foundations were vessels through which donors could identify important issues, share ideas and provide the financial support necessary to carry out these causes and produce positive, long-term change. He further explained that the new foundations would build permanent community capital in the form of endowments to create a base of stable financial support for the future of Southeast Michigan. Joe cited examples of other communities that had established similar vehicles — with Cleveland, Ohio, having created one of the largest. Many community foundations dated back to the 1930s.

Intrigued by the concept, I asked whether a president had been selected for the position — for during 1984, I was in an active search for my next job opportunity. Joe responded that the president would be Mariam Noland, who was moving to Detroit from Minneapolis. Then he remarked that New Detroit would be indirectly affected, because the organization's annual gift from the Kresge Foundation would now come from the newly established Community Foundation. This was the result of a "corpus gift" made to the foundation by Kresge in an amount sufficient to generate New Detroit's annual gift. At the time, I immediately tensed, for I instinctively knew that sooner or later the new organization might reduce the dollars that New Detroit annually received. Later, I shared my concern with my successor at New Detroit; but fortunately, my caution was not needed, as the new foundation continued to fund New Detroit and support its work in a number of other ways.

After I departed New Detroit, I was invited to join the board of the Community Foundation and got to know Mariam Noland quite well while I served on the foundation's board for the maximum term of nine years. Over its short life, the foundation has proven itself to be a terribly important community resource for numerous causes and nonprofit initiatives. Through its Donor Advisor Fund, the Community Foundation has created an important repository where Detroit donors may deposit funds that are then managed by the foundation — essentially giving donors their own personal foundation, from which they may direct gifts to purposes consistent with their dreams. As it approaches its thirtieth anniversary in 2014, the Community Foundation for Southeast Michigan now ranks nationally among the top thirty foundations in assets, and has distributed more than $300 million to support thousands of charitable activities. What a fine addition to our community it has become.

PREPARING TO MAKE THE LEAP

While I still enjoyed my work at New Detroit, I was becoming more and more convinced that I could not contribute much else; increasingly,

I began to envision my life-long dream of owning and operating a business of my own. My feelings had very little to do with New Detroit, its staff or its goals; they had much to do with how I felt about my personal future. I also felt that despite the many advocacy programs and issues promulgated by New Detroit, all in support of the city's eventual turn-around, I knew that it would take decades or more for a true renaissance to occur.

In addition, my deepening passion for golf greatly influenced my decisions about the next phase of my life. I was tired of being just a weekend golfer; I wanted to play more frequently during the week. I therefore concluded that I should seek a career that would allow for personal success while also enabling me the opportunity to play golf more often — hopefully as a member of a country club in the Detroit area. Since most area clubs refused membership to blacks, I had sought to change this contemptible practice by confronting it with the help of two New Detroit trustees — Archbishop Szocka and Frank Stella. Trustees Szocka and Stella were leading a sub-rosa effort to convince the Detroit Golf Club, one of the area's most prominent clubs, to open its membership and invite blacks to join.

The Detroit Golf Club yielded to pressure from Szocka and Stella. Most likely, others were involved as well, causing the club to change its membership practice, whereby Mayor Young was invited to become a "House" member in early 1986, shortly after I left New Detroit. This action allowed Young use of club facilities — but did not extend to him golfing privileges. (Interestingly, earlier Detroit mayors had automatically received free Club memberships that included golfing privileges.) Less than a year later, the Detroit Golf Club opened its membership to its first black golfing member, Walter Watkins, an officer of the National Bank of Detroit (now JP Morgan Chase Bank).

Also influencing the new direction of my life was the condominium that Retha and I owned at the Pinehurst Country Club in North Carolina. We had purchased the condo and a golfing membership during the late seventies as a way to stay close to our birthplaces. We had hosted Patricia's wedding there in 1979. Now, Retha and I wanted to enjoy the use of the condo and the golfing privileges of the country club more often.

The new lifestyle I wanted offered the perfect balance of all that I had seen and observed during my years at New Detroit: travel, golf, success in business, and the opportunity to serve my community as a volunteer. I felt that rather than be paid as the head of New Detroit, I was prepared to offer my skills to the community as a volunteer, a practice I had observed from the many business trustees I had worked with at New Detroit. I was fifty-two years old and knew that the time had come for my next move.

Perhaps a part of me also wanted to prove to the many publics I had worked with — the Detroit media, corporate principals, labor leaders, politicians, governmental officials, educators and community activists — that a black individual like me could become a successful business owner. Thus, I began to explore business options I felt were available to me.

Figure 14.   My daughter Patricia on her wedding day

BUSINESS OPTIONS I DECIDED AGAINST

First, I followed up on an opportunity that had been discussed with me earlier by a prominent CEO of a prestigious Detroit firm, who expressed interest in fitting me into a line position in his company. This would have been quite different at the time, as most African Americans worked in staff positions — with a rather pronounced "glass ceiling" visible to all throughout the Detroit area. However, when I approached this CEO about joining his firm, his response was that he was "in the middle of reorganizing his company," and felt "the timing wasn't right." I never pursued his opportunity further — believing that if there was not an opportunity during a period of reorganization, then none was likely to be forthcoming.

I then pursued other opportunities, including a partnership with one of Detroit's public accounting firms. That would take me along the same path that Larry had followed upon leaving New Detroit. I thought my accounting background would make public accounting a good fit. Yet, I was not a CPA; I therefore concluded that the risk was too great at my advancing age to pursue an accounting career. I knew the retirement policy of accounting firms required partners to retire at the age of sixty-two. Thus, I became even more firmly convinced that owning and operating my own business, something I felt I could do well past the usual retirement age, was my best option.

Another opportunity was presented by Peter Stroh. As a member of the Stroh Brewery Advisory Committee, I learned from Peter that his company planned to spin off what was then City Marketing, a Stroh beer distributorship in Detroit. As it turned out, Stroh Brewery sold City Marketing to Bob Holland, a former associate of Stroh's President Roger Fridholm. Subsequently, Bob invited me to join him as an investor. Although I became a partner with him in the beer distributorship, my involvement was minimal and did not fulfill my desire to own and operate my own business.

Because I lived in the Motor City and had extensive contacts and insights with the Big Three, I decided to investigate owning and operating an auto dealership.

I met first with Roger Smith of General Motors and some of his sales executives. All listened to my appeal, then they responded:

"Well we don't know if you have the aptitude for the auto industry, so why don't we administer an auto-aptitude test?"

I was not surprised that I was asked to be tested, for most corporate executives whom I had met at the time generally felt it was impossible to "cross-over" from the not-for-profit sector to the for-profit business sector. In addition to their belief that the skills gained in the nonprofit sector were not transferable, I had a sense they were questioning my innate ability to manage and operate a dealership. Knowing their feelings, I agreed to the test.

Carol Smeet, head of the Chevrolet Division, administered the aptitude test, but never told me how well I did, except to say that I passed. (I knew that I had "aced" the test!) He agreed that GM would accept me into their minority dealer-training program, during which I would receive a $3,600 monthly stipend.

I listened but came away sensing that GM lacked enthusiasm for my candidacy. Whether it was me or the GM attitude — an attitude that I and many others viewed as arrogant, insular and self-referential — I decided against pursuing an opportunity with GM.

At that point, I decided to visit the World Headquarters of Ford in Dearborn.

GETTING TO KNOW FORD

During my New Detroit years, I had met many executives at Ford Motor Company, including Henry Ford II. However, I decided to begin my exploration into owning a dealership by talking to Bob Sullivan, head of Ford's Minority Dealer Operations — unlike my approach at GM, where I started at the top. I decided I should not go over Sullivan's head.

Bob was very enthusiastic about my interest in becoming a Ford dealer. "You're just the kind of person we're looking for, a person with a track record and well-known in his or her hometown community," he said. "We want our dealers, wherever they are, to be involved in their communities. Knowing your background in Detroit

I feel that you have the requisite skills we've talked about for potential dealer candidates. So, yes, we would like to pursue an opportunity with you."

At the time, two of my children were away in college and another was about to go. I made a fairly decent six-figure income at New Detroit; yet I wasn't in a position where my family and I could live on much less than my current salary. I asked if I could work out a consulting relationship with Ford, in addition to the stipend I would receive from the minority dealer program.

"Well," Bob responded, "Tell me what you need. Put something together and get back with me." I quickly compiled a list of my monthly obligations and informed him of what I needed to cover them. Bob and Mike Erminger, who was to replace him at the end of the year, agreed to my list of financial needs. In consultation with his boss, Rusty Restucci, Bob established a consultancy arrangement in which I wrote monthly reports that evaluated the strengths, weaknesses and opportunities within Ford's minority dealer training program. Under the leadership of Bob, Rusty and Mike, Ford's Minority Dealer program became the standard of the automobile industry.

BEST EFFORTS TOWARD AN ORDERLY TRANSITION

For the months leading to my announced departure from New Detroit, I had held several conversations with the organization's chairman, Jim Aliber, to whom I told that I was looking around and had been thinking about a transition out for a year or so. As New Detroit's president, I shouldered enormous responsibilities, which covered a portentous number of issues. During my tenure with the organization, I was not afforded the flexibility of career choices offered to others in similar positions. New Detroit's president was expected to stay; upon leaving he was expected to assist the organization in finding a suitable replacement.

"If you're going to leave, who's going to run the organization?" Aliber asked. He added, "It's your responsibility to help bridge that gap. Don't leave us with an organization without a leader." I learned that volunteer chairmen do not have much stomach for having the responsibility of replacing a resigning president — especially not for an organization with the complexity of New Detroit.

As I strategized a smooth transition, I brought in S. Martin Taylor as an executive vice president. He joined the organization in early 1985. My plan was that he would succeed me as president. Not many among New Detroit trustees knew him at the time, even though he was a prominent senior government official as head of the Michigan Employment Security Commission (MESC) in Governor Jim Blanchard's Administration.

He and I had become friends while playing golf over a number of years. When I approached him, he wasn't sure he could work for me, believing it would be difficult for him to work for a close friend.

"Well, you know," I assured him, "I think it can work out. I worked for Larry Doss, and we were friends who respected each other." I remarked to Martin that the trick would be to simply do your job and not let friendship get in the way. I also reminded Martin that he had successfully worked for his long time friend Dick Whitmer at the Michigan Department of Commerce. Then I emphasized to him that the plan was for him to transition in while I was transitioning out.

Larry and I were always able to work well together, perhaps because my personality did not require that I dominate our relationship. And I had no trouble taking direction from a friend who was also my boss. While there were febrile moments between us — and our alpha-male tendencies could fur up, we were always able to work matters out.

While Martin did eventually come to New Detroit, we were never able to have a very close working relationship the way Larry and I had. For whatever the reasons, he never really acknowledged me as his boss. He did acknowledge me as president of the organization, but was clearly uncomfortable with my presence. My feeling at the time was that Martin was quite anxious for me to leave and seemed disappointed when it took more time than he thought it should. I guess that's typical of a number of people if the purpose for which they are brought in is to replace the outgoing leader who brought them in. Yet, in similar situations, others have used the transition period as a time to learn and understand the nuisances of the role they are to assume. Martin did not seem open to that arrangement.

MAKING THE BREAK

I announced my departure at New Detroit's October 1985 board meeting, drawing little surprise. Most board members knew that I was planning to leave; what surprised some of them was what I had decided to do. Rather than work in some professional opportunity created by one of the major corporations in town, here I was going to sell cars. I quickly learned that many individuals perceived selling cars as lacking prestige or continuity with what they saw as the status I had earned as the president of New Detroit.

This reminded me of many examples I had observed among blacks who valued and hyped "what one did" over the economics of "what one earned." I ignored the negative comments and innuendos I received — feeling strongly that the auto business was the perfect linkage for me. It would enable me to fulfill my desire to become a player in the capitalistic system, and if I were successful, the opportunity to play a lot more golf.

Many took my announcement well, but Janet Crawford, my executive secretary, cried. I never will forget how she just lost it. Even after returning to the office following the board meeting, she was still crying. She probably knew she didn't have any friends left in the organization. As it turned out, Janet *was* shortly pushed out; and eventually she relocated to Houston, Texas, where her children resided. I always regretted that I was unable to have her accompany me when I left. When Martin arrived, he selected his own secretary. Unfortunately, Janet lost out to Loretta Tatem, who served Martin during his tenure, then became secretary to the president of Wayne State University.

As anticipated, my bringing in S. Martin Taylor raised a debate amongst board members, particularly as the matter was discussed in New Detroit's Black Caucus — the forum where blacks raised and debated divisive issues. Thus, the focus of my replacement became the topic of debate during several caucus meetings, not all of which included me. There was the candidacy of Paul Hubbard to consider. Paul was a vice president at New Detroit; he had been there since the early seventies, and had obvious aspirations to become my successor. However, I was not convinced that Paul possessed the management and leadership skills needed to run New Detroit. Paul's candidacy for president was raised and discussed in great depth at a Black Caucus meeting that took place at my home — where Dave Bing, a very involved trustee at the time, pressed for resolution of the matter. Those present firmly deciding Martin should become president.

I was honest with Paul through this whole process and was mindful of the strain it put on our relationship. Paul and I were business partners, and I did not want my actions to change our personal relationship. I was fully aware that Paul was not happy with the outcome. Yet, I remained convinced the organization would be best served with Martin as President. I explained my position to both board members and to New Detroit's chair; and the organization elected Martin its fourth president at its December board meeting in 1985. I left New Detroit at the end of the month.

Martin's presidency went well, but I'm not so sure the organization ever fully endorsed his leadership. Martin left New Detroit after a stint of a little more than two years; Paul succeeded him with my blessings. My hunch was that Martin never joined New Detroit intending to stay for long. It was likely just a stepping-stone in his mind, and an opportunity to get away from the troubled Michigan Employment Security Commission. (At the time of his departure, the agency was battling the balky installation of a new computer system that was over budget and not proceeding well.) Yet, we all look for the best opportunities available to us; nobody can fault an individual for that.

One shift in policy disappointed me after I left: New Detroit stopped funding minority economic development during Martin's tenure. He decided to shut down the Inner City Business Improvement Forum, operated by Walter McMurtry – with some individuals second-guessing his action, I'm sure. I do not know, for I purposefully distanced myself from the organization once I left, and was not consulted when the shutdown decision was made. Minority economic development had been a very strong initiative of New Detroit; through ICBIF, many minority individuals were given their first look at business development and capital formation. Indeed, New Detroit and ICBIF had laid a foundation that helped make Detroit one of the preeminent cities in the U.S with regard to the number of successful African American-owned businesses.

Therefore, at the time, I viewed the shutdown of ICBIF as a critical blow to minority economic development in Detroit. Fortunately, other entities like the Detroit Economic Growth Corporation helped to fill the void and made the shutdown more palatable.

ONE LAST BIT OF POLITICS: THE BILL LUCAS CAMPAIGN AND MY TRIBUTE PARTY

Contentious issues always faced New Detroit, and one occurred during my waning days when Bill Lucas announced his candidacy for governor to challenge incumbent James Blanchard. At the time, Lucas was the newly elected Wayne County Executive, having run as a Democrat. Now, he was changing his party affiliation, becoming the Republican gubernatorial candidate. Many people concluded that Bill had become the Republican candidate against the well-entrenched incumbent, Jim Blanchard, because there was little likelihood for a Republican victory. Many saw Lucas' candidacy as a ploy by Republican operatives as an attempt to change their party's image among black voters.

Indeed, that was the view I held, for Jim Blanchard had been a popular governor during his first term. Many politicos felt Bill Lucas had little chance of defeating Blanchard, yet he remained convinced that he had a chance to win.

Bill Johnson, a long-time street reporter, had joined Lucas' campaign staff and visited with me to discuss Bill Lucas' candidacy. I invited Martin Taylor to join Bill and me in the discussion. What Martin and I were doing in this instance was listening to and counseling an individual who sought the views of New Detroit's leaders. This was something many candidates did when seeking elected office, much like Larry had done in the instance of Coleman Young's campaign for mayor. Martin and I listened and offered our opinions, noting the many conclusions already reached by some on Lucas' candidacy. It was a hotly debated topic, since so many Detroiters — including Coleman Young – had worked diligently to elect Bill as Wayne County's first County Executive — when he ran as a Democrat.

Martin and I predicted the eventual outcome of the gubernatorial race. Bill went down to a flaming defeat. I always liked and respected Bill and opined that had he stayed with the County, perhaps he could have enjoyed the kind of success that Ed McNamara did as his successor. McNamara had the vision to see what the County could and would become — an important entity that would rebuild and operate a successful international airport and the second largest hub for Delta Air Lines, one of the world's largest airlines. Had Bill possessed such vision, perhaps the McNamara Terminal at Detroit Metropolitan / Wayne County Airport would have been named the "Bill Lucas Terminal."

That election underscored how much I enjoyed my role of providing counsel to individuals while at New Detroit. I would miss this close involvement where so many issues would be discussed with New Detroit's president that affected the life of the city. Yet, I was ready for a new challenge, and the time was right for me to move on.

During my final month at New Detroit, I submitted letters of resignation to all of the boards on which I served, with the exceptions of the Health Alliance Plan and the Detroit Symphony Orchestra boards. I wanted the new president to serve as I had on the many boards throughout the city and suggested to them that they consider him as my replacement.

New Detroit hosted a wonderful tribute party upon my departure. Hundreds attended the affair at the Westin Renaissance Ballroom. The exception was Coleman Young, who promised to attend but did not. The next morning, Fred Martin, Coleman's deputy mayor, called to apologize. I told Fred:

"Tell Coleman to kiss my black ass."

I was definitely pissed that he did not attend my farewell reception.

I would not see or hear from Coleman for more than a year, and, at the time did not care whether or not I ever saw him again!

My final act in December of 1985 was to go into my back yard as the clock struck 12:00 a.m. and fire off my shotgun — given to me by my father shortly after the 1967 rebellion — something I had not done before and have not done since.

CHAPTER 10

FORD MOTOR COMPANY:
A GOOD FIT

JOINING FORD

When Retha and I discussed my decision to go into business for myself and to leave New Detroit, she was fine with it. Between us, the excitement was palpable. First of all, the anticipated change in career represented a new beginning. The thought of doing something different excited us even more. We talked about the potential of relocating to another city; which did not bother either of us, for neither of us was a native Detroiter. We knew that our move could be someplace else in Michigan, Ohio or even back to our home state of North Carolina. It could be just about anywhere.

However, we were not disappointed at all when the opportunity for me to become an auto dealer emerged right in metropolitan Detroit. I would subsequently purchase a majority interest in Avis Ford, on the main, north-south thoroughfare of Telegraph Road — US Route 24 — in the suburban city of Southfield. This was my dream fulfilled! I would finally own and operate a business of my own, and I would even have a shorter commute to work.

When I became a dealer, the domestic auto industry was just beginning what would be a long run of profitability and growth. The industry had come through the doldrums of the early eighties when

Chrysler nearly went bankrupt and Ford teetered on the verge of bankruptcy and sought concessions from the UAW. Yet, when I joined the Ford minority dealer training program, Ford was in the midst of introducing two new vehicles, the 1986 Taurus and Sable sedans, vehicles that became game changers and led a turnaround for Ford during the latter half of the eighties. Ford followed these sedans by introducing a rounded-shaped Thunderbird, a revamped Mustang with cat-like running lights and a restyled F-150 truck. Then in 1990, Ford introduced the all-new Ford Explorer, the best-selling SUV ever built. That put their franchise well ahead of all the domestics. Ford was on a roll and by then, I was one of their dealers, and privileged to be so.

MY MINORITY DEALER TRAINING EXPERIENCE

I began my automotive dealership training in January of 1986. The opportunity to own the Avis Dealership emerged in March. I pursued that possibility while continuing my curriculum training. Before the year's end, I and my partner, Ed Brown, walked into the Avis Dealership — on November 7, 1986 — as its new owners.

Meanwhile, however, I needed to learn how to run a dealership by attending classes convened by Ford's Minority Dealer Operations in the Westin Hotel at the Detroit Renaissance Center. This was close to Ford Division headquarters in Tower 400.

My class consisted of thirteen individuals, including: Willie Naulls, a former professional basketball player; Curtis Bunch, a former professional football player; and Dan Smith, a former Ford employee. Other classmates had worked in dealerships as salespersons or managers. One gentleman, I will never forget, had been an air traffic controller — fired by Ronald Reagan in the early eighties. He was the weakest of all candidates and quit in less than ninety days.

Bobby Jenkins, a black Ford executive, kicked off our first class session and gave us an overview of what it meant to be a Ford dealer. Bobby had been the first black district manager of Ford, having served in California and Washington, D.C. He painted an intelligent and rational vision of what we could expect in our training as dealers, provided we successfully completed the training.

Figure 15. With (L-R) Rev. V. Lonnie Peek, Jr., (center) and Michigan Governor Jim Blanchard

Chuck Royal, a recently graduated minority dealer candidate, followed him. At that time Chuck was building a new dealership — called an add-point — in Albion, Michigan. He related his experiences, citing the various steps necessary to design and build a dealership.

Next, Larry Brown gave a presentation. A recent graduate from the program, Larry had just taken over a dealership in Ottawa, Illinois — a dealership that remains successful.

Then our class got down to business.

Ford, GM and Chrysler had all started initiatives to increase the number of minority auto dealers. In 1963, Chrysler had named Ed Davis the first domestic minority dealer, but Ford took the initiative by awarding a dealership in 1967 to Ernie Banks, a Hall of Fame former Chicago Cubs baseball player (and his black partner Bob Nelson, an imports car dealer who was a retired Air Force officer), and made Nathan Conyers, brother of Congressman John Conyers of Detroit a dealer in 1970. By the time I arrived on the scene, Ford had a larger minority dealer constituent group than either of the other Big-Three. A minority dealer association had been formed and at the time was called the Black Ford Lincoln Mercury Dealer Association, later changing its name to the Ford Lincoln Mercury Minority Dealers Association (FLMMDA). The association was powerful; it met monthly with top Ford executives and placed demands before the company on the desirable number of dealerships it felt would create parity for blacks — reflecting the black population among American citizens.

As I came on the scene, I learned of an important action earlier taken by Phil Benton, at the time the president of the Ford Division. On behalf of Ford, Benton signed a "Blue Letter" agreeing that a total of over 300 dealerships would be established. A Blue Letter was used at Ford to memorialize important decisions made by the company. During the next decade or so, progress was tracked against the targeted number of dealerships established. Ford eventually reached a total of 278 black-owned dealerships, but never attained the Blue Letter target of 312. Knowing of the Blue Letter target gave me comfort as I began my sojourn with the minority dealership program. I was excited to learn the number of minority Ford dealerships outdistanced the number of minority dealer franchises established by either General Motors or Chrysler. That continues to be so, even after the severe reduction to our numbers produced by the Great Recession that began in December 2008 and persists, to some degree, as I write four years later.

Our minority dealership classes began with an introduction of dealership accounting, covering debits and credits and reviewing financial statements. It frightened the heck out of several classmates, especially Curtis Bunch. I never will forget Curtis' frantic tone when he said: "What's this? I can't do this. I'm not going to make it." Curtis was a large individual — a former defensive end who had played for the Philadelphia Eagles. So that night, I took several of my classmates to my home. We sat in my den and began to go through the mechanics of reading and understanding financial statements. From that anxious beginning, Curtis has become a very successful dealer and knows his stuff. But first, he had to get over his fear of established dealership accounting procedures and I was pleased to have helped him get started.

Dealer candidates were paired with an existing and established dealer and operated out of their dealership locations. Candidates were supposed to monitor operating processes at their assigned dealerships to get a sense of how vehicles were sold and serviced. In addition to the hands-on experiences, candidates were required to complete a classroom curriculum, including homework assignments that had to be completed between scheduled classes, which were convened about once each month. Over time, this combination of activities taught candidates the fundamentals needed to operate an automobile dealership.

My dealership laboratory was Bill Brown Ford in Livonia, Michigan, owned by Ed Brown. Ed and I hit it off right away. We found we could easily communicate and share ideas, and each of us earned the other's respect as we shared ideas and thoughts during our daily discussions. Before too long, we began to discuss the likelihood of a potential partnership. Jim Miller, the Ford Detroit District Manager, had done a great job in selecting Ed Brown — believing Ed to be an ideal dealer who would provide an excellent training experience for me. Jim knew his dealers and his belief that Ed's dealership was the best placement for me proved to be correct. As I have seen Jim over the years, I have thanked him for his clairvoyance.

After our classes, we would return to our assigned dealerships. Candidates were assigned to dealerships in California, North Carolina, Louisiana, Maryland and Michigan. We would depart from classroom sessions loaded with materials, books and the homework assignments we had to complete while we observed the day-to-day activities at our assigned dealerships. We learned as we reviewed and discussed issues and situations with dealership managers. In some cases, especially in smaller dealerships, candidates were able to gain hands-on experiences as interim managers.

Yet, in my situation, because I was assigned to a large metropolitan dealership, I sat with various managers to observe them in action and asked questions to gain an understanding of how they handled matters. Hardly ever in a larger dealership did a trainee manage a department, which was the case for me at Bill Brown's. Yet, I got to know all of Ed's managers and learned a great deal from each of them.

When I walked in, Ed's managers were all suspicious of me — because they all wanted to own dealerships themselves. Here I was, this black guy, expecting them to help develop me as part of my dealership training.

My current general manager, Jim Witmer, came from Bill Brown Ford. He was their comptroller. Ed's general manager was Bob Gunnigle, and his sales manager was Mike Schreiber — both outstanding managers. (Bob retired at the end of 2010 — nearly 25 years after we met. Mike continues to lead the sales effort at Bill Brown Ford — now ranked among the top five in the nation.) I first met these fine gentlemen when Ed introduced them to me on a very cold night in late December of 1985. We all met in Ed's office and talked about my aspirations.

From that first meeting, I've never had a reason to doubt the support or loyalty of these gentlemen. Over the ensuing years, we've played countless rounds of golf at varying venues throughout North America. We have become great friends and mutually respectful auto dealership professionals, as we have maneuvered the peaks and valleys of selling and servicing Ford vehicles in metropolitan Detroit.

Ed is a second generation auto dealer, having taken over from his deceased father in the mid-1970s. Ed also has the same interest his father had in horses. On the same cold December night that I first met his key employees, Ed invited me to accompany him to Northville Downs — where one of his horses raced and won! Of course, I placed a winning bet on Ed's horse. What followed was a succession of wins by Ed's horse, which prompted him to insist that I be present every time his horse ran from that time forward. "You know, maybe there is luck between us," he said at the time.

Since that beginning, Ed and I have had countless experiences together: attending business meetings and playing golf at varying venues throughout America and around the world; once traveling by helicopter through Scotland, where we played a number of prestigious courses before landing in front of the Road Hotel in St Andrews, Scotland. Since the early nineties, we have golfed together in my annual club invitational, the Whistler at the Detroit Golf Club — winning numerous times. Indeed, our business and personal relationships have become special.

Ed and I have also played in many events at Meadowbrook Country Club where he belongs; at his club in Las Vegas, and at many other venues around the world. Ed and I were also invited to play at Augusta National in 2001 with Ford President Steve Lyons and retired Ford CEO Red Poling, who was an Augusta National member before his death in 2012. Retha and I have visited Ed and his wife, Mary Ellen, at their home in Las Vegas on numerous occasions.

THE AVIS FORD OPPORTUNITY

Avis Ford, a large metro dealership, became available in March of 1986 when its managing partner, Richard Turner, who owned 49 percent of the dealership, died in a plane crash. At the time, fewer than ninety days had transpired since I had joined the minority dealer program. Turner's unfortunate death seemed to offer an opportunity, which I pursued immediately. I knew that the Avis dealership would be a long shot for a number of reasons. First, it was a large metropolitan dealership, for which there would be strong interest among current dealers and perhaps a few Ford executives. Then, I was a minority individual and I was not sure whether or not my candidacy would be given serious consideration. Nevertheless, I called the Ford Detroit District office and spoke with its manager, Jim Miller — the executive who had placed me at Bill Brown Ford — and expressed my interest. Jim thanked me for my call but was non-committal. I followed up with a letter to Jim, but still received no response.

Not taking no for an answer, I wrote a letter to Donald Peterson, then chairman of Ford Motor Company, and sent a copy to Ford's retired Chairman, Henry Ford II. Happily, that letter generated responses from company representatives.

But clearly, everyone recognized that as new as I was in the auto business, there was little confidence among Ford executives that I could own and operate such a large dealership with my limited experience. Ford's official response was: "We'll give you a chance to pursue the Avis Ford investment opportunity; but you must select a partner to work with you, whom we must approve."

Having already talked with Ed Brown regarding a potential partnership, he and I agreed we would begin the process of formulating a joint venture agreement. We started by having Ed's law firm, Colombo and Colombo, draft a partnership agreement — which seemed to favor Ed entirely. I decided I needed my own lawyer to balance some of the suggested language and hired Edward Dawda. Ed and I had already agreed that I would be the majority partner, but other issues needed resolution. Finding middle ground was elusive. We went back and forth; Ed's lawyer, Chuck LeFevre, was quite difficult to deal with. The agreement he had advanced gave Ed exclusive powers and almost none to me. While I would be president, I would have limited powers and authority to operate the dealership corporation.

During this process, the relationship between Ed and I became strained until we decided to take the lawyers out of the negotiations. Together we crafted a "Buy-Sell" partnership agreement we both could live with. Ed gave some and I gave some. We both knew the opportunity was too great for either of us to stand in its way. Also, while we agreed that the Avis Ford investment opportunity was fraught with problems, it offered enormous potential. Further, we knew that the dealership was undercapitalized, needed equity capital and refurbishing, and had suffered from long neglect.

"Now Walt, you're not going to flame out on me, are you?" Ed asked. "Are you prepared for the tough challenges we are going to face?"

"Ed, you can bet I won't flame out," I said. "And you can bet that I'll stand by you in this deal!"

True to my response, with all of the difficult issues we've faced through the years, we have avoided serious disagreements and have both remained focused on making the Avis opportunity work. I entered into our partnership determined that Ed would never have to worry about me, my private life, my business judgments or my commitment to our agreement. I have lived up to my promise to him and to myself; and over time I have demonstrated effective leadership. Indeed, Avis Ford became one of the first Detroit area Ford dealerships to win the coveted Chairman's Award, given for outstanding customer service. Avis Ford won ahead of Bill Brown Ford, Ed's dealership.

I'm convinced that Ed has no doubt about my commitment to the success of our joint venture — just as I have no doubt about his. Indeed, I even introduced Ed to other business opportunities. Ed became an investor in Atwater Entertainment — the casino deal promoted by Herb Strather — and walked away with a handsome seven-figure return when Atwater sold its interest to Motor City Casino.

From day one, I have maintained a winning attitude, determined not to jeopardize the dealership opportunity granted to Ed and me by Ford. Endowed with the thrilling honor to own a metro Ford dealership, I wanted nothing more than to see it become even more successful than it was when we purchased it. I have always looked for ways to improve the store's operation and have never offered excuses for the performance of the dealership.

Having trained at Ed's store, Bill Brown Ford, I had come away impressed with the high standards maintained by his dealership. During my training, I committed to myself that once in business, I wanted nothing less for the dealership I would eventually own than I had experienced at Bill Brown.

Warren Avis had been the owner of Avis Ford since 1946, which he formed with a partner by the name of A. Robert Frost, shortly after being discharged from the U.S. Army. After buying out Frost, Avis continued to maintain a fifty-one percent ownership in Avis and over time retained dealership operators whom he allowed to purchase a forty-nine percent interest.

Richard Turner had been his most recent minority partner. The question now was whether Avis wanted to sell Turner's minority interest, which reverted to his control after Turner's death, or sell the entire dealership outright. Early on, Avis indicated that he was agreeable to sell the complete dealership.

We began negotiating, with Ed handling the negotiations, which was customary with Ford not being a part of the negotiations

— unless they were intent on purchasing the dealership themselves. If a deal was struck, it would be between Avis and the purchaser, so long as the purchaser was acceptable to Ford. Ford, Ed and I agreed that my name would not surface during these initial discussions as a potential owner. All of us were suspicious that Avis might offer objections to a deal that transferred ownership of his dealership to a black owner. In effect, Ford maintained a hands-off relationship with Avis, yet, met with Ed and me from time to time. On one such occasion, Ed and I met with Al Klanke, who had responsibility for monitoring the deal for Ford. Also attending the meeting were Lee Oliphant, the Assistant Detroit District Manager and Sid Bechum, the Great Lakes Regional Manager. Al had assured us that any matters discussed during our meeting would be kept in strict confidence, and freely shared information with Ed and me about the dealership's internal operations — pointing out its weak cash position, for one thing. All of this was new to us, for neither of us had set foot inside the store since starting our negotiations.

However, the next day Ed and I learned that information we mentioned at the meeting had somehow been relayed to Avis and his staff — either directly or through someone at the Avis dealership. Someone had leaked our in-camera discussions. Ed and I began to sense that while marching orders had been received from on-high for Walt Douglas' involvement in the purchase of Avis Ford, all of the Ford minions were either not on board or one of them was a blabbermouth.

Yet, we pressed ahead, not allowing what we felt was bothersome innuendo from the leaks to hinder us. Ed continued to meet with Avis' envoy, Sid McNiece, representing his and my interests. Sid and Warren knew who Ed was, for his reputation as a successful dealership operator was well known; thus his ability to purchase the dealership was never questioned. However, the leak of our discussion had a chilling effect. It prompted Warren Avis to increase his offering price for the dealership. During Ed's initial negotiations a price had been set at $2.5 million for the entire dealership; but with the overwhelming interest by the ever-growing list of pursuers, and with the leaked information regarding my being a part of the deal, the eventual purchase price rose to $3.2 million — plus the repayment of a nearly $300,000 loan by Avis to the dealership. Avis also proposed that the dealership should be sold in two pieces: the first forty-nine percent at the cost of $1.6 million, and the remaining fifty-one percent at the same price, $1.6 million — five years later.

Ed and I began to assume that this proposition was put forth reflecting Avis' thought that perhaps we would fail and the second half would never have to be delivered. Happily, we proved him wrong!

In purchasing the dealership, Ed and I paid a premium — called blue sky — amounting close to $2.5 million over the asset value of the corporation. It was, perhaps the highest premium ever paid over asset value for a Detroit area dealership at the time. This was an enormous sum, yet because of the dealership's potential and its premier location at the intersection of Telegraph and Twelve Mile Roads, the purchase price was still considered a good buy. However, Ed and I were somewhat leery, and knew the price paid would affect the potential profitability of the dealership for a lengthy period.

Negotiations continued through the summer of 1986, and following some trepidation, Ed and I closed with Warren Avis on November 6, 1986. (It was a Thursday, and Oprah Winfrey began her national TV talk show debut the following Monday. It's amusing for me to recall that our new careers began at the same time.)

Ed and I celebrated that evening at Meadowbrook Country Club in Northville, Michigan, well into the evening. I eventually left Ed at his club around 1:00 am; and the following morning learned that Ed had to be taken to Province Hospital after experiencing chest pains. Thankfully, it was only gas; for when I mentioned Ed's problem to Avis' henchman, Sid McNiece, his first remark was, "Well, the deal is off!" In effect, Sid was telling me that they were not going to deal with me alone.

Nonetheless, Ed was released that Friday morning — November 7, 1986 — and he, Sid, and I met at the dealership in the afternoon, providing us our first opportunity to enter the dealership facility. Sid announced that we were now their partners and introduced us to the dealership's controller, Randy and his assistant JoAnne Huffman, as we took possession of the dealership. We learned in the process that the controller was leaving to join Mel Farr Ford, along with a number of sales employees — following Jimmy Athens, the dealership's general manager, who had already departed to join Farr.

Athens was legendary in the auto industry. Besides being a well-established sales veteran, he was known as an avid horse racing buff that spent a great deal of time at the tracks. Reportedly, Athens was a gruff manager who once fired off a shotgun into the dealership showroom's floor. The patched spot where the discharge entered the floor was pointed out to me in my early weeks at the store. The reason for the gun firing was never revealed to me, even though I did hear stories about the party atmosphere that reportedly prevailed at the facility.

Ed and I were blindsided by these early departures, but reacted quickly by bringing in Jim Witmer, Ed's controller, who filled this initial void. Consistent with the provisions of the closing documents, I immediately assumed the role of president and general manager. Ed became vice president.

All of the negotiations had occurred at Avis Farms, an Ann Arbor site located on State Road east of I-94. Warren Avis had developed his corporate headquarters there on a large tract of land, on which there was located an old farm house where Warren maintained his Michigan residence. Nearby, in a converted barn, were offices where his staff of professionals managed his grouping of investments — which included a fishing tackle company and other interests, in addition to Avis Ford. A nearby converted barn served as a conference center. The site was rustic, but offered an interesting venue.

My first meeting with Warren occurred on Thursday at Avis Farms — just the day before we took over the dealership. As I walked in and was introduced to Warren Avis, his first comments to me were, "So you know Henry Ford?"

My response was, "Yes sir, I do."

"Well, I know him, too!" Avis countered.

His remark startled me. It was obvious that someone had briefed him and described to him how I had come to be considered as a potential investor in the purchase of his dealership. I am sure that it surprised him that I, a black guy, had come to know Henry Ford well enough for him to support my investment in this prized venture. The conversation between us was terse. I could sense the hidden message in his tone; causing me to quickly conclude that our relationship would be both curt and rutted at best. Indeed, our initial conversation foreshadowed the malevolence that I would soon face.

But nonetheless, before Ed and I parted — after signing all the closing documents for our initial purchase of our forty-nine percent interest, Avis presented me with a dozen copies of his recently published book, "Take a Chance to be First," which chronicled his business interests — including the founding of Avis Rent a Car, the company he started shortly after his discharge from the Air Force at the end of World War II. He also related to me in an immodest fashion that he was currently a guest lecturer at the University of Michigan Business School, close by in Ann Arbor.

For the five-plus years we were partners, both Sid and Warren did everything possible to make my life miserable. They begrudgingly afforded me only a modicum of respect. However, they soon learned that despite their provocative behavior, they could neither bully me nor force me to lose control in their presence. I developed a "right back at you" way of responding to them; yet, I did it with both respect and cunning.

HEALTH SCARE

Meanwhile, during the summer of 1986 — while conducting the seemingly "non-stop-negotiations — I encountered a recurring health problem. Since my thirties, I had experienced flare-ups with my prostate, causing me to experience chills and fever. The treatment had always been a prescription of sulfur tablets, which tended to resolve the malady. This time, however, my urologist Ray Littleton at Henry Ford Hospital decided to have an ultrasound test done on my prostate. He later reported that it showed a "shaded" area, suggesting the need for a biopsy.

Here I was at age fifty-two, entering the biggest business deal of my life — facing possible prostate cancer! I was obviously alarmed.

Yet because I felt no symptoms beyond my initial reason for seeing Dr. Littleton, I simply went about my business and awaited the results of the biopsy. Fortunately, the results were negative. Dr. Littleton shared the good news on a Friday, and my birthday, August 22. How relieved Retha and I were!

This potentially life-threatening experience inspired my diligence in protecting my health, with proactive vigilance and a commitment to immediately seek medical help to investigate any symptoms that arise. Since then, I have visited Dr. Littleton routinely, had annual physicals and have had the recommended prescribed colonoscopies to make sure I know the current state of my health. Retha has done the same.

FINANCING THE DEAL

The purchase price Ed Brown and I negotiated for Avis Ford gave each of us a 24.5 percent share of the business, in return for $800,000 from each of us. Five years later, we would have to do it again — paying an additional $1.6 million for the remaining 51 percent of the business. I came up with my $800,000 by doing a number of things.

Retha and I had some money saved and used it to augment the vacation and severance pay I received upon leaving New Detroit. To that sum I added cash borrowed against my 401K — a strategy I chose to avoid the payment of federal income taxes, had I liquidated my 401K account.

We then remortgaged our home with the assistance of Charles Allen, who was president of First Independence National Bank. During that period, Charles helped many African American auto dealers with critical financing; he has since remarked that he never lost a dime supporting them! With our savings; my modest New Detroit severance; cash borrowed against my 401k and the money from refinancing our home, I was able to arrange a loan for the difference from Ford Motor Credit –all of which provided the $800,000 I needed to cover my investment. To this day, I remain partial to Ford Motor Credit, for without their initial assistance and support through the years, I would not be in business.

After giving my all to make the initial investment, and gaining ownership of one-quarter of the dealership from Day One, I knew that Avis Ford had to work — for I was "all in." Starting in November 1986, I began my Avis experience as an equal partner with Ed Brown, and a temporarily unequal partner with Warren Avis, who continued to own 51 percent.

Making the Deal Work

The dealership was in pathetic shape when we took over, but again, had great potential. Avis was a high volume metropolitan dealership that had the ability to sell cars in volume — principally because of its preeminent location; but the facility needed a serious upgrade. Ford Land, Ford Motor Company's real estate arm, owned the building at the time. Ford Land owns a great number of dealership facilities around the country — that being one of their primary purposes — to build dealerships and serve as landlord to dealers who operate the dealership business. However, their role changed under Jacques Nasser when he forced dealers to purchase their facilities from Ford to free up frozen capital.

But in 1986 and prior to our arrival at Avis, Ford Land had sent a letter to the dealership citing a laundry list of deficiencies identified during a recent inspection of the premises. Many needed immediate attention. Perimeter walls were falling down. Bricks were falling away from the building. The roof leaked, and equipment had failed or was failing, including in-ground hoists that had to be removed because of Environmental Protection Agency (EPA) violations. These were violations that we had to address immediately; however the dealership didn't have any money, for all the money we invested went directly into Warren Avis' pocket!

Thus, we were prompted to visit with Ford Land and work out a plan to correct the deficiencies their list had cited. It amounted to Ford Land lending Avis the money to correct the deficiencies, and then adding the sum of the loaned funds to their book value for the building. Rent was then adjusted to reflect the increase in dealership value.

As already mentioned, our first opportunity to enter the dealership premises in Southfield came on that Friday in November 1986, after we had already closed on the deal and suddenly learned of the departure of the store's general manager, five sales people and the office comptroller. Both Ed and I were taken aback that Mel Farr Ford, a minority owned dealership in neighboring Oak Park, hired away these employees from Avis Ford, knowing full well that I was the incoming new owner. I was learning quickly that "all is fair in war and business."

Needing a controller immediately, Ed agreed that Jim Witmer, his controller at Bill Brown Ford, would assist us in getting started. For the remainder of 1986 and all of 1987, Jim split time between Avis Ford and Bill Brown Ford. In early 1988, Jim joined Avis Ford full time, leaving Bill Brown Ford; and subsequent to our buyout in 1992 purchased some of Ed's shares — attesting to his worth to the company.

Interestingly, some of the sales people who left Avis wanted to come back awhile later. We agreed to rehire only one of the departed sales people, Caesar Punzelan, who unfortunately has since died. We brought Caesar back because he was extremely smart and we felt he could be helpful to our operation. Mel and I never discussed his pirating of Avis' employees; however, years later, he would complain when his salespeople began leaving him to join Avis. What resulted was a screaming phone conversation between he and I that prompted a slamming down of phones and the eventual suspension of dealer trading of vehicles between our dealerships. However, after a while we made amends — which was easy for me, considering that Avis continued to outperform Mel Farr Ford.

Starting as an unknown quantity, no one had any knowledge of my abilities, which were untested and unknown. I was just an unknown black guy who was taking over a dealership without a track record, save my reputation from my New Detroit years. I am sure that many Avis employees were fearful of their jobs, or worried about what to expect from the new owners. People were afraid the dealership might fail, resulting in the loss of their livelihoods. Avis' service manager at the time, Bob Skurda asked me point blank:

"Should I be concerned? Should I stay or should I go?"

I responded, "Well, you have done nothing to make me want to replace you; however, you can do anything you like."

Skurda stayed for several years and successfully managed our service department. His dedication helped us to earn our first Chairman's Award. Then he chased his dream to live in Tennessee where his wife had grown up. He continues to make his home there, but now works in the real estate industry.

Meanwhile, during our first month of operation, Mel continued to pirate our staff away, luring our service dispatcher, who later wanted to return to Avis. I refused to take him back.

Despite these early losses, we had a core of good people — some of whom remain with us today!

EARLY ADJUSTMENTS, BUSINESS SURVIVAL

But many individuals were unsure about how well we were going to fare. Indeed, we did struggle during our first year. Needing a new car sales manager, we hired Greg Marrs, an experienced "car man," as sales managers are known in the business. He was an excellent sales manager and increased our sales volume during our first year. His incompatible management style, however, forced us to let him go at the end of our first full year.

We continued to struggle before I found another proven new vehicle sales manager, Bob Morris, who began building a strong team, bringing several salespersons with him. Two of those individuals, Gary Addley and Lou Marchesi, continue as top sales producers for Avis. And another salesperson, Gene McHarris, remained after Ed and I took over and still remains at Avis: plus a majority of back office individuals, and technicians continue as tenured Avis employees.

When our business started to boom, we attracted attention from other dealers. They were amazed that we were selling more vehicles than the dealership had historically sold. In fact, during the nineties, our new vehicle volume increased from the high 2,000s to end the decade at nearly 4,000 annually. I was thrilled!

Although Avis' employees initially did not know me or my business style, they soon learned I would insist upon high performance standards. I also set "stretch" goals, seeking to grow the dealership's performance and ranking, especially in the treatment of our customers. I always wanted our customers to view us as a successful and caring business that offered no excuses for the sales or service experiences they encountered. I began by following an old adage: "Managers do things right; leaders do the right thing."

Avis' employees quickly adapted to my style of leadership and that of Jim Witmer, which has resulted in limited turnover of personnel since our arrival. We continue to replace employees only for cause or when their performance dictates such action.

To ease our need for capital, we borrowed working capital from Ford Motor Credit. That enabled us to operate and meet our obligations. As we sold more vehicles, more working capital was needed. Our scariest moment came about a year after we had taken over operation of the dealership. Standard financial procedure at Ford dealerships calls for Ford Credit to come in every six weeks and count the dealership's new vehicle inventory. Ford Credit inventories vehicles on the premises and those recently sold, to reconcile with pay-offs the agency has received. At the end of the inventory count, Ford Credit requires a check for any vehicles that have been sold but not paid off.

At this particular moment, we did not have enough money to pay Ford Motor Credit. We had been doing what a lot of dealers do: we'd write checks to pay off vehicles sold, but kept them in our possession, knowing there was not enough money in the bank to allow these checks to clear. It was at this juncture that Ed Brown stepped in and made the dealership a working capital loan. That was our scariest moment because we were essentially broke: out-of-trust with Ford Credit.

Thereafter, the dealership accrued interest on Ed's loan and paid him just as we paid Ford Motor Credit. We struggled, but fortunately, the business cycle was "up," making it easier for us to make strides and remain profitable.

Other money problems plagued us. First, I had a note with Ford Credit, payable each month. Can you imagine having to pay Ford Credit $15,000 every month? I was quite mindful we had to make money, but more importantly, we needed cash to make my Ford Credit payments. There were other obligations such as federal and state taxes, which, of course, needed to be kept current.

Yet, before we bought him out, our majority partner Warren Avis was insistent on receiving quarterly profit distributions, consistent with our deal. He was not sympathetic to our cash flow problems. Something had to give. I had always surmised that Avis believed Ed and I would not be able to make the dealership operation work, and would either default on our deal with him or come to him "hat in hand" and ask for a modification of our deal. I was determined that we would do neither.

Thus, it became my responsibility to report our cash flow difficulties to Warren Avis, advising him that we were unable to make the anticipated quarterly distributions. I looked him straight in the eye and told him, "We're only going to do what the business can afford to do. We're not going to bankrupt the business by paying out money we don't have."

Then I met with Ford Credit and requested that they allow me to pay "interest only" on my personal loan, explaining that the dealership was strapped for cash, although we were making money. They agreed, suspended my principal payments and allowed me to pay only the monthly interest due on my note, which allowed the dealership to reduce the distributions we had to make.

After a year, the dealership was healthier and allowed for the resumption of larger distributions; thus, I was able to resume making principal payments to Ford Credit. Interestingly, while this was going on, the Detroit community thought that I was rich and constantly prodded me to participate in every fund raising event imaginable. But I lived through that period and the trying cash flow problems we faced. Thank God!

COMPLETING THE PURCHASE

Five years passed and it became time to purchase Warren Avis' 51 percent of the dealership. That's when Sid McNiece's irritating stalling tactics and attempts to discourage us from closing the deal began — a draining process described at the beginning of this book. As I indicated, it all culminated in my verbal showdown with Sid two days before the scheduled closing. When he realized that I was truly ready to take back all of my money and walk away from the deal, he finally relented — and the deal closed on time.

What I didn't mention in my earlier telling of that final confrontation underscores how debilitating meanness and pettiness can be in business or any other part of life. Once I stood over Sid and delivered my ultimatum in a threatening manner, I knew I had frightened him and changed his attitude toward me. I noticed two days later, at the deal closing, a slight lisp in Sid's speech. It was later reported to me that he had had a slight stroke. Following the Avis sale, Sid retired from Avis Farms, moved back to Texas and died within two years.

Years later, in 1996, when we invited Warren to the dealership to celebrate its fiftieth anniversary, Warren confessed to me that he had made a mistake in selling the dealership. Nonetheless, he congratulated us on the job we were doing, and I appreciated that kind gesture.

FROM NONPROFIT TO BUSINESS OWNER

The purchase of Avis and the ensuing five years had proved beyond a shadow of doubt that I could successfully make the transition from not-for-profit to the for-profit sector. If there had been doubters, they were now convinced that Walt Douglas had skills beyond those he had employed as an advocate for social change during his career at New Detroit. I was demonstrating that I could manage a profitable business that produced over a $100 million in annual sales. Furthermore, not only was the business breaking sales records, it was achieving success in customer service rankings.

I was proud that Avis achieved membership in Ford's Hundred Club, whose membership was predicated on a national ranking among the top one-hundred dealers in vehicle sales and customer service. Being a Ford Hundred Club member placed Avis Ford among the elite Ford dealerships in America. We were the first black Hundred Club dealer, for before our achievement, no other minority dealer had met the sales volume and customer service criteria. Thus, we stood out among the otherwise all-white dealer group awardees at annual gatherings in prestigious resort venues like La Quinta in Palm Springs, California; The Ritz Carlton in Naples Florida; the Turnberry Isle Resort in Miami; The Broadmoor in Colorado, and others, causing many stares and whispers by the attendees. Yet, it was not long before other black dealers began to win the coveted award.

Avis also began to be recognized on numerous occasions as President's Award Winners — those dealerships with the highest customer satisfaction index ranking within their geographic market area. In other words, President's Award winners are considered to be the best of the best dealerships.

Avis achieved "triple threat" status when we won Ford Credit's "Partners in Quality" dealership award — a program created by Edsel Ford when he was president of Ford Credit. The award gave recognition to dealerships for their financial loyalty and the quality of credit services extended to customers. Earning the Partners in Quality award made Avis one of a few dozen among more than 3,100 Ford dealerships that have received all three awards in the same year.

I was also proud of the fact that Avis Ford was included among the President's Circle of dealerships, an entity that operated until the end of 2006. The President's Circle was composed of a grouping of 150 dealerships selected worldwide with whom Ford maintained close relationships to gain feedback and business insights.

CHAPTER 11

BOARD WORK AND NEW BUSINESS VENTURES

LIFE AS A BUSINESSMAN AND COMMUNITY LEADER

It was not long after I purchased my interest in Avis Ford that the community began to recognize me as a business leader and sought my involvement as a board member to help address a number of community issues, as I had during my years at New Detroit. I was asked to join the Oakland University Foundation Board, the Boy Scouts Board and a number of others as well.

However, I was trying to devote my time and energies to Avis Ford, as we struggled to stabilize our business operations. Thus, I had to say "no" to some requests; otherwise, I would have been overextended.

I continued my involvement with the Detroit Symphony Orchestra, yet I did not attend all board meetings. I had been asked to join the DSO board during the early eighties when the organization went through a difficult period and when the black community criticized it for its lack of diversity amongst its staff and orchestra. Back then, the DSO asked me to join its executive committee, where I would become its first black member.

As I contemplated their request, knowing that other blacks were just as suited as I, if not more suited, I concluded that placing me alone on the DSO's executive committee would not be sufficient. I countered that I would agree to serve only if in addition to me; federal Judge Damon J. Keith and Wayne State University Vice President Dr. Arthur L. Johnson were asked to join as well.

The DSO agreed and the three of us joined and served for many years. I never mentioned my suggestion to anyone, for my request that Damon and Art join with me was meant solely to achieve greater diversity. That would result in giving stronger support for the initiatives that needed attention by the DSO's executive committee and board. The community was pressing for black musicians in the orchestra and for a stronger interface between the DSO and the Detroit Public Schools. During that period, none of us could understand why it was so difficult for blacks to gain access to positions in the orchestra, for we knew of the rich history of blacks in music, dating before the turn of the 20th century.

As it was explained, musicians had to audition behind a screen where their identity would not be disclosed. The inference was that orchestra selections were completely fair and based only on the talent of the musician. Even still, progress was slow in seating the first black musician — leaving many blacks with lingering suspicion.

Finally, as the orchestra diversified, other initiatives included a youth orchestra and an intern program allowing talented young black musicians to sit-in on occasions with the DSO. Indeed, much progress was made in the DSO and I enjoyed my association with many music lovers and supporters as I served. I still serve on the DSO board and enthusiastically support their fine work. In the late eighties, I served on the search committee that selected Deborah Borda as the DSO president. I have also enjoyed working with her successors, Mark Volpe and Ann Parsons. Of course, during the three decades I have served, the Detroit community has enjoyed fine music under music directors Gunther Herbig — brought to Detroit during the mid eighties from behind the Iron Curtain, Neeme Jarvi and Leonard Slatkin, who began his service in 2008.

HEALTH ALLIANCE PLAN AND HENRY FORD II

I also remained active with the Health Alliance Plan, where in 1985 I was named Chair of its Board. This followed the resignation of the HAP's original Chair, Jack Shelton, who resigned to join the Blue Cross Blue Shield Board. Jack, a Ford Motor Company healthcare expert, had been placed in charge by Henry Ford II when the alliance was formed between the Metro Detroit Health Association and the Henry Ford Hospital, creating the Health Alliance Plan (HAP).

Following Jack's departure, I was asked by various board members to run for the vacated chair position. Ray Majerus, Secretary Treasury of the UAW was also interested in becoming HAP's chair. However, hearing of my interest and board support, Majerus stepped aside and endorsed me. My sense was that Majerus was running just to protect the interest of the UAW, which had become partner to the alliance when Henry Ford II of Ford Motor Company and Douglas Fraser, then President of the UAW, originally established HAP.

As it turned out, I was to play a major role in affecting a merger between HAP and the Henry Ford Hospital, with Ford assuming ownership of HAP. And once the merger was completed in 1986, I — as HAP's chair — was to become an ex-officio member of the Ford system's holding company board. My tenure as HAP's chair ended after thirteen years, resulting in the election of Jack Martin, who was then followed by N. Charles Anderson — as Jack again assumed the chairmanship. Indeed, except for HAP's founding chair, Jack Shelton, all of the organization's chairs have been African Americans!

Henry Ford Hospital had seen the potential in HAP, a health maintenance organization (HMO) that was growing, and believed that controlling it would position the Ford system to become a major player in the managed care market. HAP had earlier struggled; but was now profitable. Under the Presidency of Jim Walworth, many saw its potential to dominate the Detroit HMO market.

At the time, Stan Nelson was President and CEO of the Ford system, but had announced his plans to retire. His planned successor would be an in-house senior officer named Doug Peters. However, I learned at my first meeting at the holding company's January 1987 meeting in Florida that Henry Ford II, the hospital's chair, had decided to simultaneously conduct a study of both the hospital's organizational and governance structures and mount a search for Nelson's successor, deciding not to select Doug as president.

Henry presented his plans to the hospital's Holding Company Board, which consisted of Nelson, Board Chair Bob Vlasic and Dr.'s Roger Smith and Bruce Steinhauer of Ford Hospital's Medical Group plus a number of his cronies that included Wendell Anderson, E. Paul Casey, Carlton "Bud" Higbie, J. Edward Lundy, Robert Valk, Ken Herrick and me — the lone black in attendance. I later learned that the site of the meeting had been changed when the hospital's board secretary Anita Watson reminded the chair that their usual meeting place did not allow blacks. Thus, we met at the local Hyatt hotel. All of Henry's cronies had run their own companies with the exception of J. Edward Lundy, who had been CFO of Ford Motor Company.

Hearing that Henry had decided not to select Doug as Nelson's successor, I expressed support for Doug, whom I had known as a New Detroit trustee, hoping that Ford might reconsider. However, not wanting to be disagreeable, especially at my first board meeting and hearing no dissenters, save Bob Vlasic — I said little else. The deal was sealed.

Henry's concerns were not just about Doug. He worried about the governance of the hospital, citing the advancing ages of his fellow trustees in attendance — all of whom, like Henry were well on in age, with most nearing or over seventy. He announced that he had engaged Booze-Allen, a healthcare consulting firm, to conduct an assessment of the hospital's governance and organizational structures and make recommendations. They were to report back at the May holding company board meeting, five months later in Detroit. Simultaneously, a search began for Stan's successor.

The night before the holding company meeting in Florida, Bill Breech — a non trustee — hosted a dinner meeting for the hospital trustees at the Palm Beach Club. After the meal, Bill rose and offered a toast to Henry and his wife, Kathy. Henry stood, faced the group and thanked Bill. Henry then recalled his experiences with Bill's father, Ernie Breech, who helped him save the Ford Motor Company when he took over from his grandfather, Henry I, upon his death in 1945. Henry became quite emotional as he recounted his visit to Breech's office at Bendix Corporation in Detroit, where he asked him for assistance. He described how Ernie Breech had agreed to help; emphasizing that he hoped someone would help his son in a similar situation.

I have often pondered Henry's remarks that evening, recalling the account of his and Breech's turn-around efforts that were chronicled in a *Fortune* magazine article that I had read during the early fifties while in college. The article reported how Breech had helped Henry revive the company; and here I was, listening to Henry recount in oral-history fashion the events that had occurred.

COMING FULL CIRCLE AT AVIS FORD:
HENRY FORD II AND COLEMAN YOUNG

At the conclusion of the trustee meeting the next morning, I approached Henry and thanked him for his efforts that assisted me in my acquisition of Avis Ford. I reported how well things were going and asked whether he would attend a grand opening I was planning. Henry said yes, but indicated that he would not return to Detroit until May. I assured him that May would be just fine.

I returned to Detroit and began to prepare for the grand opening at Avis Ford. In late March, while planning the event, I called Henry, who answered the phone himself, reviewed his calendar and gave me a date in May.

The date for the Avis Ford Open House was set for Thursday, May 7, 1987. Later that spring, while attending the reopening of the remodeled Westin Hotel's lobby in downtown, I ran into Mayor Coleman Young, whom I had not seen since leaving New Detroit. Without mentioning my comment to his deputy when he did not attend my party upon my leaving New Detroit, I informed him of my planned open house and that Henry was to attend. Coleman's response was, "I'll be there — and for you, I'll cross Eight Mile Road!"

I was pleased, for his remark brought us full circle and I knew there was no lingering bad blood between us.

Avis Ford's Open House was a grand affair. Henry surprised us all with his early arrival — not in a limo for which we were watching, but in a Sable sedan. Coleman arrived shortly thereafter and was followed by the arrival of founder Warren Avis.

I had planned a short program and asked Lou Lataif, president of the Ford Division, to make remarks. Lou Lataif congratulated my partners and me for our success during our first seven months in business, when sales increased fifteen percent. I followed Lataif with remarks, thanking all for attending, including Henry, Coleman, the plethora of Ford executives and the several hundred others.

Neither Henry nor Coleman spoke, but availed themselves for dozens of photo opportunities. The event became an opportunity for the two of them to revisit old times, as they had been quite close in the seventies — when Coleman often referred to Henry as the "Deuce"; and in 1979, upon his retirement from Ford, gave him a private party at the Manoogian Mansion, the Detroit mayor's official residence (and invited Larry Doss, Art Johnson, Judge Damon Keith and me, along with a few others). Coleman and Henry were the life of my open house party. Henry departed first, having expressed to me earlier that he was not well.

A week later, I attended the Ford Hospital Holding Company's board meeting and heard the report from Booze-Allen. Their recommendations were adopted. Later we heard the results of the search for Stan Nelson's successor. The search committee unanimously recommended Gail Warden who succeeded Stan, joining the hospital in midsummer. The spring trustee meeting in Detroit would be Henry's last.

Henry passed away in September of 1987 at the age of seventy. Henry's funeral was held at the Cathedral Church of St. Paul on Woodward Avenue at Warren in Detroit. I was invited by Stan Nelson to accompany him and Bruce Steinhauer, Henry's personal physician, to the funeral in a private car. I invited my partner Ed Brown to join us. All in attendance — including a cadre of local Ford dealers — were touched by the emotional services and the recessional that followed, where a New Orleans-style band played "When the Saints Go Marching In."

BOARD POLITICS AT HENRY FORD HEALTH SYSTEM

Following Henry Ford's death, Gail Warden immediately began to tangle with Dr. Bruce Steinhauer, who proposed that as head of the system's medical group, he should report directly to the board of trustees, bypassing Gail. Gail would have none of it, forcing Steinhauer to resign from the system.

While I did not take part in the active hiring of Gail Warden, I quickly began to work closely with him during my tenure as chair of the Health Alliance Plan. Gail brought national recognition to Henry Ford Health System, as he was a prominent national leader, serving as chairman of the American Hospital Association board of trustees and at a point was ranked fourteenth by Modern Healthcare amongst the 100 most powerful people in health care.

Gail showed sensitivity to diversity — a first among Henry Ford CEOs — and steered the organization away from its traditional practices of limiting roles for black professionals and treating black patients insensitively. Gail brought in Henry Ford's first black officer when he hired Dennis Dowdell as vice president of human resources.

Part of Gail's legacy will be that he brought in Nancy Schlichting, his successor, and spearheaded a nearly twenty-year effort to justify the required Certificate of Need that allowed the system to build a state-of the-art hospital in West Bloomfield, Michigan

I was a member of the search committee that elevated Nancy to CEO and consider my one-on-one interview with her (via telephone) to be the greatest interview I ever experienced. Speaking with Nancy from Florida, as I was unable to attend the search committee meeting in Detroit, Nancy blew me away with her candid assessment of what would be required to fix the system, which was hemorrhaging red ink. Once selected, she did indeed fix the system — turning a profit in her first month as CEO and a profit of over $100 million in her first year. She has subsequently produced profits every year since, one of many outstanding achievements in her stellar career.

I give Nancy high marks for her diversity efforts. She empowered women in unique ways to build support teams throughout the health system, and has remained committed to increasing African American participation at all levels throughout the organization. Nancy has never been afraid of setting "stretch" goals. A few years back, she decided that the health system should apply for the prestigious Malcolm Baldrige Quality Award, determined to make the hospital a national role model from which others could learn. After a national site visit in early October 2011, she received word in November from U. S. Commerce Secretary John Bryson that Henry Ford had been named a 2011 Baldrige National Quality Award recipient — one of three health-care providers among the year's four award winners. What an honor for Nancy and the Ford System. More recently, Nancy has led the effort to merge the suburban Detroit William Beaumont Health System with the Ford System — combining the two systems into a new organization. This is yet another bold action that is a testament to her exemplary leadership — the best I have ever observed in a CEO. At the end of 2009, I left the health system's board. I am honored that in April 2010, the Henry Ford Health System board named the HAP board room the Walter Douglas Board Room.

A BUSINESS DEAL AT METRO AIRPORT

Larry Doss called one day during the late eighties and asked me to join him and Clarence Daniels, a vice president of Host Marriott, a subsidiary of the Marriott Corporation. Clarence was investigating with Larry the opportunity for Disadvantaged Business Enterprises (DBEs) to join Host in bidding at Metro Airport for food and other concession opportunities that would also include news and gift items, plus the sale of duty-free merchandise.

Clarence had asked Larry to organize a group of Detroiters to bid for the concession rights, and Larry asked me to introduce several individuals to the group. I brought along Paul Hubbard, Sam Thomas (our former partner at DHT), and Howard Sims. Larry had already asked Janice Frazier, a former associate of his at Coopers and Lybrand;, Dave Lewis of Lewis, White and Clay (now Lewis and Mundy); Attorney Charles Brown;, New Detroit staffer Anna McCune; and Don Barden (although Barden declined to participate). Clarence suggested that Tom Fox and Gloria "Brandy" Atchison be added.

The group explored two promising prospects. One was the pending bid opportunity to handle news and gift stores at the airport; the other was the pending bid to handle duty-free merchandise. Agreeing that the group needed to be divided in two, Larry offered to take half of the group and bid for the news and gift stores in partnership with Paradies Merchandising. He suggested that I, with the other half, go after the duty-free opportunity. I agreed and took those I had introduced — Paul, Howard and Sam — adding Brandy and Tom to increase our group to six.

Each of us agreed to own one-sixth of any proposed venture we were successful at securing. Later, Tom Fox offered half of his interest to his associate, Dr. Glen Hatcher, an ophthalmologist. That increased the number of our partners to seven. Both groups were successful bidders and entered into partnership agreements — Larry's group with Paradies, to handle "news and gifts"; and my group with Host Marriott and Northwest Airlines, to handle duty-free sales.

Figure 16. Our Avis Ford Grand Opening, 1987. With (L-R) Ford Division President Lou Lataif; my partner Ed Brown; Henry Ford II; Avis Ford founder Warren Avis and Ford Division General Manager Bob Rewey.)

Figure 17. A greeting from Coleman at our 1987 Grand Opening

Figure 18. With (L-R) Judge Damon Keith, Henry Ford II and Mayor Coleman Young at The Deuce Party we held for Henry at the Manoogian Mansion in 1979

We named our company "Nico Ventures" and negotiated a 36 percent ownership of the venture, with Northwest Airlines owning 11 percent and Host retaining the balance of 53 percent. I was named President of Nico and hired Don Walter, a Host employee, to manage the operation. Walter had been earlier brought to Detroit from Denver where he had gained experience in the management of airport retail establishments. The partnership had to build out the space for the duty-free store, which required an investment of $1.2 million — with each investor entity responsible for its share of the cost. Once built, the store did very well and operated from the early nineties until 2002, when the new McNamara Terminal opened and forced a rebid of the venture.

Knowing how profitable the venture had been for our group prompted competitors to out-bid Nico and Host by $10 million in pursuing the duty-free opportunity in the new terminal! Northwest, which was playing a principal role in building the McNamara Terminal, declined to remain a partner. The airline said it would be a conflict of interest, as each dollar of rent paid by airport vendors reduced landing fees for airlines.

Unfortunately, the winning bidder was quickly confronted with shrinking international passenger travel following 9/11. That made us thankful that we had not won the contract.

My Involvement with The Skillman Foundation

In 1989, I was invited to serve on The Skillman Foundation board. Already aware of its fine work, I was pleased to join. I first learned of Skillman while at New Detroit when Mrs. Rose Skillman passed away. Her estate, consisting mostly of Minnesota Mining and Manufacturing (3M) stock, was then "poured" into The Skillman Foundation. The value of her 3M stock was more than $200 million!

By the time I joined the Foundation, its assets exceeded $300 million. Under the presidency of Leonard Smith, the Skillman Foundation had fashioned a strong programmatic presence in the Detroit community. It principally funded programs and projects that assisted the growth and development of children and youth. I served as the organization's chair for three years during my tenure, which ended in 2005 as I reached their mandatory retirement age.

I was proud to facilitate the hiring of William Beckham, who replaced Leonard Smith when he retired. The board had selected a prominent national firm to conduct the search for Leonard's successor. We were consistently unhappy with the applicants they presented — predominantly "Easterners in pastel suits."

"Did anyone ever talk to Beckham?" I asked.

"I would be quite happy with Bill Beckham," answered fellow trustee Alan Schwartz. Others agreed that we should talk to him about the Skillman vacancy. I was given the assignment to contact Bill.

I immediately called him and inquired of his interest. In an insightful manner, Bill chuckled but quickly remarked, "What about New Detroit?" as he was their president and deeply immersed in issues they were pursuing, one of which involved the Detroit School System. Yet, with my urging, Bill agreed to be interviewed. He impressed the Skillman board with his candor, insight and vision of what he felt the Foundation could be. In short order, Bill was hired and joined Skillman following our November meeting in 1999. I was elected chair at the same time. One of my first acts as chairman was to ask an old friend, Edsel Ford, to join the Skillman board — on which he continues to serve.

Bill completely revamped the organization's internal reporting relationships. He opened up its access to many more in the community who were seeking funding assistance. And he became the organization's spokesperson, exciting and generating interest for new and innovative funding requests wherever he went.

Unfortunately, Bill passed away suddenly in the spring of 2000, after serving the organization for less than six months. Karen Schlauchtenhaufen replaced Bill and served for a short period. She was succeeded in 2004 by Carol Goss, Skillman's current president and CEO. After a very active tenure, Goss announced in 2012 that she will retire at the end of 2013 — and that the Skillman Board of Trustees has selected Tonya Allen, Chief Operating Officer and Vice President of Program, to replace her as president and CEO.

Figure 19.   At the HAP Board Room named for me with Henry Ford Health System CEO Nancy Schlichting

Figure 20.   Children, spouses and grandchildren with Retha and me at the Walter E. Douglas HAP Board Room Dedication

JOINING THE BOARD OF THE AUTO CLUB GROUP

In 1991, I was invited to join the Auto Club of Michigan board, where I served until 2006. During my time of service, AAA Michigan grew from a single state auto club association with fewer than two million members to a seven-state entity serving more than four million members.

Having changed its name to The Auto Club Group, the Michigan-based entity now serves Wisconsin, Minnesota, Iowa, Illinois (The Chicago Motor Club), Nebraska and North Dakota. In addition to providing road service to all of its members, The Auto Club Group sells insurance in all seven states where it operates, plus offers insurance products to customers in Indiana, Ohio, Pennsylvania and Florida. I was pleased to have served as the chair of the Auto Club's Michigan subsidiary, AAA Michigan, as well as chair of the seven-state holding company board, before stepping down in 2006. However, I have remained active with the Auto Club Group, chairing the board of their subsidiary bank, The Auto Club Trust, which currently has offices in Dearborn, Michigan, and Omaha, Neb. I have summarily watched the organization grow and merge with Auto Club South (Florida), more than doubling the size of the association — now close to nine million members.

I was pleased to have been asked to serve by CEO Ron Steffens during the early nineties. It was an honor to work with many fine executives, including Ron's replacement, Chuck Podowski; Senior Vice Presidents Ann Federici, Steve Monahan and Terri McElroy; General Counsel Richard White; President of AAA Michigan, Linda Woolwine before her untimely death and many other fine AAA executives.

Also, it was during my years of service that board member Charles Allen became AAA Michigan's first black chair, and subsequently the first black chair of the national AAA headquartered in Heathrow, Florida.

SERVING ON THE BOARD OF THE CHARLES H. WRIGHT MUSEUM

After becoming mayor of Detroit, Dennis Archer appointed me to the board of the Charles H. Wright Museum of African American History. When asked to serve, I was somewhat apprehensive, for I knew of the uneven history of the museum, dating to the many meetings I had attended over the years with its founder, Dr. Charles H. Wright. The noted obstetrician and gynecologist had been my wife's physician when our third child, Mark, was born.

During the sixties, Dr. Wright had envisioned an institution to preserve black history after visiting a memorial to Danish World War II veterans in Denmark. He started the institution in partnership with thirty Detroiters in a home on West Grand Boulevard. In 1978 a relocation and expansion process began when the City of Detroit agreed to lease to the museum land between John R and Brush Streets, in order to build a larger facility.

During this period, while at New Detroit, I worked with Dr. Wright and supported his "Buy a Brick" campaign that helped complete the 28,000 square-foot facility that opened in 1987. Wright was not easy to work with; he was a somewhat contentious individual who many described as able to "extract defeat from the jaws of victory" on any given issue. I personally mused at his many flaying actions as he attempted to press forward his vision for the museum. Once at a luncheon with his friend and mentor, Judge George Crockett, Dr. Wright dressed me down for not providing more resources from New Detroit. We wrangled through our discussion, and it ended with my promise to assist more in ways that I could. Despite his caustic manner, which at times caused reverberations, I continued to work closely with him.

The new museum was delightful, but almost immediately proved to be too small to house its ever growing collection. This prompted Mayor Young to ask the citizens of Detroit to authorize a construction bond issue to build a larger facility: a 120,000 square foot, state-of-the-art showplace that opened shortly after Mayor Archer appointed me to the board in 1995.

My appointment occurred shortly after the arrival of Kimberly Camp from the Experimental Gallery in Washington, D. C., and a new unit of the Smithsonian Institution. She oversaw the completion of the construction of the Museum's new home. It would become the largest African American historical museum in the world, featuring a domed structure with a "ring of genealogy" embedded in its rotunda floor. Surrounding the central rotunda are exhibition galleries and meeting facilities, including a research library and retail store.

Early during Camp's tenure, she initiated a strategic planning process with the professional assistance of Sandy Duncan, a consultant who specialized in that sort of work. Camp wanted to prepare the board to meet the governance challenges for the much larger facility, whose budget would increase several-fold over the size of the budget at the site on Frederick Douglass Drive.

Once the new museum opened, facing Warren Avenue, it drew large crowds, tripling its earlier attendance numbers. However, its operating budget had more than quadrupled in size. As board members, we tussled with the challenge of meeting the financial needs of the new organization — and were then faced with the loss of Camp, who was recruited away. A national search produced Christy Coleman, a museum cultural expert who had spent years at Colonial Williamsburg, the nation's largest living history museum.

By this time, the museum's board chairman, Dr. Arthur Jefferson, former superintendent of Detroit Public Schools, asked me to chair the Museum's development committee, responsible for generating operating and endowment funds. I first demurred, then accepted the challenging assignment. I insisted that Roderick Gillum, vice president of General Motors, and W. Frank Fountain, vice president of Chrysler, agree to join me in steering the organization through its governance challenges. They both agreed, with Rod replacing Jefferson as board chair and Frank taking the important role of chairing the board's finance committee. The three of us braved the challenge of stabilizing the organization that found itself with a commanding deficit under Coleman's presidency. While we ultimately mounted a Legacy Campaign that generated more than $42 million, the Museum's immediate need was to erase its growing deficit, which threatened its survival.

This crisis was overcome when federal Judge Damon J. Keith convened a series of meetings in his chambers that garnered commitments from Detroit-area black business owners. It produced more than $1 million in cash and pledges in less than sixty days — a feat never before accomplished by an individual African American in any U.S. city. This accomplishment makes us all proud that Judge Keith is a citizen of our community.

Meanwhile, Christy Coleman had begun to assess the Museum's core exhibit — a display depicting the Middle Passage of slaves in the hull of a ship. This poorly executed exhibit had drawn the ire of many museum supporters, as they felt it did not reflect anything close to the true Diaspora of black Americans. Coleman, an expert in the area, began the arduous task of conducting focus group sessions with local citizens. She also elicited the knowledge of cultural experts of the African American experiences, both in America and Africa, to guide the development of a more reflective exhibit to anchor the Museum's permanent core exhibition space. Ultimately, at a cost of more than $12 million, a new, far more reflective core was built. It opened to rave reviews at the end of 2004.

Figure 21. With Bill Beckham (L) and Larry Doss

Figure 22. AAA Michigan Board, top row (L-R): Charles Allen; Larry Johnston; William Baer; Bill James; Joe Stewart; Steve Ewing; Bob Naftaly; Stephen Polk. Bottom row: W. Douglas; Shirley McFee; Chuck Podowski; Rick Inatome; Yousif Ghafari; Tom Duke; Hans Schuler

Figure 23. With Retha and Detroit Mayor Dennis Archer after he appointed me to the Charles H. Wright Museum of African American History Board, 1994

Christy Coleman departed in 2006 and was replaced by Juanita Moore, the Museum's current president, who has brought enormous strengths in management and leadership.

In 2007 the museum concluded its successful, $42 million Legacy Campaign, raising the impressive total from area individuals, businesses, government agencies and foundations. This occurred under the leadership of Nick Scheele, former president of Ford Motor Company, whom I recruited to lead the campaign. We all owe Nick and his co-chair, Don Coleman of GlobalHue, a great deal of gratitude.

I have been quite proud to serve the Charles H. Wright Museum of African American History and continue to support it with my financial support and with my time as a volunteer board member.

CASINO GAMBLING IN DETROIT

It was Larry Doss — again — who inquired in the late 1990s of my interest in meeting with him and Herb Strather, a real estate developer in Detroit who suggested that there was merit in pursuing casino gambling in the Motor City. He believed it was possible to gain passage of enabling legislation. At the time we met, Herb had already done most of the preliminary work and was selling shares of ownership in Atwater Entertainment, named after Atwater Street, where casino facilities would likely be placed in Detroit.

Herb, Larry, Charles H. Brown — a partner of Larry's in his Paradies investment — and I met to discuss the business venture. I immediately wrote Herb a check and became an avid supporter and investor, introducing Herb to my Avis partner Ed Brown, who also became an investor.

Governor John Engler appointed a casino study group, composed of prominent Michiganders who researched the issue and presented a report to him. Engler reviewed their detailed report, and then concluded that the issue should not be forwarded to the Michigan Legislature for its consideration. Many believe that Engler's reasoning was likely prompted by the little known fact that his brother had earlier sold land to a casino development group that was building a casino near their hometown in Mt Pleasant, Michigan.

Strather then led an initiative to collect sufficient signatures to place the casino issue before the Michigan electorate. The ballot initiative was approved in a statewide referendum in 1998, providing for the development of three casinos in Detroit. What had been Strather's belief was now law, and led to the construction of three permanent casino sites in Detroit. Those of us who invested in Atwater, a firm which later partnered with Motor City and the Las Vegas based firm Mandalay Bay — becoming Motor City Casino — were handsomely rewarded.

MY YEARS ON THE TIGER WOODS FOUNDATION

In 1996, I joined the Tiger Woods Foundation, upon the recommendation of Dr. Robert Sims, a prominent Detroit physician and avid golfer. Bob, who knew Earl Woods and watched Tiger grow up, knew of my experience in foundation work and asked for my assistance and advice when Tiger and Earl were establishing the Tiger Woods Foundation.

As Bob and I discussed options that needed to be explored, he suggested that I join the foundation. I quickly agreed, and for the next several years, I helped establish expense and program policy guidelines and controls. For example, I suggested that board members pay their own expenses to avoid any hint of impropriety involving the use of corporate assets, as the foundation grew from its infancy. Also, working with Wilmer Cooks, a former NFL player and foundation board member well known to Earl and Tiger, we developed program funding policies and investment guidelines. Wilmer and I also established benchmarks to monitor the foundation's portfolio performance. In finalizing our work, he and I traveled to New York, where we interviewed and selected a number of money managers who were each allocated a portion of the foundation's assets. We were assisted in this effort by George Hubbard, who had been hired by Chris Hubman, chief financial officer of ETW Corporation (which stands for Eldrick T. Woods, Tiger's real name), the asset management firm for Tiger's personal portfolio. Hubman had left International Management Group (IMG), the behemoth sports management firm, to join Tiger. [IMG represented Tiger when he signed his initial Nike contract, and manages the business affairs and marketing of many professional athletes, including Arnold Palmer (its first client); tennis stars Rafael Nadal and Roger Federer; and many others. In recent years, IMG has become a global producer and distributor of televised sports events, and the leading holder of licensing rights for U.S. colleges, universities and football bowl games.]

As a Woods Foundation board member, I served as chairman of its investment committee and oversaw the organization's portfolio performance, which by the time of my departure had grown to well over $50 million. I was pleased to serve with Bob Sims, Wilmer Cooks and other board members, including: Earl and Tiger; Mike Johnson of the Williams Companies; Mark Steinberg of IMG; Chris Hubman; Gail Dorn of the Target Corporation; the honorable Deane Buchanan, a Cleveland Heights, Ohio, municipal judge; John Hayes of American Express; and Rob Light of the Creative Artist Agency, based in Beverly Hills, Calif.

During my tenure, I enjoyed my work with Earl, Tiger and the foundation's president, Greg McLaughlin and his staff. We had a number of successful accomplishments, including the launch of "Start Something," a program — based on a book written by Earl Woods — that encourages leadership and community involvement among young people. From his professional start, Tiger hosted clinics in various cities, including Detroit, where youngsters received golfing instructions from him and Dennis Burns, an African American PGA professional whom the foundation hired to run the clinics. The foundation also built the innovative Tiger Woods Learning Center in Anaheim, California. At the time I stepped down from the Board, the foundation's grants program continued to utilize the funding guidelines that Wilmer and I developed in the early years to handle distribution of more than a half million dollars given annually to not-for-profit agencies throughout America. The foundation continues to thrive, enjoying an international presence in China and Taiwan, and has established a second learning center in Washington, DC.

Tiger was never close to foundation board members; we had limited face time with him. I remember Tiger from the earliest days as being quite shy, yet forcible enough to articulate his strong desire to make a difference through the work of his foundation. My sense was always that his introverted personality and shy manner caused him to avoid one-on-one contacts whenever possible. He distanced himself from event sponsors as well as board members, leaving the details of events to his handlers while he played golf. He never seemed comfortable talking about much else but golf and the program efforts of his foundation. But I also sensed that his age was a factor in the early days.

Tiger generally left the work of fleshing out his thoughts to his father, Earl, or foundation staff and board members. During my years of service, board members from AT&T and the Target Corporation played key roles in the program work of the foundation.

Because of Earl Woods' debilitating illness, he stopped attending foundation board meetings in late 2005. He missed the grand opening of the Tiger Woods Learning Center in February 2006, where former President Bill Clinton and Maria Shriver Schwarzenegger — then First Lady of the state of California — were guest speakers. Earl Woods passed away in May 2006. His absence from the board produced a major void, for it prompted the closing of ranks by those closest to Tiger — Mark Steinberg, Chris Hubman and to a lesser extent Greg McLaughlin — forming a virtual blockade around Tiger. Earl had fought hard to balance the diversity of those who made contact with Tiger and helped to maintain access to him. But with Earl's absence and subsequent death, Steinberg, Hubman and McLaughlin made it almost impossible for board members or others to talk one-on-one or have direct contact with Tiger. Their actions cemented my decision to leave the board in December 2006.

Their cloistering actions reminded me of an experience a few years earlier, when I had been asked by Clark Durant, a prominent Detroit attorney and educator, to invite Tiger to an event that would celebrate the fiftieth anniversary of Arnold Palmer's 1954 U. S. Amateur win at the Country Club of Detroit in suburban Grosse Pointe Farms, Michigan. To commemorate the historic win, Clark had gotten Palmer to agree to host an event at the Country Club of Detroit, with the proceeds going to Cornerstone Schools in Detroit, a private, faith-based K-12 school system that graduates 95 percent of its students. (Clark co-founded Cornerstone Schools in 1991 with Detroit's Catholic Archbishop Cardinal Adam Maida.)

Dozens of U. S. amateur winners had already agreed to appear and play in the event, which was to take place in September 2004. Because of my association with the Tiger Woods Foundation, I was asked to make the invitation to Tiger; his attendance was eagerly anticipated. To make it worth Tiger's while, Clark and I met with William Pulte of Pulte Homes, Inc., who agreed to guarantee an appearance fee of $2 million — payable to the Tiger Woods Foundation.

When I attended the December 2003 Woods Foundation board meeting, I was armed with the commitment of this gift, plus the knowledge that Tiger would be free of conflicts for the event's scheduled date. His own tournament — the Deutsche Bank Championship in Boston — would be the week after the Country Club of Detroit event. The Deutsche Bank event had a Friday start, which would give Tiger more than enough time to attend Palmer's event on the preceding Monday. I made my request with vigor and emotion, and Tiger responded, "Can I do this?" — all the while looking toward Mark Steinberg. I sensed that Tiger wanted to attend Palmer's event, but also wanted Mark's OK before responding to my request.

Steinberg responded, "Walt, let me get back with you." When he contacted me a day or so later, his answer was that Tiger could not attend. The fact that Tiger's nonattendance would cost his foundation $2 million was totally ignored. However, even with Tiger's absence, the event was a resounding success — raising more than $6 million.

I quickly learned that Tiger would do what IMG — or Mark Steinberg — wanted Tiger to do; and, generally did appearances only when *IMG* got paid! Mark's brush-off of the Detroit event was very similar to Tiger's earlier snub of President Clinton following his first Major tournament win at Augusta in 1997. The president invited Tiger to accompany him on the following Monday to the fiftieth anniversary celebration commemorating Jackie Robinson's breaking of the color barrier in professional baseball. IMG declined on Tiger's behalf at that time, as well. The organization's failure to appreciate Tiger's importance to people of color and his stature as a symbol of hope to urban communities was a blind spot that damaged Tiger's image — making him appear more aloof, arrogant and untouchable than he really is.

On the personal side, I regret that as an amateur who can hold my own with some of the best golfers in the country — even at my age — I never played golf with Tiger. I have often wondered why that did not occur during the ten years that I was involved with his foundation. Yet, Tiger was always quick to embrace me with a warm hello. I'm sure that the timing of board meetings, which were usually scheduled to coincide with one of his tournament appearances, made it difficult for Tiger to play with board members.

Retha and I met Tiger's former wife, Elin, shortly after her engagement to Tiger in 2003, while we attended Tiger's annual tournament at the Sherwood Country Club in Thousand Oaks, Calif. I remember Elin as being shy, but engaging. She seemed both excited and expressive about her engagement to Tiger as we chatted briefly on the Wednesday afternoon before the tournament's Thursday morning start, meandering through the buffet line in the country club's mixed grill. Later that evening, Elin and Tiger were the center of attention at a festive banquet which featured a brief appearance by jazz saxophonist Kenny G.. Many — including me — sought photo opportunities with Elin and Tiger that night.

Figure 24. With Retha, Tiger Woods, Evelyn Sims and Dr. Bob Sims, a fellow Tiger Woods Foundation board member

While Tiger's alleged philandering may have wrecked his marriage, tarnished his image and hurt his golf play in the year that followed those revelations, I continue to hold him in high regard and only wish him well. Hopefully, his embarrassing experiences have taught him important lessons that will help him emerge even the stronger golfer and person. Perhaps these experiences will help him peer over the veneer wall that those closest to him have built — allowing him to rebuild his image, manage his life affairs and become all he can be. I still see Tiger as a "phenom" — not only because of his amazing golfing ability, but also because of his fundamental intelligence and potential for leadership and positive impact, as his once-spotless image clearly demonstrated.

Despite my disappointment with how Tiger's handlers influenced him, I enjoyed my involvement with the Tiger Woods Foundation. When I retired from the foundation board in December 2006, I was presented with a thoughtful resolution. Tiger was gracious enough to provide his personal quote below regarding my years of involvement:

> *"At my Foundation, we teach that anything is possible. Walt Douglas' tireless efforts on behalf of the children helped make that a reality."*
>
> — TIGER WOODS

CHAPTER 12

WORTHY REFLECTIONS AND CLOSING THOUGHTS

REFLECTIONS ON THE DOMESTIC AUTO INDUSTRY

My first quarter-century as an auto dealer has been part of a personal odyssey not unlike several million others experienced by people my age. Most Americans have something of a love affair with the American automobile — especially those of us who grew up in the 1930s and forties.

That was certainly true in my case. As a child, I remember going downtown in my hometown of Hamlet, North Carolina, to get a peek at the new vehicles at introduction time. We were all anxious to note the differences between the new and older models. We could distinguish them from one another, noting design and feature changes, and identifying most makes and models by sight.

Growing up, I also observed the ebb and flow of the auto industry, starting when I picked up my first *Fortune* magazine. That's when I read the article chronicling the rebirth of the Ford Motor Company under the leadership of Henry Ford II, which followed the introduction of the re-styled 1949 Ford sedan. Ford had taken over the helm of the company from his grandfather Henry Ford I following his death. It was Henry Ford I who put "America on Wheels" and then announced the "five dollar work day," an action that started the migration of thousands of Americans to Detroit. Indeed, no other industry has stirred economics and created jobs as has the automobile industry — a stirring that changed the lives of countless immigrants and poor Americans. Mr. Ford's actions had a momentous effect on the lives of countless blacks in America.

As a young man I paid special attention to the design and engineering leadership of domestic manufacturers in vehicle features; recalling the first V-8 engines and automatic transmissions; and new vehicle offerings with the introductions of the Corvette by GM and Thunderbird by Ford during the fifties. Indeed, I was never more proud than I was when I drove my father's new 1957 Bel-Air Chevrolet (with turbo-drive transmission) to Miami as Retha and I celebrated our delayed honeymoon in 1958, months after our marriage. Taking along her brother Jimmy and his wife, Ida, how proud we were to drive this four-door, hard-top sedan! We had no idea that it would become a collector's item years later. However, my father — being a true Ford man — eventually traded the Chevy and purchased a 1959 Ford Station Wagon.

In addition to loving cars, I paid close attention to many other aspects of the auto industry early in life. At the time, I had no hint that my family would eventually move to Detroit and I would become an auto dealer. Because no African American dealers existed at the time, such a thought was far removed from my mind. How proud I remember being in the fall of 1963, when I read in *Jet* magazine the announcement of Ed Davis having become an auto dealer with Chrysler, making him the first black auto dealer to sell new cars for one of the Big Three. Davis had earlier — in 1939 — become the first African American to own an auto franchise, as a Studebaker dealer.

I also remember February 1, 1956, when Ford Motor Company shares went public. On that day, a fellow Edward Waters College instructor asked me whether Ford shares were a good buy. I remember opining that they might be, hedging my response. Then, as discussions regarding the need for smaller vehicles emerged, prompting the eventual introduction of the Nash Rambler, the Ford Falcon, the Chrysler Valliant and Chevrolet Corvair, I paid close attention.

This focus continued after I moved to Detroit, where GM's chairman James Roche was quoted during a public gathering that he was "free, white and twenty-one." That statement drew the ire of many people.

Back then, most acknowledged that the U.S. auto industry was at the "top of its game" and was generally without criticism. Senior auto executives seemed to be the highest paid of any industry; the local press announced their compensation annually. And, until Ralph Nader attacked the Chevy Corvair — alleging that the four-door sedan was "unsafe at any speed" — the Big Three enjoyed almost completely favorable public opinion. Perhaps Ford did suffer somewhat from the quick demise of the Edsel — introduced in the late fifties and named after Henry's father Edsel. The sedan quickly became a complete flop — rare for a well publicized, major product introduction.

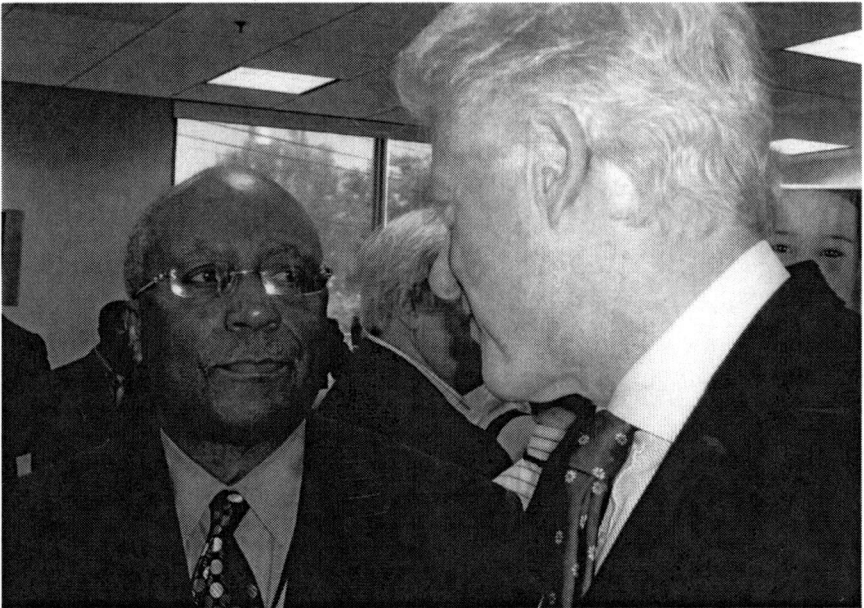

Figure 25. With President Bill Clinton at Tiger Woods Learning Center Dedication

The seventies ushered in an era when the seeds of change began to appear — first with the oil embargo; then with stricter emission standards adopted by the U. S. Congress. Catalytic converters were introduced. By the end of the decade, Detroit was repenting for years of producing poor quality, "gas-guzzling" vehicles. This ushered in massive job cuts during the early eighties, as the energy crisis persuaded many Americans to purchase smaller, more fuel-efficient foreign vehicles. The Big Three struggled during this period. In 1980, Chrysler asked the federal government for a loan guarantee. Ford teetered on the verge of bankruptcy, closing some plants. GM, the strongest of the three, under the leadership of Roger Smith, toyed with changes in its operating paradigm. First it established the Saturn brand, and then attempted diversification by purchasing Hughes Aircraft Corp and Electronic Data Systems.

During this period, I recall commenting to my wife how glad I was that I was not in the auto industry, especially as dealers were going out of business and sales were down. I recall a Sunday news article during the early eighties that asked editorially: "Would the last person who leaves Detroit please turn out the lights?" Indeed, many individuals were leaving Michigan, heading for far-off destinations like Texas, where the economy seemed stronger.

However, by the mid-eighties, the Big Three seemed healthier as Ford introduced the Taurus and Sable sedans. Ford displayed them in the foyer of the Renaissance Center in downtown Detroit; crowds several rows deep seemed to suggest that the models would indeed become popular. Seeing this, I began to change my mind about becoming an auto dealer.

I also noted that the Big Three's dealer body was beginning to include minority dealers, with Ford dealers Ernie Banks and Nathan Conyers leading the way. Back when I joined New Detroit in the early seventies, the Big Three employed no black officers. However, GM became the first to hire a high-level African American. Otis Smith, the first black Michigan Supreme Court Justice, was hired into GM during the late sixties and eventually became their vice president and general counsel. Otis remained until he retired in 1984.

It was not until the eighties that Ford and Chrysler followed the GM lead by hiring their first African American officer. First, Chrysler hired Leroy Richie, who became general counsel — recruited from the Federal Trade Commission in New York. Then Ford hired its first black officer, Elliott Hall — also a lawyer — plucking him from the Dykema Gossett legal firm in Detroit to head their government affairs office in Washington. Other blacks would soon follow. Roy Roberts joined GM from the Lear Corporation, where he had been an officer. He first managed a GM plant in New York before moving to Detroit, where he became GM's vice president of human relations; but soon left to join the Navistar Corporation in Chicago. He was replaced by William (Bill) Brooks — also an African American. Interestingly, Roberts is one of the few officers of the Big Three to leave their employ, then return. GM's CEO Roger Smith persuaded Roy to come back to GM to manage its Cadillac assembly operation in southwest Detroit.

Roy tells the story of an incident that occurred during the time of his return to GM. Deciding to check out the site of his new assignment; Roy arrived in Detroit on a Sunday afternoon and drove to the city's southwest section to find the Cadillac plant that he would manage. Not knowing just where the Cadillac plant was, Roy stopped in a small party store to ask directions. There, behind a counter enclosed by bullet-proof glass, sat a black woman dozing with a handgun at her side. Roy introduced himself as the plant's new manager and inquired where the Cadillac plant was.

"Nigger, how the hell you gonna run the son of a bitch?" she demanded. "You can't even find it!"

"When I find that son of a bitch," Roy said, slowly backing out the door, "I'm gonna run it!"

Indeed, Roy successfully ran the Cadillac plant before moving on to broader responsibilities. After leaving the Cadillac plant, Roy rose to the highest position of any black in the auto industry — becoming Group Vice President for sales and marketing of the GM car divisions before he retired a decade ago. Roy and his lovely wife, Maureen, are dear friends, despite the fact we have our roots in crosstown rivals, GM and Ford. (In May 2011 Roy took on a new challenge as Emergency Financial Manager of the Detroit Public Schools, employing broad authority to restructure and reform the city's public school system.)

Other blacks that either joined or were promoted to officer-level positions among the Big Three include GM officers Barbara Mahone, Roderick Gillum, Eric Peterson and Edward Welburn Jr. All were promoted up through the ranks, with Welburn becoming GM's chief of global design. Frank Fountain was promoted to senior vice president at Chrysler, and was later followed by Ralph Gilles — the designer of the Chrysler 300, who now leads Chrysler's Dodge Division in addition to his design duties. Before his retirement, Don Goodwin was also a Chrysler officer. At Ford, Ron Goldsberry followed Hall — becoming vice president of Ford's Parts and Service operation. Then, in a stellar career that involved a varying number of assignments, Darryl B. Hazel became general marketing manager of the Ford Division, and later was promoted to president of Ford's Lincoln Mercury Division. Prior to retiring, Darryl rose to corporate senior vice president and president, Ford Customer Service Division.

Joe Laymon joined Ford from Xerox, becoming senior vice president of human relations; he was joined by Tony Brown, hired to head up Ford's global purchasing. However, Joe left Ford early in 2008 to join Chevron Corporation, where he became senior vice president for human resources. Laymon was replaced at Ford by Felicia Fields, an African American woman.

Others who have emerged at Ford include Deborah Coleman, since departed, and Bennie Fowler. Both officers directed Ford's quality operations, with Fowler following Coleman. Fowler, now Ford's Group Vice President for global quality, has raised Ford's quality to equal that of Honda and Toyota — generally considered to be the best in the world.

Clearly, progress is being made with both blacks and women piercing the notorious glass ceiling among the domestic automakers. Other officers of note would include: Sue Cischke, who emerged at Ford becoming their senior vice president for sustainability, environment and safety engineering (Sue retired in January 2012 and was replaced by Robert D. Brown); Barbara Samardzich, Product Development; Kathleen Ligocki, who was vice president of Ford's Parts and Service Division, before leaving Ford to pursue other interests; plus Frederiek Toney, who is a Ford vice president and president of Ford's Global Customer Service Division. I am sure that there are others at GM and Chrysler whom I do not know.

Perhaps the time has arrived among the Big Three where performance is measured more objectively. This undoubtedly created fissure in the glass ceiling that for too long only allowed white males to gain entry. Indeed, with the global reach of nearly all auto companies, diversity has become a buzz-word. Acronyms have emerged to describe the global nature of the industry. Emerging markets in countries such as Brazil, Russia, India and China have helped form the term "BRIC" — a shorthand acronym that reflects these hot new markets with diverse populations that didn't register on the industry radar just a few years ago.

During the eighties, other changes were occurring as well. Vehicle manufacturers challenged dealers, insisting that they treat their customers more fairly. The domestic Big Three then measured dealers' customer satisfaction scores — thus establishing standards for acceptable dealer/customer relationships. Dealers initially howled, complaining that their low customer relation scores resulted from faulty parts and poor vehicle assembly. They blamed low scores back on vehicle manufacturers. But over time, dealers accepted the notion that improved treatment of customers had become a necessity. When auto manufacturers tied incentives to satisfaction scores, dealers had little choice but to improve customer service. In fact, dealers could not participate in company-sponsored events if their dealership scores were low.

Once that trend was in place, manufacturers began to turn their attention toward measuring the differences in quality of vehicles manufactured — a measure based on the number of "things gone wrong" in the manufacturing process that required correction at the dealership level. Not surprisingly, these numbers — compiled by J. D. Power and Associates — showed import vehicles repeatedly outpacing domestic manufacturers in vehicle assembly quality. Thankfully, domestic manufacturers began closing the gap with improved vehicle quality that now equals or exceeds that of many import makes.

Yet, market trends and manufacturing costs have positioned domestic manufacturers behind Asian imports. In the early 90's, domestic manufacturers began a trend of building trucks and SUVs — vehicles which had become quite popular and were more profitable than cars — while importers developed a specialty in building high quality sedan vehicles. Not surprisingly, with the increase in the price of gasoline since September 11, 2001, truck and SUV vehicle sales began to decline. This brought favor to the well-designed and more fuel-efficient import vehicles that were "tried and tested," and ushered in an era that began to favor these vehicles. Then came an unsettling period when manufacturing and legacy costs began to weigh down domestic manufacturers — creating a "perfect storm" that resulted in unprecedented losses for the Big Three in the decade that followed.

In 2001, Ford began to question the leadership of its CEO Jacques Nasser. Nasser, a hard-driving executive who arrived in Dearborn during the late 1990s, after serving a stint in Australia and other international Ford assignments, started off by making common sense decisions. Those included eliminating the long-in-the-tooth Thunderbird. He was somewhat controversial, but forceful. Thus, he became a favorite of Ford's board of directors and was promoted to CEO, replacing the retiring Alex Trotman. Initially, Nasser and his wife, Jennifer, were popular with dealers and many of us bought into his vision.

However, before long, his leadership style and vision for Ford, along with his questionable investment decisions, began to raise questions. His investments in two European ventures resulted in major losses when they were eventually sold. One was for a network of vehicle repair facilities, which actually competed with established Ford dealer repair shops. The other was for a vehicle salvage operation. Jack purchased these as part of his grand scheme to control all facets of the transportation industry. Jack used to say that Ford was not in the auto manufacturing business, but the transportation business.

Nasser also led Ford into vehicle retailing by establishing the Ford Retail Network through Ford-owned dealerships; but the

Network competed head-to-head with established Ford dealers. Again, the effort failed. During this period, Ford also experienced a major recall to replace defective tires, costing the company billions of dollars.

The end result was that Nasser was fired in the fall of 2001 and Ford quickly discovered that it was nearly broke. It also needed to replace its aging vehicle line-up and address credit woes in its company-owned financing arm, Ford Motor Credit. Many Ford dealers feel strongly that Ford's board of directors was asleep at the switch. Instead of providing appropriate oversight and governance over many of Jack's follies, they simply nodded in agreement. What a shame!

The spillover of the spending excesses under Nasser limited dollars needed later to redesign many of Ford's vehicles, including the Jaguar S Type. This resulted in a sharp sales reduction for that vehicle and produced huge losses for the Jaguar franchise. That was the flagship vehicle of Ford's Premier Auto Group, whose volume Ford had planned to grow. However, instead of growing sales for the brand, sales plummeted, affecting the viability of Jaguar dealers in the process. I became one of the affected dealers.

Having been offered a Jaguar Land Rover franchise during the first decade of this century, my son Edmond and I purchased land and built a facility in Toledo, which was completed in late 2005. This coincided with the worst sales experience for the Jaguar S Type. As a result, the dealership never produced sufficient new Jaguar vehicle sales to make the operation profitable. We agreed with Ford in September 2007 to close down the dealership.

Beginning in 2008, all three domestic manufacturers renegotiated their UAW contracts. Agreements called for the off-loading of health care costs through the establishment of VERBAs (volunteer employee retiree benefit associations) to be funded by the Big Three, but owned and operated by the UAW. This move was made to reduce recurring legacy costs among the Big Three and hopefully increase sales and profitability.

For a time, I watched Ford's CEO Alan Mulally closely. He who started as an outsider to the industry, but has signaled an end to the "car-guy" idée-fixe that plagued the auto industry for years — with his Boy Scout leader image, complete with blue blazer and khaki pants. My view is that, after relying upon his gut instincts and his Boeing experience, Mr. Mulally has set the company on a course that bodes well for its future. Instead of continuing business as usual and accepting warmed-over product design suggestions, he has set the bar high for both design and quality performance levels.

Since his arrival, all are beginning to recognize Mulally's leadership and corporate vision. In May of 2009, he was quoted in *Fortune magazine* as saying "I am here to save an American and global icon." Veteran auto writer David E. Davis Jr. reported in the September 2009 issue of *Car and Driver*: "Mr. Mulally has now demonstrated beyond all doubt that he is the real thing, and his revamped Ford Motor Company, with a terrific portfolio of new products, is rolling proof." Indeed, we dealers think so as well, and in our opinion his performance is stellar. He employs an easy-going, eclectic leadership style that has driven Ford to produce exciting vehicles with outstanding design features and creature comforts, plus, superior quality. As I mentioned earlier, Ford vehicle quality is now equal to or better than that of vehicles produced by Toyota and Honda, firms generally touted by J. D. Powers as among those producing the highest quality vehicles in the industry. Also, under Mulally, Ford has avoided bankruptcy — unlike GM and Chrysler, which had to avail themselves of government loans to survive.

Undoubtedly, with insightful fiscal planning — coupled with leadership quality, exciting vehicle design and technology benchmarks — Mr. Mulally has placed Ford at the head of the class. His market-wise decisions helped Ford emerge from a product famine that made life very tough for dealers by the year 2005. At Avis Ford, for instance, that year our volumes fell to less than half of what we were used to annually. But Mulally's product revival initiatives helped us to come back stronger and survive the severe economic downturn at the end of the decade. As a Ford dealer, I believe that Alan has the right stuff to fix our ailing problems!

Figure 26. A golf outing with Ford dealers Buzz Holzer (far left), Doug North (far right), and President and CEO Alan Mulally (who inscribed a personal note)

The Great Recession of 2008-10 had a devastating effect on the auto industry, certainly evidenced by the bankruptcies of General Motors and Chrysler — which were made mandatory, of course, as part of the federal government's rescue and reorganization of those two iconic companies in 2009. While I am thankful for and proud of the fact that Ford avoided a government bailout and endured the recession with excellent cars and trucks to sell, the wreckage the recession caused for black-owned auto dealerships hit painfully close to home. *Automotive News* magazine, the leading trade publication for the industry, reported in July 2011 shocking figures compiled by the National Association of Minority Automobile Dealers: that the number of African-American owned auto dealerships in the U.S. was slashed almost exactly in half in only three years: from 523 on Jan. 1, 2005, to only 261 on Jan. 1, 2008 — a catastrophic loss of jobs, talent and capital. The *Automotive News* article noted that the loss of black dealers was so severe that *Black Enterprise* magazine reduced its annual listing of the 100 largest dealers to 75 in 2009, and then dropped the number down to only 60 in 2010 and 2011.

As a result, when *Black Enterprise* named Avis Ford as its "National Dealer of the Year" in June 2010 — with a five-page feature story in its much-anticipated, annual "BE 100s" issue, we could have viewed it as a diminished honor. However, we appropriately saw it as a rewarding recognition of the fact that we were survivors, largely due to our dedication to solid business fundamentals. The honor was especially gratifying as we prepared to celebrate our 25th anniversary as owners of Avis Ford in 2011. I was pleased that the *BE* feature story quoted Alan Mulally, who noted not only our positive presence in the community, but also the fact that Avis Ford was the 11th largest Ford dealer in the nation in 2009.

One of the principal themes of the *Black Enterprise* coverage of Avis Ford, and one that brought me considerable pleasure, was its emphasis on the fact that my sons Edmond and Mark are active in the management of the dealership, and that a succession plan is fully in place to pass ownership of the business to them once I retire from active involvement in its operation — and ultimately, when I'm no longer around. I made Mark president of the company in January 2005, with responsibility for day-to-day operations. Edmond is vice president and business development manager. The three of us posed together in the *BE* article's main, full-page color photo.

The experience of being profiled prominently in a national magazine, combined with my quarter-century anniversary at Avis Ford the following year, prompted me to considerable reflection. It reminded me not only how much I love and value my immediate and extended family, but also how important family, reliable friends and strategic networks are for everyone, particularly African Americans. The black community's development and forward progress in the 21st century will depend upon a renewed commitment to strong families and visionary, socially active black institutions.

Figure 27. With Earl Graves, Sr., Chairman of Earl G. Graves Ltd., and founder of Black Enterprise magazine. Standing (L-R) are my sons Edmond and Mark, and Earl "Butch" Graves, Jr., President and CEO of Black Enterprise.

THE REWARDS OF PARENTING

On the morning of May 27, 2010, Retha and I attended a breakfast at the tony Townsend Hotel in Birmingham, Michigan, a classy meeting place and favorite spot for celebrities who visit Detroit. The breakfast was sponsored by The Yes Foundation, an organization that promotes academic achievement and leadership training among K-12 students — especially in the urban communities of Detroit, Highland Park and Pontiac, Michigan. The foundation held the breakfast to present its first Distinguished American Award; and the distinguished American honored that morning just happened to be me!

The honor was slightly misplaced and the award was probably misnamed, in my opinion. Foundation founder, President and CEO Julia Richie made it clear the purpose of the award was to celebrate someone who had been married a long time, had never been divorced and whose children had become successful adults. I therefore viewed the YES Foundation's honor as a tribute to good marriages and strong parenting, and I was proud to share the recognition with Retha.

I have since reflected often on how special that award was, and noted that the kind of marriage and family Retha and I have been able to build has become rare, indeed. So many factors have contributed in the past few decades to the decline in long-lasting marriages and two-parent families, and the rise in divorces. Certainly one of the primary factors has been the economic change in America that makes it more difficult for young people to marry, start a family and gradually build wealth. Jobs with a definable career path that require no advanced education or special training have all but disappeared. In other words, the American Dream of my youth — especially one that allows one spouse to focus on the household while the other works fulltime — seems to be a thing of the past for most families.

Of course, the best solution to our economic challenges is educational achievement: staying aware of career and economic trends and preparing oneself for immediate and future opportunities. Nevertheless, I also believe that when possible, more couples should consider making the sacrifice we made early in our marriage: to live on one income once the children arrive — at least while the children are very young. Retha and I realized early on that we were blessed to have had the opportunities we had to have gotten off to such a good start. Ever since we decided she should stay home and oversee the raising of our three children, I have been a contented soul. I believed strongly that that was the right decision for us to make, for it helped us begin to control the variables that inevitably influence the raising of children.

We essentially raised Petra, Edmond and Mark by ourselves, always living apart from close relatives. To the extent we could, we limited the outside influences they received while growing up, save school, church and neighborhood experiences — all of which were with few troubling incidents, except for a period when Petra and Edmond were in elementary school. Because we lived east of Livernois Avenue in Detroit's

Green Acres neighborhood, both Petra and Edmond had to walk to Pasteur Elementary, which was west of Livernois. Because of cultural clashes, children living west of Livernois and along the Livernois boundary bullied the two of them at times — causing Retha to intervene, picking them up from school, etc. Retha was a regular school volunteer and because she was available, the bullying matter was handled mostly without any lasting effects — except that both Petra and Edmond recall them vividly and feel that the bullying later affected their selection of friends in middle and high school. Mark came along later and seems to have had no problem with being bullied.

Early in our marriage, we visited our parents at least once annually, but they were far away, in North Carolina. Thus, during holidays and special family occasions, we celebrated together in Detroit with just our nuclear family and a handful of close friends. Tom and Sarah Diggs, who moved to Detroit with us from D.C., were our closest friends in the city. Retha and Sarah grew close, with Sarah at times serving as a surrogate mother to our children. Our children consider Janet — Tom and Sara's only child — to be like a sister.

There was never ranting or raving in our home, and our children's interaction with us was a model of respect and pleasantness. Retha and I never fought, and when we disagreed or discussed differences, it was not in front of the children. I believe we set good examples as parents and employed both love and logic in our responses to their inquiries. Our children followed regular rules: nothing elaborate, just logical things, like regular to-bed routines and study times. But we never had to put a limit on TV. We did little paddling, but when it was necessary, it was done mostly by me. We did not scold our children; we talked to them firmly and directly when necessary. They were never made to do things they were uncomfortable doing. Petra tells the story of getting squeamish on one occasion when she was supposed to perform at the famous Detroit Institute of Arts in front an audience, but got cold feet. She recalls with appreciation that I never made her feel badly about it, or said anything more about it.

While I was quite busy during my New Detroit years — the years our children were growing up — Retha was home with them, reading to them, making meals and doing the countless little things involved with mothering. My sons and I attended sporting events on a regular basis — primarily Lions, Pistons and Tigers games; sometimes Retha and Petra attended also. Our children grew up knowing they were middle class, but nothing more. They were never deprived of anything; yet, they were not treated with lavishness. They were taught to respect the rights of others. They were not members of Jack and Jill, the Co-ettes, or any other elitist group. Race was discussed in family settings, but color differences or preferences were not. Our kids grew up with mostly black friends, but knew a handful of white kids — met mostly at our church, Central Methodist.

Ours was a quiet home with few visitors. However, there were lots of conversations around meals, with me always in attendance when my schedule permitted. In-depth discussions took place — eventually leading to the establishment of formal "Family Meetings" which we have held annually for more than two decades. At these meetings, everyone has input and can freely discuss any problem or issues they might wish to raise. It was at one of these meetings that Retha and I announced the gifting of our Motor City Casino interest, acquired in 1998, to our three children. At yet a subsequent family meeting, we announced the gifting of Avis Ford shares to them.

Education was always stressed in our home. The children knew early on that we were planning for them to attend the college or their choice, and were setting aside what resources we could for that eventuality. We are very proud that they have all graduated from college and incurred little or no debt for their undergraduate training, which was paid for by their parents.

Petra graduated from Oakland University in Rochester, Michigan, with a degree in Nursing, then went on to Detroit's Wayne State University and received her master's as a nurse anesthetist. Today, she is assistant director at the University of Detroit Mercy's Anesthetist Program, where she is heavily involved in the selection and admission of graduate students. She also employs her anesthesia skills at Saint Joseph Mercy's Hospital in Pontiac, Michigan and at Crittenden Hospital Medical Center in Rochester, Michigan. Occasionally, she serves on evaluation teams, which visit anesthesia programs around the country to assess their level of compliance with national standards.

Figure 28. L-R) Mark, Walt and Edmond Douglas at Avis Ford
(Photo courtesy of Howrani Studios)

Edmond received his degree in finance from Wayne State University later in life. At Avis Ford, Edmond is an officer responsible for a plethora of tasks, including the wholesaling of used vehicles, information technology and serving as our representative to the Twenty Group to which our dealership belongs. (Twenty Groups are groupings of twenty or more dealership executives who meet periodically in order to compare performance results of their respective stores).

Mark graduated from Howard University in electrical engineering, and then received his MBA from the University of Michigan. Mark has served as president of Avis since 2005. I cannot say often enough how gratified I am that both of my sons are active, knowledgeable managers of Avis Ford, and will be well-prepared to lead the dealership into the future.

Seeing our children productive, prosperous and making their own contributions to the metropolitan community and the nation is the ultimate reward of parenting. There's no doubt that being a parent is a complex and sometimes thankless responsibility. But there is a delightful bonus: grandchildren! Retha and I thoroughly enjoy being grandparents. We don't mind spoiling the six of them, then sending them back to their parents.

EXTENDED FAMILY

I recall that The Wire Road was the name locals gave a rural road in Northern Marlboro County, South Carolina, where my father, Frederick Weldon Douglas, grew up at the turn of the 20th century. The road was the first to be electrified in that remote rural community, which earned it the name it carries to this day. The Wire Road begins near Cheraw, South Carolina, about mid-state, then winds east, just south of the North Carolina line, for twenty-five miles. It stretches into North Carolina's Scotland County, where it ends at a small town called Wagram. The Wire Road intersects Highway 38, a north-south artery running though Bennettsville, South Carolina, to my hometown of Hamlet, North Carolina.

Some of my fondest childhood memories center on times in my early youth when we visited my father's brothers Ernest and Arch, who lived close to the Wire Road, and his sister Ethel, who also lived not far away.

Today, both my home and my business border another "wire road" that has become very significant in my life. It is U.S. Highway 24, also known as Telegraph Road, a main artery of Southeastern Michigan. Telegraph Road took its name from the time that the main telegraph lines for the region ran along it, more than likely linking the cities of Monroe and Pontiac, Michigan. Avis Ford is located on Telegraph Road at its intersection with Twelve Mile Road in South-field, Michigan. My home is in a quiet, slightly wooded subdivision just off Telegraph, about five miles north of the dealership.

The symbolism of Telegraph and The Wire Road as historically important arteries of commerce, technology and economic development is not lost on me. Just as real is the connection between my family's livelihood and those two similar commercial corridors — early in our history and today.

Figure 29. Family Portrait at YES Foundation Award Ceremony: (L-R) Edmond, Van, me, Retha, Detroit Mayor Dave Bing, Petra, Derek, Mark, Tiff, Jaxson and Jamesyn

Figure 30. (L-R) Edmond, Petra and Mark

Thinking about those parallels reinforces for me the perspective that comes with keeping in touch with one's roots. I have taken an active role in the Douglas family's annual reunion since 1970, the year after the tradition began, and my nuclear family has attended each one since, with the exception of 1981. By the early eighties, nearly one hundred family members attended annually. I served as reunion president from 1984 until the mid-1990s, and with the help of our children, we have hosted the reunion in Detroit four times — in 1974, 1985, 2002 and 2012.

These annual gatherings not only reconnect me to my extended family and my ancestors, they produce priceless memories — such as my last visit in 1973 to Marlboro County, South Carolina, and Aaron's Temple, a United Methodist Church and cemetery on the grounds where my grandparents and uncles are buried. We began that memorable weekend in Charleston, South Carolina, where we picnicked on Saturday at the home of Matthew McCollum, our reunion's president at the time. His aunt — a McCollum — was my grandfather Scippio's second wife. On that Sunday morning, we motored from Charleston to Aaron's Temple, where we attended emotional church services that were followed by a wonderful picnic luncheon and fellowship.

Another memorable reunion took place in 2009, when we celebrated the one-hundredth birthday of my mother's youngest sister Mary. Her centennial celebration followed an earlier testimonial bestowed on her by the city of Newark, New Jersey, for her longevity and the many contributions she had made to her hometown. Tony McDonald, Mary's grandson, had just become reunion president the year before.

FRIENDS AND NETWORKS

Throughout my life, positive relationships with good people have been the most valuable resource of all. Whether men or women; black, white, or members of other ethnic groups; a plethora of caring, kind-hearted and generous people have shared an immeasurable wealth of knowledge, friendship and opportunities. Retha and I credit our hundreds of friends and associates with blessing us as we have experienced a fascinating and fulfilling lifetime journey.

I must acknowledge that many of these individuals have congratulated me and expressed pride in what they observe as my accomplishments of one type or another. I have always been appreciative of their kind words, praise and encouragement; and in the few instances where some have been critical or seemingly resentful, I have taken both the criticisms and resentments in stride, attempting to learn from them without firing back.

Our memberships in many social groups and civic organizations have facilitated these relationships. Retha's sorority and my fraternity have enriched our lives beyond measure. Since college, Retha has been a member of the Delta Sigma Theta sorority and I've been a member of the Omega Psi Phi fraternity. Other outstanding social organizations have added tremendously to our lives. Retha is a founding member of a Detroit chapter of The Links, which is a national service organization composed principally of African American women. She also belongs to a similar organization called the "Smart Set" — a group that introduced us to a wonderful couple, Pat and Gil Fisher.

★ ★ ★

America's black community is a many-layered, multifaceted network that includes additional fraternities, clubs and social organizations — both formal and informal — that operates locally, regionally and nationally. Two of these organizations are The Boule and The National Association of Guardsmen. I asked my friend Wilson Copeland to describe these two organizations:

The Boule — whose formal name is Sigma Pi Phi Fraternity, Inc. — is the oldest black fraternity in the United States. Founded in Philadelphia in 1904 by a group of black professionals, with the primary requirement for proposed members being a college degree, it has quietly grown to a selective nationwide organization of almost 4,500 members. A college degree is still the hallmark of membership, but success in one's field of endeavor and recognized service to the community is the unwritten secondary requirement.

As for The Guardsmen, founded in Brooklyn in 1933, its eighteen chapters are now spread across the country — with membership capped at 540. Although there is much cross membership with The Boule, the requirements are not nearly as stringent: a love of golf, good food, laughter and appreciation for the presence of a skilled bartender are paramount!

Membership in both groups is by nomination from within. You do not apply, you are invited to join; and the invitations are cherished.

Walt Douglas is an outstanding member of both groups, having fully met the requirements for both; and each group is better off for his being carried on their rosters.

In other words, he does more than sell cars!

— WILSON A. COPELAND II, ESQ.

Indeed, my life is fuller than merely selling cars, although one associate of mine — Leroy Richie, formerly of the Chrysler Corporation — once reminded me that I was "just a car dealer."

The social organizations and activities we enjoy have allowed us to maintain relationships with many fine individuals, their spouses and partners. These wonderful acquaintances include some of the most active and influential business and social leaders of metropolitan Detroit and America: my partner Ed Brown and his wife, Mary Ellen; Cynthia and Edsel B. Ford II; Nancy Schlichting and Pam Theisen; Michelle and Charles Allen; Trudy and Dennis Archer; Lynette and Kendrick Adkins; Sara and Tom Diggs; Vivian Carpenter and Jon Barfield; Darrell Burks; Jennifer and Paul Edwards; Paul Hubbard and Robin Barclay; Sharon and John James; Judy Doss; Carol and Tom Goss; Linda and Rod Gillum; Debbie and Jerry Jorgensen; Lisa and David Lewis; Bettye and Jack Martin; Jean and Aubrey Lee; Lois and Eddie Munson; Maureen and Roy Roberts; Yvonne and Horace Rodgers; Sherry and Phil Saunders; Judy and Howard Sims; Carrie and Hayward Maben; Linda Forte and Ty Davenport; Helen and Melvin Jefferson; Diane and George Richards; Kathi and O'Neil Swanson; Harriet and Walt Watkins; and

JoAnn and Al Washington — all of Detroit; Helena and Cullen Dubose; Joel Ferguson and his friend Anna Strong; Rita and Clint Canady, III, and Noreese and Clarence Underwood — all of Lansing, Michigan; plus Earline and Curtis Richardson of Greensboro, North Carolina; and Vivian (now deceased) and Julius Chambers of Charlotte, North Carolina. Four additional Guardsmen are great friends as well: Barbara and Robert (Bob) Holland of New York; Cheryl and Cleve Christophe of Greenville, South Carolina; Veronica and Franklin Biggins of Atlanta and Gloria and Thad Mumford of Washington, D.C. And of course, the Copelands, Debbie and Wilson — two iconic Detroiters who typify the heritage of our fine city!

My friend C. Mason Quick of Fayetteville, North Carolina, now deceased, first introduced the Guardsmen to me and suggested that I join. His suggestion came years after we were first introduced by his friend, Dr. Michael Vick, whom I met during my first visit to the Pinehurst Country Club with Claude Reese and Howard Sims of Detroit. During that introduction in March 1974, I learned C. Mason and his wife, Beulah, became the first black members of the Pinehurst Country Club in 1972. Meeting C. Mason prompted Retha and me to subsequently become Pinehurst members in 1978. I later learned C. Mason was a distant relative on my mother's side, a fact that helped to cement a long and close friendship between the two of us and our wives. He and I shared many golf games during our nearly forty-year friendship. Once I expressed interest in becoming a Guardsman, he personally introduced me to the Detroit Guardsmen Chapter through then-president Waldo Cain. What a wonderful and caring gentleman C. Mason was — and what a great example of the value of networking!

These club and membership associations — including my status as a Thirty-Third Degree Mason — have helped Retha and I plant deep roots in Detroit, and have provided meaningful life experiences and cherished moments.

Retha and I have also made lasting friendships amongst a number of couples that we have met during our winter stays in Florida. They include Kim and Curtis Artis; Debbie and Woodie Brittain;

Ella and John Cornish; Michele and John Davidson; Grace and Ted Martin; Ben and Maxine Miller (our next-door neighbors); Cynthia and Mamon Powers; and Carol and Carey Tucker — all wonderful individuals who have enriched our lives.

Also, we have traveled extensively throughout America and the world as we have gotten to know many of our auto industry colleagues on a personal level. Most of these travels were with groups of fellow auto dealers and their wives, who like Retha and I had successfully competed for and won travel awards in one contest or another. We were always joined by Ford executives and their wives and got to know them all over time.

In recent years, we have slowed our travels as the control of our dealership operations has been transferred to our sons. However, we fondly recall trips to Bermuda, the Bahamas, Nevis and many other Caribbean countries; Mexico, our only Central American visit; Spain, Italy, Greece and other Mediterranean countries; Great Britain, including Scotland and Ireland; France; Northern Africa; South Africa; Zimbabwe; China (Hong Kong); Taiwan; Korea; Australia; the Polynesian islands — including Tahiti and Bora Bora; the Fiji Islands; Malaysia; Singapore; and Jakarta, Indonesia.

Perhaps our fondest experience was the time we spent on the African Continent where we visited Zimbabwe, Botswana and South Africa. We spent time with its varied citizens, viewed animals in the wild as part of a photo safari, and finally looked down upon the magnificent Victoria Falls from a circling helicopter.

Early in my tenure as a dealer, Retha and I were among the first blacks to attend many of the Ford meetings and travel award trips. White dealers and their wives were not initially warm or receiving. Yet, over time, Retha and I became traveling companions with many of them on recurring trips. Friendships blossomed and we have stayed in touch. Our experiences have taught us that if given the opportunity, "people will be people" and seek relationships with like-minded individuals.

LEGACY

Leaving a legacy means many things to me. This book will be part of my legacy. People will be able to read about me and get some insight as to who I was and where I came from, what inspired me and what roles I played during my time. Hopefully, these words might inspire someone.

One of my main goals with this book, and a significant aspect of my legacy, I believe, is proving that despite its many challenges, anything is possible in America. I want young people to learn my story and realize that yes; tremendous personal and professional success is possible, no matter how modest one's beginnings might be. I want them to know the tools required for attaining such success are simply a vision and the determination to bring its grandeur to fruition.

Even if, early in life, that vision conjures up only modest achievement, believing in oneself and applying persistent efforts will attract opportunities that can lead to achievement and success far beyond any that might have been earlier envisioned. Indeed, starting out, it is impossible to know one's innate potential for success. Becoming a high achiever requires continuous growth. Otherwise, how does a person become President of the United States if he or she does not believe that one can be bigger than what was possible while a child growing up?

Certainly, my legacy will be one that endures if Avis Ford or other businesses with which I have been associated continue after my demise and become the springboard for my family to ascend to greater heights in the business world. I'm not suggesting that my children need to be auto dealers, but if the economics of being an automobile dealer can generate something greater, then I say go for it! I do hope that knowledge of the keys to building successful businesses will become part of my legacy.

High achievement is not something someone else talks you into. It's something that you must envision independently. Just observing what others do — how they get up every morning and dress themselves — you can muse, "You know what? That's not so hard to do." Believing in yourself and not setting limits on your vision and goals allows the impossible to come into view. No one should limit his or her vision or potential; yet, one must also realistically set concrete goals, while in the process of fulfilling that potential.

Leaving a legacy became important to me early on. I've always been critical of myself and I've always followed good examples. Had I died at a young age, and thank God I didn't, I think there still would have been some things about me that people would have observed as exceptional. (Of course, this is where Mrs. Chapman, my teacher back in Hamlet, would disagree!)

Those closest to you will always know whether you have lived up to your potential. Hopefully, by the time I retire or otherwise become disengaged, I — and those who know me best — will feel that I have done everything possible to break glass ceilings and reach individual successes that I earlier envisioned. Certainly, I want my legacy to be so significant that others will want to emulate it.

★ ★ ★

Of course, at the most practical level, leaving a legacy means leaving a will and assigning assets to be distributed at one's death. Each of us has to eventually face death. "It is a lucky person who gets out alive!" a fellow IRS employee said to me in the late 1960s, while I was on an assignment in Washington, D.C. None of us at the time could have imagined that this individual would be dead in less than a month.

A will of trust instrument should be executed as early in your adult life as possible, and updated as life progresses — always with your chosen estate administrator clearly identified. Finally, since no one knows exactly the time or the hour, it is most important to be prepared for a long life. Try not to outlive your assets!

Sooner or later, we all suffer the emotional devastation of losing a loved one. When we are lucky, we are protected from the emotional trauma of death until we are older and more emotionally mature; however, all of us are not so lucky. Fortunately, my parents lived well into their eighties before passing away, providing parenting to me, my wife and children for many loving years.

Retha was not quite so fortunate; her mother passed at the age of sixty. Soon thereafter, Retha's older brother, Jimmie, died in his early forties from complications related to injuries he received in the U.S. Air Force. Those deaths in the early 1970s were traumatic to Retha, our children and me. Her father, in his late seventies, passed in 1988. A year later, I lost my older brother Freddie.

In recent years, Retha has lost both her older sister, Esmeralda (Boot), and her younger brother Eddie, making her the only remaining sibling of her family. I believe that each of these deaths brought our family closer together; they also reinforced for me that preparing for the inevitable is an important part of life. Indeed, once I lost my parents, I almost immediately began to realize that I was now part of the oldest generation in my family. It was important that I first assume the role of a patriarch, then prepare for my own inevitable death.

The first rule of preparing for death is to not put off for tomorrow those tasks or matters that you either want to do, should do or have visions of doing. These include making peace with yourself, coming to closure regarding your personal accomplishments, and making every attempt to finish important open items needing completion. Second, it is important to make peace with individuals you care for — resolving or setting aside old grudges, and showing those individuals your love and affection.

★ ★ ★

Ultimately, a legacy is the impact of a person's values, as demonstrated by the quality of his or her relationships with a spouse, children, neighbors, friends, and with complete strangers. What about those relationships became memorable in the annals of one's life? That is what legacy means to me. I hope I have passed my values on to my children and others I have mentored by example, through my own consistent conduct. For instance, I have always fashioned myself as a giver rather than a taker. Because of my many successes, I have been able to bring others along with me — helping here and there, opening a door or putting in a favorable word; at times, just doing some deed because I could. I'm sure I sometimes raised the question in the minds of others: "Why is he extending this kindness to me?" In my own mind, I always tried to keep the reason for such actions simple: "because I could" — always using my influence to help others. That left me with few regrets about giving back and opening doors along the way.

Values affect the political and economic philosophy one follows — a fact that has become more evident in the dangerously polarized atmosphere of today's American politics. I have generally supported office holders and candidates only when I consider them committed to and representative of policies favorable to ordinary Americans who look to their governments to educate their children and stabilize the quality of their lives. In politics and all other endeavors, I have tried to adhere to the basic tenets of my upbringing — maintaining the principles taught to me by my parents and others who influenced my early development.

THOUGHTS ON POLITICS, WITH AN EYE ON THE FUTURE

Many business colleagues and political operatives have suggested that I change my political persuasion, opining that business owners are more suited to the tenets of Republicanism. But I have preferred to continue to call myself a Democrat — albeit a conservative one. There was one exception to my support of Democratic policies and politicians, which occurred during my tenure as president of New Detroit. Republican Bill Milliken was governor of Michigan; I got to know him and supported him unabashedly. (So did Coleman Young.) Later, during my tenure as an AAA board member, I got to know Bill and his wife, Helen, even better, as she and I both served on that board. I was saddened to hear of Helen Milliken's passing on Nov. 16, 2012.

With the election of Barack Obama, America's forty-fourth President and its first black Commander in Chief, my resolve to prefer an association with the Democratic Party was reaffirmed. Considering the monumental problems we faced at the end of 2008, the election of Senator John McCain, in my view, would have been a terrible mistake. Many believe that a President McCain and his Republican colleagues in Congress would have destroyed the domestic automobile industry as we know it today — a prospect that would have had devastating consequences for my business, for metropolitan Detroit and for the national economy.

Figure 31. With President Barack Obama

Despite the many obstacles President Obama has encountered —
from day one! — I am most enthusiastic about his presidency. His
leadership is a breath of fresh air. President Obama exudes a cerebral
approach to addressing the many problems that beset our country
and the world. My view is that America is blessed to have such a
committed and honest president to lead us through a difficult period
of economic strife that is not only affecting America but also other
quarters of the world. Yet, it troubles me how quickly and easily
President Obama's opponents criticized him and blocked many of
his initiatives through his first term. Let's be honest: the mere
presence of a black president in the White House is an immutable

offense to the most hardcore of Mr. Obama's opponents. I'm convinced that many among them do not want the recorded history of our nation to reflect on his presidency in a positive way.

I also consider Obama's election as America's first African-American president to be an affirmation of the conviction shared for decades by me and millions of other African Americans: that we must never give up or lower our sights toward achieving extraordinary successes in life; we must continue to reaffirm that one's vision, preparation, determination, integrity and excellence in performance are the best ways of responding to the injustices of racism and bigotry. Yet, I am appalled that despite the assertion of whites who have constantly proffered that all "you people" have to do is educate yourselves and reflect high character, and you too can live the American Dream — now that one of us has become President of the United States, many of those same individuals have gone out of their way to excoriate him, demean his motives and create trumped-up arguments that question his birthright as an American. Still others have openly displayed bumper stickers and protest posters that depicted President Obama as a monkey or a lion, or have lynched him in effigy — all actions that reflect either a stagnant or growing racist sentiment within American society.

Despite these sickening comments and assertions, Obama comfortably won reelection over Mitt Romney, the Republican nominee whose plastic persona many found suspicious and unsettling. He and his Republican colleagues overlooked the voting power of blacks and Hispanics, and were wrong-headed on women's issues and other subjects that many forward-thinking Americans — including a number of blue-collar white males — view as important. Even their initiatives to limit voter turnout failed. The Republicans have set themselves on a course for further failure, in my view. Unless their party ceases its use of tawdry phrases and becomes more inclusive and centric, they will lose more national elections — notwithstanding all the good and bad arguments they will make in Manichaean debates preceding those elections.

My business and travel associations have taught me to look upon the controversy produced by race as a constant in American life and as a problem we all must confront and neutralize, if possible. I can state, without belaboring the point, that while racial and gender preference continues to exist in many aspects of American life — a preference that generally favors white males — women and nonwhites are succeeding on many fronts and creating the diversity needed to make America's future better than its past. In addition, while I continue to acknowledge the role that race has played in the lives of most black Americans, including myself, I have tried not to allow difficult racial encounters to poison my mind, misshape my personality, or embitter me. Indeed, when I reflect on my own racial encounters, occasionally looking at incidents that were demeaning or troubling at the time, I wonder where the offending individual, or group of individuals, are now. Have they fared as well in life as I have? After all, at the time, they seemed to have had the upper hand. But I have mostly taken such incidents and encounters to be lessons learned, or teachings in tolerance and anger management. They have developed in me the ability to accept occasional insults, racial or otherwise, and move on — strengthening my resolve and character in the process.

★ ★ ★

I often think of my life and legacy in terms of the low expectations and outright scorn directed toward me at the time I left New Detroit. I can recall the innuendos of some who believed I was all done. The sub-rosa expressions proffered that I had performed well as the organization's third president, but upon leaving, would ride off into the sunset to live out my remaining years in a marginalized existence. But no! To the contrary, I have stayed right here, become a success-ful businessman and continued to make a contribution to the Detroit community that Retha and I have grown to love. I've broad-ened my horizons, traveled the world, and played countless rounds of golf — some at exotic places like Augusta National, Pine Valley, Pebble Beach Golf Links and Saint Andrews in Scotland. Along the way, I have scored eight-holes-in-ones; and shot many rounds at or below my age — my best being a 69! I have enjoyed watching our children grow up to become successful adults. And I am savoring the great joy of seeing my grandchildren every week, watching them as they grow toward adulthood.

I am blessed, too, that my beloved wife, Retha, and I are still in love with each other as we celebrate more than fifty years of life together.

Meanwhile, I continue to pursue a vision of my future beyond my past achievements — hopefully embellishing a legacy that will become all the richer in the years ahead.

Index

INDEX

INDEX

INDEX

WALT DOUGLAS is chairman and majority stockholder of Avis Ford, an automobile dealership in Southfield, Mich. *Black Enterprise* magazine named Avis Ford its National Dealer of the Year in 2010.

Douglas is a native of Hamlet, N.C., who earned an accounting degree and an MBA from North Carolina Central University. He worked as a computer programmer for the Internal Revenue Service early in his career, and became active in community development organizations after the IRS transferred him from Washington, D.C., to Detroit in 1966. By 1972, Douglas joined the staff of New Detroit Inc., which, as one of the nation's first urban coalition organizations, addressed economic inequities that contributed to the 1967 civil disturbance often known as the Detroit Rebellion. Douglas served as New Detroit's president from 1978 to 1985, when he became a Ford dealer trainee.

Douglas has been a director of numerous local and national organizations, including the Tiger Woods Foundation; Henry Ford Health System; and the Skillman Foundation. He is an avid golfer who regularly shoots rounds in the low-to mid-70s. Walt and Retha Douglas enjoy regular interaction with their daughter, two sons and six grandchildren.

waltdouglasonline.com

CPSIA information can be obtained at www.ICGtesting.com
Printed in the USA
BVOW07*2230110813

327622BV00001B/1/P

9 780988 226203